Allen Hayden Weld, Sidney A. Norton

Norton's Edition of the Progressive English Grammar

Allen Hayden Weld, Sidney A. Norton

Norton's Edition of the Progressive English Grammar

ISBN/EAN: 9783337779153

Printed in Europe, USA, Canada, Australia, Japan

Cover: Foto ©Thomas Meinert / pixelio.de

More available books at **www.hansebooks.com**

NORTON'S EDITION

OF THE

PROGRESSIVE ENGLISH GRAMMAR,

ILLUSTRATED WITH COPIOUS EXERCISES IN

ANALYSIS, PARSING, AND COMPOSITION.

ADAPTED TO SCHOOLS AND ACADEMIES

OF EVERY GRADE.

By ALLEN H. WELD, LL. D.,
AND OTHER EXPERIENCED TEACHERS.

REVISED BY

SIDNEY A. NORTON, A.M., M.D.,
PROFESSOR OF CHEMISTRY,
Ohio Agricultural and Mechanical College.

PORTLAND, ME.:
PUBLISHED BY BAILEY & NOYES.
OGDENSBURG, N. Y., H. F. LAWRENCE.

QUACKENBOS'S PREFACE.

TEN years have elapsed since Weld's "New English Grammar," revised by its author, was presented to the public. Well received as it has been from its first appearance, and still enjoying an extended circulation, the Publishers have felt it due to the large circle of intelligent teachers who have made it their standard text-book on Grammar, to render it still more deserving of their confidence by subjecting every part to a critical revision, improving the plan wherever the experience of the school-room showed it to be necessary, and incorporating with it such meritorious features as the recent advances in school-book literature have developed.

This work has been intrusted to the undersigned, and in performing it he trusts that he has contributed to the usefulness of the book, and removed some of the difficulties which always obstruct the young learner's path when entering on the study of language. The fundamental features of Weld's system, such as the number and divisions of the parts of speech, the technical nomenclature employed, &c., it was not his province, as editor, to touch; but for the present arrangement, the system of analysis introduced, the new matter added to make the work in his view complete, and the general character of the whole as regards adaptation to the school-room, he alone is responsible.

No teacher, of course, will use this book without previously examining it; and it is preferred that its distinguishing features should speak for themselves on such examination, rather than be heralded in a lengthy Preface. Suffice it here to say, that the chief aim throughout has been to present the subject in a clear, simple, and intelligible light; to make a text-book on Grammar which could be understood by the youthful beginner, while it should be sufficiently comprehensive for advanced classes. It has been sought to command the pupil's attention from the outset, by showing him that he is not dealing with dry abstractions, but with familiar realities which he uses every moment; to interest him in words by means of the thoughts that they express; and to make him, to a certain extent, comprehend their relations as combined in sentences, before considering them separately. This is the object of the simple Lessons with which the volume commences.

In the rules and definitions, clearness is aimed at, and verbiage avoided. Exercises of a practical character have been introduced wherever opportunity offered; and in these, the principles laid down are applied synthetically as well as analytically, from the conviction that it is chiefly for synthetic application — that is, the construction of sentences spoken or written — that a knowledge of Grammar is needed. With the same view of enhancing the practical value of the work, the portion relating to Punctuation has been extended, and particular attention given to the department of False Syntax. The importance of saving the teacher time and labor, by presenting everything so distinctly as to require little or no oral explanation, has been kept in view throughout. It is hardly necessary to say, that the best authorities have been consulted, and that a proper use has been made of whatever seemed good in other systems.

Should an extended course of Parsing be desired, it will be found in Weld's Parsing-Book, which has been adapted to the present volume; but it is trusted that this Grammar will, of itself, be found to cover the ground completely and satisfactorily.

GEORGE PAYN QUACKENBOS.

NEW YORK, August 1, 1859.

CONTENTS.

INTRODUCTION.

LESSON		PAGE
I.	The Use of Words	7
II.	The Use of Words (*continued*)	9
III.	The Use of Words (*continued*)	10
IV.	Division of the Subject	11

PART I. — SENTENCES.

V.	Declarative Sentences. — Interrogative Sentences	13
VI.	Imperative Sentences. — Exclamatory Sentences	15
VII.	Exercise on Sentences	17
VIII.	The Subject	18
IX.	The Logical Subject. — The Grammatical Subject	20
X.	The Predicate	22
XI.	Exercise on Subject and Predicate	23
XII.	Simple Sentences. — Complex Sentences. — Compound Sentences	24
XIII.	Different Kinds of Compound and Complex Sentences	26
XIV.	Copula. — Attribute. — Logical Predicate. — Grammatical Predicate	28
XV.	Models of Analysis	30
XVI.	Exercise in Analysis	32
XVII.	Review Questions	33

PART II. — WORDS.

CHAPTER		
I.	Classification of Words	34
II.	The Noun	40
III.	The Pronoun	59
IV.	The Adjective	70
V.	The Verb	85
	Participles	97
	Conjugation of the Verb	111
	List of Irregular Verbs	120

CONTENTS.

CHAPTER	PAGE
VI.— The Adverb	131
VII.— The Preposition	137
VIII.— The Conjunction	140
IX.— The Interjection	143

PART III.— COMBINATION OF WORDS IN SENTENCES.

X.— The Elements of Sentences	146
Classification of Clauses	150
Classification of Phrases	153
Contracted Elements	154
Modification of Words	155
Forms for Parsing and Analysis	157
XI.— The Rules of Syntax	166
General Exercises	218
XII.— Punctuation	224

PART IV.— LETTERS.

XIII.— Classes, Sounds, and Combinations of Letters	233
XIV.— Spelling	239
List of Prefixes	240
List of Suffixes	242

PART V.— COMPOSITION.

XV.— Exercises in Description	246
Exercises in Essay-writing	256

PART VI.— PROSODY.

XVI.— Kinds of Verse	261
Iambic Verse	263
Trochaic Verse	265
Anapestic Verse	266
Amphibrachic Verse	267
Dactylic Verse	268
XVII.— Figures	268
SYNOPSIS OF GRAMMATICAL RELATIONS	274
APPENDIX	276

ENGLISH GRAMMAR.

INTRODUCTION.

LESSON I.

THE USE OF WORDS.

Adam and Eve, our first parents, were placed by their Creator in the beautiful garden of Eden, but soon lost it by their disobedience.

Learn the words given above.
Of whom is something said?
Of *Adam* and *Eve*.
Who were Adam and Eve?
Our first parents.
Whose first parents?
Our first parents; the first parents of you and me and all mankind.
What is said of Adam and Eve?
They *were placed* somewhere.
Where were they placed?
In *the garden.*
In what garden?
In the garden *of Eden.*
What kind of a garden was it?
A *beautiful* garden.

What further is said about Adam and Eve?
They lost it.
What did they lose?
It, the garden of Eden.
When did they lose it?
They *soon* lost it.
How did they lose it?
By disobedience.
By whose disobedience?

By *their* disobedience,—that is, Adam and Eve's disobedience.

Repeat the words that stand at the commencement of the lesson.
Why are the words *Adam* and *Eve* used in this sentence?
To tell us who were placed in this garden.
Why is the word *and* used?
To connect *Adam* and *Eve*.
Why are the words *our first parents* used?
To tell who Adam and Eve were.
Why are the words *were placed* used?
To tell what was done with Adam and Eve.
Why are the words *in the garden* used?
To tell where Adam and Eve were placed.
Why are the words *of Eden* used?
To tell what garden they were placed in.
Why is the word *beautiful* used?
To tell what kind of a garden it was.
Why are the words *by their Creator* used?
To tell by whom they were placed in this garden.
Why are the words *lost it* used?
To tell something more about Adam and Eve.
Why is the word *soon* used?
To tell when they lost it.
Why are the words *by their disobedience* used?
To tell how they lost it.

LESSON II.

THE USE OF WORDS (CONTINUED).

Washington, the father of his country, was born in Virginia, in 1732.

Learn the words given above. Of whom is something said? What was Washington? The father of what? The father of whose country? Whose country is meant by *his* country?

What is said of Washington?

Where was he born? When was he born?

Repeat the words that stand at the commencement of the lesson.

Why is the word *Washington* used?

To tell us who was born in Virginia in 1732.

Why are the words *the father of his country* used?

To tell us what Washington was.

Why are the words *his country* used?

To tell us what he was the father of.

Why is the word *his* used before country?

To tell us whose country he was the father of.

Why are the words *was born* used?

To tell us a fact about Washington.

Why are the words *in Virginia* used?

To tell us (what?)

Why are the words *in 1732* used?

To tell us (what?)

Has every word a use and meaning of its own?

It has.

Why do we use words?

To express thoughts.

How may we express any thought that occurs to us?

By combining words.

Questions similar to the above may be put on the following sentences:

Learning is a chaste ornament in prosperity, a safe refuge in adversity.

Rome, once the metropolis of the world, but now only a shadow of its former self, was founded by Romulus and Remus, twin brothers, 752 years before the Christian era.

> There is a world above,
> Where parting is unknown;
> A long eternity of love,
> Formed for the good alone.

LESSON III.

THE USE OF WORDS (CONTINUED).

Let us now endeavor to employ words to express our thoughts. If I say *Flowers grow*, or *Flowers are growing*, I have a complete thought, although I have used only two or three words. We may extend this thought in various ways. I will ask several questions and answer them. Ask yourself the same questions, and write down at least three different answers to each.

What flowers grow?
White flowers are growing.
What kind of flowers grow?
Large flowers are growing.
How many flowers grow?
Two flowers are growing.
Where do the flowers grow?
Flowers *on my rose-bush* are growing.
When do the flowers grow?
Flowers are growing *every moment*.
How do the flowers grow?
Flowers are growing *rapidly*.
Why do the flowers grow?
Flowers are growing *on account of gentle showers*.

We may now combine these in one expression; as,

Two large white flowers on my rose-bush are growing rapidly every moment on account of gentle showers.

In the following examples, select the simple thought, and tell what questions are answered by the other words.

Many strong sailors in my brother's boat are now rowing vigorously down the stream to reach their ship.

A flock of beautiful blackbirds, being scared by a small boy early this morning, flew, with many outcries into the forest.

A rude boy, being found by an old man in his apple-tree, was gently desired by him to come down.

Extend the following simple thoughts by asking the questions what? what kind? how many? how? when? where? why? whose?

Horses ran.   Ships are sailing.
Dogs bark.   Scholars study.
Boys play.   Soldiers are marching.

LESSON IV.

DIVISION OF THE SUBJECT.

Can brutes talk to each other?
Can men talk to each other?
What great advantage, then, do men possess over brutes?

They can make known their thoughts to each other.

What do they use for the purpose of making their thoughts known?

Language.

Of what does language consist?

Of words, each of which represents some idea. Thus the word *horse* represents the animal so called.

What do we call such a collection of words as expresses a complete thought?

A Sentence.

Give some short sentences as examples.

Time flies. — Are you industrious? — Always do right. — How pleasant it is to learn!

Make up four short sentences of your own as examples.

How are sentences constructed?

According to certain rules and principles, which constitute the science of GRAMMAR.

How may a person learn to write and speak correctly?

By mastering the rules and principles of Grammar.

In studying Grammar, with what do we have to deal?

In studying Grammar, we have to deal, —

1. With Sentences, which express complete thoughts.

2. With Words, which represent the separate ideas that make up the complete thoughts.

3. With Letters, or characters that represent the sounds of words.

What is the meaning of the word Analysis?

Some bodies are made up of several different things; water, for instance, is composed of two gases, oxygen and hydrogen. *Analysis* implies the separation of such a compound substance into the parts that compose it. A chemist would *analyze* water by resolving it into oxygen and hydrogen.

When, then, we separate a sentence into the parts that compose it, what is the process called?

Analysis.

What are parts into which we analyze a sentence called?

Elements.

When we put together words to form sentences and express our thoughts, what is the process called?

Composition.

Of what is Composition the opposite?

Composition is the opposite of Analysis.

On what are the principles of Composition based?

On the principles of Grammar.

In studying Grammar, with what are we to commence?

With SENTENCES.

PART I.

SENTENCES.

LESSON V.

DECLARATIVE SENTENCES. — INTERROGATIVE SENTENCES.

What is a Sentence?

A Sentence is such a collection of words as expresses a complete thought.

Show the origin of the different classes of sentences.

In expressing a thought, we may either, —
1. Declare something.
2. Ask something.
3. Command, entreat, or permit something.
4. Exclaim something.

This gives rise to four different classes of sentences.

What are the four kinds of sentences called?

Declarative Sentences, Interrogative Sentences, Imperative Sentences, and Exclamatory Sentences.

What is a Declarative Sentence?

A Declarative Sentence is one in which something is declared; as, "The sun shines." "You may be a good scholar."

Make a declarative sentence containing the word *fire*.

What mark stands at the end of the two sentences given above, and all other declarative sentences?

A little dot (.) called a Period.

What is an Interrogative Sentence?

An Interrogative Sentence is one in which a question is asked; as, "Does the sun shine?" "Are you a good scholar?"

Ask a question about *snow*. What kind of a sentence have you made?

Life is short. What kind of a sentence is this? Turn it into an interrogative sentence.

Is life short?

What mark stands at the end of the sentence last given, and all other interrogative sentences?

An Interrogation Point (?).

When you turn a declarative into an interrogative sentence, in writing, what mark must be changed?

The period (.) at the end of the declarative sentence must be changed into an interrogation point (?).

In such sentences as these, "*He asked how the world could be round,*" "*They inquired whether you were well,*" is a question asked?

No direct question is asked; we simply declare that a question was asked.

What kind of sentences, then, are the above?

Declarative sentences.

Read each of the following sentences, and tell whether it is declarative or interrogative: —

Who knocked? — Did anybody knock? — I asked whether anybody knocked. — Somebody knocked. — Where is he who can say, "Perfect happiness is mine"? — What is truth? — Pilate asked what truth was. — "What is truth?" asked Pilate. — United, we stand. — If Columbus had listened to his men, he would have abandoned his voyage, and America might not yet have been discovered.

Lives there a man with soul so dead,
Who never to himself has said,
"This is my own, my native land"?

EXERCISE

I. Make each of the following declarative sentences interrogative.

1. Love conquers all things.
2. Charity covers a multitude of sins.

3. Cairo is the largest city in Africa.
4. There is no man that sinneth not.
5. Napoleon might have lived happily and reigned gloriously.
6. When Victoria dies, her eldest son will ascend the throne.

II. Make each of the following interrogative sentences declarative.
1. Is the Atlantic Telegraph cable 1,640 miles long?
2. Are there parts of the earth where it never rains?
3. Have you learned that the Volga is the longest river in Europe?
4. Was Newton the greatest philosopher of his age?
5. Might he have learned this, had he been more attentive?
6. Must all men die?

III. Make six declarative sentences, each of which shall contain one of the following words: —

MODEL. — *Honey.* Bees make honey.

steamboats	are	love
happy	brothers	grass

IV. Make six interrogative sentences, each of which shall contain one of the following words: —

MODEL. — *Thunder.* Did you hear it thunder?

did	were	sweet
where	who	clouds

LESSON VI.

IMPERATIVE SENTENCES. — EXCLAMATORY SENTENCES.

What is an Imperative Sentence?

An Imperative Sentence is one that is used in commanding, entreating, or permitting; as, "Let the sun shine." "Do not hurt me." "Go in peace."

When you say, "Let the sun shine," do you command, entreat, or permit?

When you say, "Do not hurt me," do you command, entreat, or permit?

When you say, "Go in peace," do you command, entreat, or permit?

What mark stands at the end of each of the three sentences given above, and all other imperative sentences?

Suppose you had a brother Robert, and wanted to tell him to study his lesson, what would you say? What kind of a sentence would that be?

Make an imperative sentence containing the word *go*.

What kind of a sentence is this? — *It rains.* Turn it into an interrogative sentence. Turn it into an imperative sentence.

Let it rain.

What is an Exclamatory Sentence?

An Exclamatory Sentence is one used in exclaiming; as, "How it rains!" "What a studious boy!"

What two words often stand at the commencement of exclamatory sentences, as in the two examples given above?

How and *what.*

Make an exclamatory sentence beginning with *How.* Make an exclamatory sentence beginning with *What.*

What kind of a sentence is this? — *Pope wrote fine poetry.* Turn it into an exclamatory sentence.

What fine poetry Pope wrote!

What mark stands at the end of the last sentence, and all other exclamatory sentences?

An Exclamation Point (!).

When you turn a declarative sentence into an exclamatory sentence in writing, what mark must be changed?

The period (.) at the end of the declarative sentence must be changed into an exclamation point (!).

Read each of the following sentences, and tell whether it is declarative, interrogative, imperative, or exclamatory: —

Nero, the Roman emperor, was a monster of wickedness. — Was Nero, the Roman emperor, a monster of wickedness? — What a monster of wickedness Nero was! — Let Nero, that monster of wickedness, be abhorred by all good men. — O reputation, dearer far than life! — Where was George Washington born? In Westmoreland County, Virginia. — Be just and fear not. — Know thyself. — There is no city in America as far north as Paris. — "How fortunate it is that ice is lighter than water!" "Why so?" "Because, were it not so, the streams would be frozen in winter from bottom to top, and all the fish would be killed."

LESSON VII.

EXERCISE ON SENTENCES.

I. Make each of the following declarative sentences imperative : —

MODEL. — *Declarative.* We must not think too highly of ourselves.
You must depart.
Imperative. Let us not think too highly of ourselves.
Depart.

1. No one loves bad men.
2. You ought to be diligent, like the little ant.
3. You are not hard-hearted.
4. No man should despair, however unfortunate he may be.
5. They prize virtue more than gold.
6. You will not keep bad company.

II. Make each of the following declarative sentences exclamatory : —

MODEL. — *Declarative.* It rains hard. Education is a treasure.
Exclamatory. How hard it rains! What a treasure education is!

1. The birds fly prettily.
2. Dr. Kane boldly explored the Arctic regions.
3. The peacock has ugly feet.
4. Very little is known about the interior of Africa.
5. It is exceedingly warm in the torrid zone.
6. Chicago has a fine situation on Lake Michigan.

III. Make six imperative sentences, each of which shall contain one of the following words : —

MODEL. — *Give.* Give alms to the poor.

| walk | studies | always |
| look | cheerful | rise |

IV. Make six exclamatory sentences, each of which shall contain one of the following words : —

MODEL. — *Kind.* How kind my teacher is!

| graceful | books | character |
| sweetly | writes | farmers |

LESSON VIII.

THE SUBJECT.

What kind of a sentence is this?— *Cinnamon is produced in Ceylon.*
What is my object in writing this sentence?
To tell something about cinnamon.
What, then, is the leading word in the sentence, about which I say something?
The word *cinnamon.*
What is the leading word, about which something is said, in each of the following sentences?
Gunpowder is said to have been invented by the Chinese.
We never lose anything by industry.
Is not the Amazon the largest river in the world?
Shall we cross the ocean?
What do we call this leading word, about which something is said?
It is called the *Subject* of the sentence.
Can there be any sentence without a subject?
Make a declarative sentence with *gold* for its subject.
Gold is found in California.
Make another sentence like the above, with *gold* for its subject.
Make an interrogative sentence with *lion* for its subject.
Is not the lion the king of beasts?
Make another interrogative sentence with *lion* for its subject.
Make an imperative sentence with *thou* for its subject.
Be thou happy.
Make another imperative sentence with *thou* for its subject
Make an exclamatory sentence with *men* for its subject.
How unwise some men are!
Make another exclamatory sentence with *men* for its subject.
When a sentence is given, how can you find the subject?
By asking a question with *who* or *what.* The word that answers the question will be the subject.
Give an example.
Cinnamon is produced in Ceylon. To find the sub-

ject of this sentence, ask the question, *What is produced in Ceylon?* Answer, *cinnamon.* Then *cinnamon* is the subject.

Give another example.

Lions are found in Asia and Africa.
Question.—What are found in Asia and Africa?
Answer.—Lions; *lions* is the subject.

Give an example with an interrogative sentence.

Were Cæsar and Alexander great generals?
Question.— Were who great generals?
Answer.— *Cæsar* and *Alexander;* *Cæsar* and *Alexander* are the subject.

May a sentence, then, have more than one word for its subject?

Yes, it may have a number of words.

Give a sentence which has several words for its subject.

Cats and dogs are foes to mice.

What words are the subject of the sentence last given? Make a sentence of your own, like the one just given, which will have more than one word for its subject.

EXERCISE.

I. Select the subject in each of the following sentences. If you are at a loss, ask the question with *who* or *what*, as you have been shown above.

1. The rose-geranium is a native of Arabia. 2. Are not the Himalaya Mountains the highest range in the world? 3. Few know the value of a friend. 4. Grammar teaches us how to speak and write correctly. 5. How happy we are when we do right! 6. Let the sinner turn from his wickedness and live. 7. He and she and I go to school. 8. Hills and valleys, fields and farm-houses, meet the eye.

II. Make six sentences which shall have the following words for their subjects in order:—

1. sun
2. anger
3. gardens
4. father and mother
5. day and night
6. apples, plums, and peaches

LESSON IX.

THE LOGICAL SUBJECT. — THE GRAMMATICAL SUBJECT.

What is the difference between these two sentences? —
    Solomon built a temple.
    The wise Solomon built a temple.

The first sentence has *Solomon* for its subject; the second, *the wise Solomon*.

In the second sentence, why is *Solomon* modified by the words *the wise?*

To tell what kind of a man Solomon was.

In the expression, *the wise Solomon*, what is the leading word?

Solomon.

What are the other words, *the wise*, called?

Modifying words.

What are modifying words?

Modifying words are words joined to some leading word, to describe or limit it.

Join some modifying words to the word *day*, to describe it.

A cold day. — The words *a cold* tells us what kind of a day is meant.

Join some modifying words to the word *day*, to limit it.

The fifteenth day. Day before yesterday. Here the modifying words are joined to *day* to limit it, that is, to tell us what particular day is meant.

What do we call the leading word in a sentence, about which something is said, together with the words that modify it?

The Logical Subject.

What is the logical subject in the sentence, *The wise Solomon built a temple?*

The wise Solomon.

What do we call the leading word, *Solomon*, without the modifying words joined to it?

The Grammatical Subject.

LOGICAL AND GRAMMATICAL SUBJECT.

Select the logical and the grammatical subject in the following sentence: *The best printing-presses are made in America.*

The logical subject is *the best printing-presses;* the grammatical subject is *printing-presses.*

Select the logical and the grammatical subject in each of the following sentences: —

    The latest news from India is favorable.
    The man who does his duty will be rewarded.
    The Declaration of Independence was adopted July 4, 1776.
    Wine is made from grapes.

In this last sentence, is there any difference between the logical and the grammatical subject?

Are there sentences, then, in which the grammatical subject may be the same as the logical subject?

Yes. When the logical subject consists of but one word, without any modifying words joined to it, it will also be the grammatical subject. When, however, the logical subject contains modifying words, we must take them away from the leading word in order to get the grammatical subject.

When the grammatical and the logical subject are not the same, which is the shorter of the two?

EXERCISE.

I. Select the logical and the grammatical subject in each of the following sentences: —

1. Mercy is twice blessed. 2. O that my enemy would write a book! 3. He that would have his work well done, must do it himself. 4. Let the dead bury the dead. 5. Who was the oldest of men? 6. Were not Adam and Eve our first parents? 7. Certain peace is better than hoped-for victory.

II. Make six sentences, each of which shall have one of the following words for both its grammatical and its logical subject: —

    oxen   silver   money
    ice   fisherman   summer

III. Make six sentences, each of which shall have one of the above words for its grammatical, but not for its logical subject.

LESSON X.

THE PREDICATE.

The wise Solomon built a temple. What is the logical subject of this sentence?

What do we call that part of the sentence that remains when the logical subject is taken away?

The Pred'-i-cate.

What is the predicate in the sentence given above?

Built a temple.

Now let us define these words.— What is the subject of a sentence?

The subject of a sentence is that about which something is said or written.

What is the predicate?

The predicate is that which is said or written about the subject.

Select the subject and the predicate in this sentence: *The bible of the Mohammedans is called the Koran.*

The subject is *the bible of the Mohammedans.*

The predicate is *is called the Koran.*

Select the subject and the predicate in this sentence: *In the battle of Bunker Hill the noble Warren fell.*

The subject is *the noble Warren.*

The predicate is *fell in the battle of Bunker Hill.*

Select the subject and the predicate in the following sentences:—

Within a few years, several fine carriage-roads have been constructed across the Alps.

Among Spanish authors, Cervantes, the author of Don Quixote, holds the highest rank.

Where can we find a greater mind than Sir Isaac Newton's?

Into how many elements may every sentence be divided?

Into two, Subject and Predicate.

What is the process of dividing a sentence into these elements called?

Analysis.

Analyze the sentence, *Arabian horses will travel nearly a hundred miles without stopping.*

EXERCISE ON SUBJECT AND PREDICATE.

This is a declarative sentence. *Arabian horses* is the logical subject; *horses* is the grammatical subject; *will travel nearly a hundred miles without stopping* is the predicate.

Analyze this sentence:—*My friend, have you heard the news?*

This is an interrogative sentence. *You, my friend,* is the logical subject; *you* is the grammatical subject; *have heard the news* is the predicate.

EXERCISE.

Analyze each of the following sentences according to the models just given, mentioning,—1. What kind of a sentence it is. 2. The logical subject. 3. The grammatical subject. 4. The predicate.

1. The red coral of which trinkets are made is found in the Mediterranean Sea. Its cells are the abode of a little insect, by which it is formed. Who would suppose that creatures so small could make such extensive beds of this beautiful substance?

2 At the North Cape, in Norway, the sun does not go down for several weeks. How strange it must seem, to go to bed by daylight! Would you like to travel there?

3. An ungrateful man is like a hog eating nuts under a tree, without ever looking up to see whence they come.

LESSON XI.

EXERCISE ON SUBJECT AND PREDICATE.

There can be no sentence without a subject and a predicate.

I. Below are six subjects. Make with them six sentences by supplying a predicate to each.

1. The color of the sea
2. Whether we shall go
3. Ground that is barren
4. The Rocky Mountains
5. Columbus
6. Working in the sun

24 SIMPLE, COMPLEX, AND COMPOUND SENTENCES.

II. Below are six predicates. Make with them six sentences by supplying a subject to each.

1. come from South America
2. are shot on the prairies
3. was born in Virginia
4. make good men
5. is disgraceful
6. would be wrong

LESSON XII.

SIMPLE SENTENCES. — COMPLEX SENTENCES. — COMPOUND SENTENCES.

How many distinct parts are there in the following sentence? — *Poverty afflicts us; vice disgraces us.*

Two parts: — 1. Poverty afflicts us.
2. Vice disgraces us.

What is each of these parts called?

A Member.

Does each of these members express an independent thought? What is the subject of the first member? What is its predicate? What is the subject of the second member? What is its predicate? Are their subjects and predicates the same or different?

What is a member of a sentence?

A Member of a sentence is such a part as expresses an independent thought and has a distinct subject and predicate of its own.

How many members are there in the following sentence, and what are they? — *Cork is light; air is lighter; hydrogen is lightest.*

Pick out the subject and the predicate of each member.

What do we call a sentence like the above?

A Compound Sentence.

What is a Compound Sentence?

A Compound Sentence is one that contains two or more members.

What do we call a sentence that contains only one assertion?

A Simple Sentence.

SIMPLE, COMPLEX, AND COMPOUND SENTENCES. 25

Is the following sentence simple or compound, and why? — *The harvest is past.*

Is the following sentence simple or compound, and why? — *The harvest is past, the summer is ended.*

Make a simple sentence of your own. Make a compound sentence.

What do we call a sentence that contains a leading assertion modified by one or more dependent assertions?

A Complex Sentence.

What are the dependent assertions of a complex sentence called?

Clauses.

What kind of a sentence is this, and why? — *Solomon was the son of David.*

What kind of a sentence is this, and why? — *Solomon, who built the temple, was the son of David.*

What kind of a sentence is this, and why? — *Solomon, who built the temple, was the son of David, but he neglected the worship of his God.*

Make a simple sentence of your own. Make a complex sentence. Make a compound sentence.

Is the following sentence simple, complex, or compound, and why? — *Rome, which had conquered the world, fell before the northern barbarians.*

Complex: because it contains the leading assertion *Rome fell before the northern barbarians*, and the dependent assertion *which had conquered the world.*

Analyze it.

It is a complex declarative sentence. *Rome, which had conquered the world*, is the logical subject. *Rome* is the grammatical subject. *Fell before the northern barbarians* is the predicate.

Is the following sentence simple or compound? — *The best life-boats and agricultural implements are made in America.*

It is a simple declarative sentence. *The best life-boats and agricultural implements* is the logical subject. *Life-boats* and *implements* are the grammatical subject. *Are made in America* is the predicate.

EXERCISE.

Make eight simple, eight complex, and eight com-

pound sentences, each of which shall contain one of the
following words: —

ships	swift	run	beauty	while
business	and	handsome	rapidly	if
but	give	have	and	who
blow	eyes	stoves	Europe	that

LESSON XIII.

DIFFERENT KINDS OF COMPOUND AND COMPLEX SENTENCES.

When a declarative sentence contains two or more members, what is it called?

A Compound Declarative Sentence.

When an interrogative sentence contains two or more members, what is it called?

A Compound Interrogative Sentence.

When an imperative sentence contains two or more members, what is it called?

A Compound Imperative Sentence.

When an exclamatory sentence contains two or more members, what is it called?

A Compound Exclamatory Sentence.

Give an example of a compound declarative sentence.

Genius accomplishes much, but industry does more.

Why is this a declarative sentence? Why is it compound? What two members does it contain? What are the subject and predicate of each?

Give an example of a compound interrogative sentence.

Has he said it, and shall he not do it?

Why is this an interrogative sentence? Why is it compound? What two members does it contain? What are the subject and predicate of each?

Give an example of a compound imperative sentence.

Let Flora be your jeweller; let rose-buds be your rubies.

Why is this an imperative sentence? Why is it compound? What two members does it contain? What are the subject and predicate of each?

Give an example of a compound exclamatory sentence.

How noble was Washington, how exalted was his character, how exemplary was his career!

Why is this an exclamatory sentence? Why is it compound? What three members does it contain? What are the subject and predicate of each?

What kind of a sentence is this?—*Americus Vespucius gave his name to the Western Continent; but did he deserve the honor?*

It is a compound sentence.

What word connects the two members?

But.

What is the first member? Is it declarative, interrogative, imperative, or exclamatory?

What is the second member? Is it declarative, interrogative, imperative, or exclamatory?

When a compound sentence has members of different kinds, like the one just given, what is it called?

A Compound Mixed Sentence.

Make up a compound mixed sentence.

On what does the class of a complex sentence depend?

On its leading assertion.

What kind of a sentence is this, and why?—*Since you request it, I will assist you.*

A Complex Declarative Sentence; because the leading assertion, *I will assist you*, is declarative.

What kind of a sentence is this, and why?—*Shall I instruct a class that will not hear?*

A Complex Interrogative Sentence; because the leading assertion, *Shall I instruct a class?* is interrogative.

What kind of a sentence is this, and why?—*Let him go, if he dare!*

A Complex Imperative Sentence; because the leading assertion, *Let him go*, is imperative.

What kind of a sentence is this, and why? — *How faithless was the man in whom I trusted!*

A Complex Exclamatory Sentence; because the leading assertion, *How faithless was the man*, is exclamatory.

Tell what kind of sentence is each of the following; that is, whether it is simple declarative, complex declarative, compound declarative, simple interrogative, &c.

Must you go, and must I remain?
How pleasant it is in summer, but it is not always healthy.
Let me go to school, and I will try to learn.
Forgive me, will you not?
War and Love are strange compeers.
War sheds blood, and Love sheds tears;
War has swords, and Love has darts;
War breaks heads, and Love breaks hearts.
I saw him, when I came home.
No one knew that he was a traitor.

LESSON XIV.

COPULA. — ATTRIBUTE. — LOGICAL PREDICATE. — GRAMMATICAL PREDICATE.

What kind of a sentence is this? — *Horses are strong.*
What is the subject? What is the predicate?
If we leave out *are*, and say *Horses strong*, do we assert anything?
No.

What word, then, in this sentence, asserts?
Are.

What do we call *are?*
The Copula.

What does *strong* express?
It expresses a quality that belongs to horses.

What do we call *strong?*
The Attribute.

LOGICAL AND GRAMMATICAL PREDICATE.

What is an attribute?

It is any word that expresses the quality, state, or condition of the subject.

Taken together, what do the copula and the attribute make up?

Are is the copula; *strong* is the attribute; taken together, they make up the predicate.

Mention some words that are used as the copula in sentences.

Am, is, are, was, were, has been, have been, shall be, may be, &c.

In the sentence *Horses are very strong*, what is the subject? What is the copula? What is the attribute? What is the predicate?

Does the predicate contain any other words than the copula and the attribute?

It contains, besides them, the modifying word *very*.

What is the whole predicate, including the modifying word or words, called?

The Logical Predicate, or the Modified Predicate.

What are the copula and attribute taken together, without any modifying words, called?

The Grammatical Predicate. In the sentence *Horses are very strong*, the grammatical predicate is *are strong*.

Is the grammatical predicate ever the same as the logical predicate?

It is, when the logical predicate does not contain any modifying words.

Give an example.

Scholars should be diligent. Should be diligent is the logical predicate, and, since it is not modified by any words, it is also the grammatical predicate.

Does every predicate have separate words for the copula and the attribute?

No; in some predicates they are united in the same word. Thus, *time flies; flies* is both copula and attribute.

Prove that it is both copula and attribute.

Time flies is the same thing as *time is flying*. In

the latter sentence, *is* is the copula, *flying* is the attribute; therefore *flies*, which is equivalent to *is flying*, is both copula and attribute combined.

In each of the following sentences, name the copula; name the attribute; if they are combined in one word, state in what word they are combined.

Vice is degrading. Virtue is ennobling. Ships sail. Ships are sailing. James writes. James is writing. Boys play. Boys are playing. Stars twinkle. Stars are twinkling.

RECAPITULATION.

Sentences.
- Forms.
  - Simple.
  - Complex.
  - Compound.
- Uses.
  - Declarative,
  - Interrogative,
  - Exclamatory,
  - Imperative,

or Mixed.

LESSON XV.

MODELS OF ANALYSIS.

In analyzing a sentence,—

1. Mention whether it is simple declarative, complex declarative, compound declarative; simple, complex, or compound interrogative; simple, complex, or compound imperative; simple, complex, or compound exclamatory; or compound mixed.

2. If the sentence is simple, mention its grammatical subject, logical subject, grammatical predicate, copula and attribute, logical predicate.

3. If the sentence is complex, mention its leading

assertion, name each of the clauses and state the office of each; mention the grammatical and logical subject, the grammatical predicate, copula, and attribute, and the logical predicate of the leading assertion, and of each clause.

4. If the sentence is compound, select each member: say whether it is declarative, interrogative, imperative, or exclamatory; mention the grammatical and logical subject, the grammatical predicate, copula and attribute, and the logical predicate of the first member. Do the same with each remaining member in turn.

Learn the following models of analysis.

MODEL I. — *Simple Sentence.* How many evils war brings on a country!

This is a simple exclamatory sentence.

The grammatical subject is *war.* The logical subject is *war,* the same as the grammatical subject, because there are no modifying words.

The grammatical predicate is *brings;* copula and attribute are combined in the word *brings.* The logical predicate is *brings how many evils on a country.*

MODEL II. — *Complex Sentence.* Alonzo, who was a youth of great promise, found an early grave.

This is a complex declarative sentence; the leading assertion is *Alonzo found an early grave;* the clause is *who was a youth of great promise,* and it introduces an additional fact respecting *Alonzo.*

The grammatical subject of the leading assertion is *Alonzo;* the logical subject is *Alonzo, who was a youth of great promise.*

The grammatical predicate is *found,* which includes copula and attribute; the logical predicate is *found an early grave.*

The grammatical subject of the clause is *who,* which, being unmodified, is also the logical subject.

The grammatical predicate is *was youth,* consisting of the copula *was* and the attribute *youth;* the logical predicate is *was a youth of great promise.*

MODEL III. — *Compound Sentence.* Napoleon escaped from Elba; but how little did he foresee the consequences of that act!

This is a compound mixed sentence: the first member is *Napoleon escaped from Elba*, which is declarative; the second member is *how little did he foresee the consequences of that act*, which is exclamatory.

The two members are connected by *but*.

The grammatical and logical subject of the first member is *Napoleon*.

The grammatical predicate is *escaped*, which includes copula and attribute; the logical predicate is *escaped from Elba*.

The grammatical and logical subject of the second member is *he*.

The grammatical predicate is *did foresee*, which includes copula and attribute; the logical predicate is *how little did he foresee the consequences of that act*.

LESSON XVI.

EXERCISE IN ANALYSIS.

Analyze the following sentences according to the models given above: —

1. The largest library in the world is at Paris; it contains over 800,000 volumes.

2. How balmy is the air, and how sweetly the birds sing in the groves!

3. The kangaroo and the black swan are found only in Australia and Van Diemen's Land.

4. I know that the stars are shining in the sky.

5. In what manner does the diamond act upon glass, so as to cut it?

6. If the lama is struck by his master, he lies down and looks up towards heaven; large tears flow from his beautiful eyes, and in less than an hour he expires.

7. Let the slothful beware, and let the wicked tremble.

8. The poet Burns was habitually a hard drinker; what a pity it was that he gave way to this vice!

9. A good scholar excels his master.

LESSON XVII.

DIRECTION TO TEACHERS. — Young students should now write at least one composition a week after the models given in Part V. This exercise will enable them to apply the principles of grammar as fast as they have learned them, and will, at the same time, lead them to make intelligent selection of their thoughts.

Advanced pupils may now take up the study of Chapter X. before entering Part II.

REVIEW QUESTIONS.

[The numbers prefixed to the paragraphs refer to the Lessons from which the answers may be obtained.]

IV., V. What is a sentence? How many kinds of sentences are there? Name them. What is a declarative sentence? What is an interrogative sentence? What is an imperative sentence? What is an exclamatory sentence? Give an example of each.

VII., VIII. What is the subject of a sentence? What is the logical subject? What is the grammatical subject? In what sentences is the grammatical subject the same as the logical subject?

IX. What is the predicate of a sentence? What is analysis?

XI. What is a member of a sentence? What is a simple sentence? What is a complex sentence? What is a compound sentence?

XII. What is a compound declarative sentence? What is a compound interrogative sentence? What is a compound imperative sentence? What is a compound exclamatory sentence? What is a compound mixed sentence? Give an example of a compound mixed sentence. On what does the class of a complex sentence depend? What is a clause? What is a complex declarative sentence? What is a complex interrogative sentence? What is a complex imperative sentence? What is a complex exclamatory sentence?

XIII. What do we call that word in the predicate which simply asserts being, such as *am, is, are, was, were*, &c.? What do we call that word in the predicate which stands after the copula and generally expresses quality? What is an attribute? What is the logical predicate of a sentence? What is the grammatical predicate? When are the logical predicate and the grammatical predicate the same?

XIV. Give the directions for analyzing sentences.

According to Model I., analyze the sentence, "How many evils war brings on a country!"

According to Model II., analyze the sentence, "Alonzo, who was a youth of great promise, found an early grave."

According to Model III., analyze the sentence, "Napoleon escaped from Elba; but how little did he foresee the consequences of that act!"

PART II.

WORDS.

ENGLISH Grammar teaches the principles and usages of the English language. These relate,—
1. To letters and the manner of combining them in words;
2. To the classification and derivation of words;
3. To the arrangement of words in sentences;
4. To the arrangement of words in verse.

The first is called Orthography; the second, Etymology; the third, Syntax; and the fourth, Prosody.

CHAPTER I.

CLASSIFICATION OF WORDS.

SECTION I.

WORDS DISTINGUISHED AS PRIMITIVE, DEIVATIVE, AND COMPOUND-DECLINABLE AND INDECLINABLE.

1. A Word is what is spoken or written as the sign of an idea, or a sign to denote the relation between ideas.

Thus in the sentence *Horses are strong*, the words *horses* and *strong* are used to represent ideas, and the copula shows the relation between them. Notice how the relation is changed when the copula is changed to *have been* or *will be.*

2. Etymology is that department of grammar which treats of the derivation, classification, and accidents of words.

3. Words have been formed in different ways. To distinguish them according to their formation, we divide them into three classes:—

CLASSIFICATION OF WORDS. 35

I. Primitive Words, or such as are not formed from any simpler words in the language; as, *sun, flower, garden.*

II. Derivative Words, or such as are formed from simpler ones, by the addition of one or more letters not separately used as words; as, *sunny* (from *sun*), *flowery* (from *flower*), *gardener* (from *garden*).

III. Compound Words, or such as are formed by putting together two or more primitives or derivatives; as, *sun-flower, flower-garden, fire-man, laughter-loving.*

When you are in doubt whether a word is a derivative or a compound, try whether each of the parts of which it is made up, when used by itself, has meaning. If so, it is a compound word; if not, a derivative. — *Manly* is composed of *man* and *ly: ly*, by itself, means nothing; therefore, *manly* is a derivative. — *Man-servant* is composed of *man* and *servant:* each part, used separately, means something; therefore *man-servant* is a compound.

4. Some words may be changed in form; as, *boy, boys; walk, walks.* Such words are said to be Declinable.

Some words do not admit of any change of form; as, *quickly, alas.* Such words are said to be Indeclinable.

EXERCISE.

Tell whether the following words are primitive, derivative, or compound. When you come to a derivative word, tell from what primitive it is formed. When you come to a compound, tell what words unite to form it.

Fire, thirsty, ever, nightly, nevertheless, boatman, books, bookstore, frequent, frequently, house, houses, ice-house, act, action, transact, transacted, write, writing, writing-book, hangman, storehouse, laughter, sugar-loaf, dromedary.

CLASSIFICATION OF WORDS.

SECTION II.

WORDS DISTINGUISHED ACCORDING TO THEIR USES.

5. There are nearly 100,000 words in the English language.

5. Each word has its own part to perform in a sentence, and is placed there for a certain use, as you found in the first two lessons of this book.

I. Some words are used as the names of objects; as, *bird, horse, apple.*

These words are called NOUNS. Any word that denotes an object that we can speak of or think of is a noun. Any noun may be the subject of a sentence.

Pick out the words that are used as the names of objects in the following expressions: — ripe cherries — in London — man is mortal — reading and writing are taught in school.

Mention all the nouns in the seventh exercise on Composition in this book.

Name five other nouns that are the names of things.
Name five other nouns that are the names of animals.

II. Some words are used instead of the names of objects.

I, thou, he, she, it, we, you, they, who, which, &c., are used instead of the names of objects.

These words are called PRONOUNS. They are not very numerous; but they are very useful, because they can take the place of any noun.

Washington was the father of his *country.* We mean Washington was the father of *Washington's* country; but we use *his* instead of the name *Washington's.*

Language would seem very strange to us if there were no pronouns. To express the thought, *Mary has studied* her *lesson, but* she *does not understand* it, we should be obliged to say, *Mary has studied* Mary's *lesson, but* Mary *does not understand* the lesson.

Mention all the pronouns in the seventh exercise on Composition.

III. Some words are used to express the quality of objects, or to limit their meaning. — *A good horse; good* expresses the quality of the horse, or tells what kind of horse is meant. — *Seven days; seven* limits the number of days.

These words are called **ADJECTIVES**. They are generally used with nouns, and are said to *belong* to them.

Pick out the words that qualify, or limit, in the following expressions: — graceful women — three weeks — the ocean — a beautiful sight — in this room — steamboats are useful.

Mention all the adjectives in the seventh exercise on Composition, and state whether they qualify or limit.

In the same exercise, write down all the qualities of the *piece of glass*. Which of the words that you have used are adjectives?

IV. Some words are used to assert. — *Lambs play ; play* asserts that an act is performed by lambs. — *Man is happy ; is* asserts a state respecting man.

These words are called **VERBS**. No assertion can be made without them, and hence they are very important. Most verbs are capable of forming by themselves the predicate of a sentence; as, Time *flies*. The copulas *am, is, are,* &c. mentioned in Lesson XIV. are also verbs. When the attribute expresses quality, it is always an adjective; as, The apples are *sour*. When it expresses condition, it is a noun; as, Franklin was a *philosopher*.

Pick out the words that assert in the following sentences: — Time flies. Pompey was defeated. We shall see. I may be wrong. Look before you leap.

In the seventh exercise on Composition, mention all the verbs that form complete predicates. Mention all the copulas. Mention all the attributes that are adjectives. Mention all the attributes that are nouns.

V. Some words are used to tell when, where, or how an action is performed, or the degree of a quality. — *Yesterday he went there very willingly ; yesterday* tells *when* he went, *there* tells *where* he went, *willingly* tells *how* he went, *very* tells the *degree* of his readiness.

These words are called **ADVERBS**. They are used to modify the meaning of verbs, adjectives, and other adverbs.

Pick out the words that tell when, where, and how an action is performed in the following sentence: — Come here; listen attentively to-day, and you will understand perfectly to-morrow. It is exceedingly sour.

Mention five more words of this kind.

Mention all the adverbs in the seventh exercise on Composition, and state whether they modify verbs, adjectives, or other adverbs.

CLASSIFICATION OF WORDS.

VI. Some words are used to express relations of various kinds; as, *at, in, by, with, for, from, of, out, down, to, up,* &c.

These words are called PREPOSITIONS. They are so called because they are *placed before* nouns. When taken with the nouns with which they are associated, they constitute *adjuncts;* as, *in England.* Adjuncts often take the place of adjectives and adverbs to denote the relations of place, time, manner, possessor, &c.

In exercise seventh on Composition, mention all the prepositions. Mention all the adjuncts. Mention five other prepositions.

VII. Some words are used to connect other words; as, bread *and* cheese.

These words are called CONJUNCTIONS. They have no other office than to connect words and sentences.

And, or, if, but, although, because, for, yet, unless, whether, nor, &c. are used as conjunctions. Some adverbs are frequently used as connectives. They are then termed conjunctive adverbs; as, *when, while, where.*

Mention the conjunctions in exercise seventh on Composition. Mention the conjunctive adverbs. Are there any words in the exercise which you have not mentioned in some one of the preceding classes? If there are any, to what class do the omitted words belong?

VIII. Some words are used to express sudden feelings, such as grief, joy, wonder, disgust, &c.

Oh, ah, alas, hurrah, hark, pshaw, &c. are words of this class.

These words are called INTERJECTIONS. They do not bear any grammatical relation to other words in a sentence.

7. Thus we have eight different classes of words, distinguished from each other by their use, that is, the part they perform in a sentence.

The different classes into which words are divided according to their use are called Parts of Speech.

There are eight Parts of Speech: the Noun, the Pronoun, the Adjective, the Verb, the Adverb, the Preposition, the Conjunction, and the Interjection.

Some words have several different uses; hence the same word may be one part of speech in one sentence, and another in another.

PARTS OF SPEECH.

8. The relations which words bear to each other are denoted either by other words, or by changes in their endings.

Inflection is a change in the termination of a word. When carried through their different inflections, nouns and pronouns are said to be *declined;* adjectives, to be *compared;* and verbs, to be *conjugated.* Some adverbs are *compared,* but prepositions, conjunctions, and interjections are *indeclinable.*

Accidents are the different properties and inflections of the parts of speech.

9. Parsing is the process of telling what part of speech a word is; stating its grammatical properties; and showing its relations to other words.

10. Analysis is the process of separating a sentence into its elements, and defining the office of each element.

RECAPITULATION.

Etymology.	Forms of Words.	Simple; as, *man.* Derivative; as, *manly.* Compound; as, *seaman.*
	Uses of Words.	Noun; as, *bird.* Pronoun; as, *it.* Adjective; as, *good.* Verb; as, *fly.* Adverb; as, *very.* Preposition; as, *above.* Conjunction; as, *and.* Interjection; as, *alas!*
	Accidents of Words.	Person, Number, Gender. Voice, Mood, Tense. Positive, Comparative, and Superlative Degrees.

CHAPTER II.

THE NOUN.

11. A Noun is the name of an object; as, *George, Manchester, tree.*

12. To determine whether any given word is a noun or not, ask whether it is the name of anything that can be thought of or spoken of; if so, it is a noun. We can think of *virtue, vice, goodness, time, light, darkness;* these words, therefore, are nouns. We can speak of *persons, places, rivers, mountains,* &c.; therefore the names that designate these, such as *Cæsar, Paris, Rhine, Andes,* &c., are nouns.

We can think of a *word,* or *letter, figure,* used merely as a term, without reference to its usual meaning; as, *me* is a pronoun; *a* has four sounds; 9 is an odd number. In these sentences, *me, a,* and 9, as well as all words, letters, and figures used in the same way, are nouns.

A noun is sometimes termed a *Substantive,* from a Latin word denoting that which *stands under,* or that which is the *substance* of our thought, whether obtained through the senses or the understanding. Several words jointly performing the office of a noun are termed *Substantive elements.* Phrases and Clauses may be thus used.

EXERCISE.

Mention the *names* of the objects in a school-room.
Mention the *names* of the animals in a farm-yard.
Mention the *names* of the flowers in a garden.
Mention the *names* of the persons and places which you can see or think of.

What part of speech is each of the names you have mentioned? Why?

Place a noun before each of the following predicates, in place of the dash: —

Model. — — is hard.		— are sweet.	
Marble is hard.		*Figs* are sweet.	
— is pleasant.	— is kind.	— are sour.	— run.
— walks.	— reads.	— write.	— mow.
— is high.	— studies.	— play.	— shine.

SECTION I.

Classes of Nouns.

13. The same name may be applied to many different objects belonging to the same class; as, *man, river, mountain.*

If we wish to distinguish an individual belonging to the class, we give it a particular name; as, *Adam, Amazon, Mont Blanc.*

The name *man* may be applied to every male human being, and distinguishes men as a class from every other class of animals, from monkeys, horses, &c. It does not, however, denote any individual; that is, it does not tell us what man is meant. For this a particular name is necessary; as, *Adam, Stephen, Washington.* This gives rise to a division of nouns into two classes.

14. Nouns are divided into two classes, Common and Proper.

A Common Noun is the name that distinguishes one class of objects from another; as, *woman, city, nation.*

A Proper Noun is the name that distinguishes one individual of a class from others of the same class; as, *Victoria, London,* the *Greeks.*

A Complex Noun is a Proper Noun with some title added to it; as, *Mr. James White; Judge Wild; Dr. E. Smith.*

15. When an object without life, or a quality, is spoken to or spoken of as if it had life, it is said to be *personified.* The name of an object personified ceases to be a common noun and becomes a proper noun; as, "O *Time,* how few thy value weigh!" "*Peace* and *Plenty* smile upon the earth."

16. A common noun also becomes proper, when, with the word *the* before it, it denotes some particular place, object, or event, remarkable above others of the same name; as, the *Bar,* the *Park,* the *Common,* the *Deluge.*

17. A proper noun becomes common, when it is used to denote, not an individual, but a whole class having the same general character, properties, or profession as the individual to whom the name belongs; as, "He

is the *Cicero* of his age," — that is, the *great orator* of his age. "He will never become a *Washington*," — that is, *a person with the character of Washington*. In these sentences, *Cicero* and *Washington* are common nouns.

18. Common Nouns embrace Collective, Abstract, and Verbal Nouns.

A Collective Noun is the name of a body or collection of individuals; as, *people, flock, council, assembly.*

An Abstract Noun is the name of some quality; as, *cheerfulness, vanity, goodness, frailty.*

A Verbal Noun is the name of some action or state of being, and ends in *ing;* as, "the *cheering* of the multitude," "the *singing* of birds."

EXERCISE.

Analyze the following sentences according to the models on page 31. Select the nouns, and tell whether they are common or proper; if collective, abstract, verbal, or complex, mention it in addition.

Cambyses, the son of Cyrus, led an army against Amasis.
The Thebans commenced hostilities with the Athenians.
The thoughts of the diligent tend only to plenteousness.
Slothfulness casteth into a deep sleep.
Genius and learning walk in the train of virtue.
In reason and in fact, character goes before scholarship.
Steamboats and railroads are inventions of the present century.
Lord Bacon says, "Conversation makes a ready man; writing, an exact man."
Cabral, a native of Portugal, discovered Brazil.

SECTION II.

Accidents of Nouns.

19. Accidents are the different properties and inflections of the parts of speech.

The accidents of the noun are Person, Number, Gender, and Case.

Person.

20. Person is that accident that distinguishes the speaker, the object spoken to, and the object spoken of.

21. There are three Persons, known as the First, the Second, and the Third.

The First Person denotes the speaker.
The Second Person denotes the person spoken to.
The Third Person denotes the object spoken of.

22. When you wish to know whether a noun is the first, the second, or the third person, ask whether it is the name of the speaker, a person spoken to, or an object spoken of. Thus:—" I, Alexander, make this decree;" *Alexander* is the name of the speaker, and is therefore first person.—" O men, why will ye die?" *men* is the name of the persons spoken to, and is therefore second person.—" All men are mortal;" here, *men* is the name of the objects spoken of, and is therefore third person.

In one of the sentences just given, *men* is *second* person, and in another *third* person; a change in person, therefore, makes no change in the form of the noun.

23. Persons only can speak or be spoken to; therefore, strictly speaking, the names of persons alone can be first or second person. Sometimes, however, animals and things without life are spoken to as persons, and in that case they are second person; as, " O *Death*, where is thy sting?" *Death* is personified, and is second person.

Any noun, no matter what it is the name of, may be third person, because any object can be spoken of. Almost all the nouns that we meet with in sentences are third person.

24. Sometimes a speaker or writer, instead of using his name in the *first* person, uses it in the *third;* as, " Mr. Lewis sends his compliments to Mr. Gray, and requests the pleasure of his company on Wednesday evening." Here *Mr. Lewis* is the speaker; but instead of saying *I send*, or *I, Mr. Lewis, send*, he uses the third person, *Mr. Lewis sends*. This is a polite form of address often employed in invitations.

So, the third person is sometimes used for the second, as a more respectful form of address. In asking my father's forgiveness, instead of saying, " Father, forgive me!" (in which case, *father* would be second person), I may say to him, " I hope my father will forgive me." In this case, *father* is third person.

NUMBER.

EXERCISE.

Analyze the following sentences according to the models given. Point out the nouns; name their class and person.

Thou, a worm, and I, another worm, will soon pass away from earth. Captain S. R. Jones will be happy to see Mr. I. Dewitt at his office on board of the Commodore as soon as convenient. O Grave, where is thy victory? He is full of charity, and does not charity cover a multitude of sins? I, James Porter, hereby leave my brother Robert all my houses and lands, steamboats and railroad stock.

Number.

25. Number is the accident that distinguishes one from more than one.

26. There are two Numbers, the Singular and the Plural.

The Singular Number denotes one.
The Plural Number denotes more than one.

Boy is in the singular number, because it denotes one; *boys* is in the plural number, because it denotes more than one.

27. *Rules for forming the Plural Number.*

RULE I.— The plural of nouns is generally formed by adding *s* to the singular; as, road, *roads ;* mountain, *mountains.*

Annexing *s* to a word, to make it plural, often gives it an additional syllable. This is the case when the *s* does not unite in sound with the syllable to which it is added; thus, the plurals of *horse, house, page, rose,* &c., have two syllables; as *hors-es, hous-es,* &c.

RULE II.— Nouns ending in *x, z, ss, sh,* or *ch* soft, form their plural by adding *es* to the singular; as, fox, *foxes ;* glass, *glasses ;* adz, *adzes ;* lash, *lashes ;* church, *churches.*

RULE III. — Most nouns ending in *f* or *fe* form their

plural by changing these letters into *ves;* as, wife, *wives;* loaf, *loaves.*

Except the following nouns, which, with their compounds, form the plural regularly by adding *s:*—*strife, fife, safe, brief, chief, grief, kerchief, mischief, dwarf, scarf, turf, surf, gulf, roof, proof, hoof, reef, serf,* and all nouns ending in *ff.* Wharf has two plurals, *wharves* and *wharfs.*

Staff, as a military term (the *staff* of a general, that is the body of officers attending him), makes *staffs* in the plural. *Staff,* a cane, makes *staffs* and *staves* (the *a* in this latter word must have the same sound as in the singular, *staff*). The compounds of *staff* add *s,* to form their plural; as, distaff, *distaffs,* flag-staff, *flag-staffs.*

RULE IV.— Nouns ending in *y* preceded by a consonant form their plural by changing the final *y* of the singular into *ies.* Nouns ending in *y* preceded by a vowel form their plural regularly; as, cry, *cries;* study, *studies;* valley, *valleys;* boy, *boys.*

RULE V.— Nouns ending in *eo, io, oo,* and *uo* form their plural by adding *s* to the singular; as, cameo, *cameos;* folio, *folios;* bamboo, *bamboos;* duo, *duos.*

Nouns ending in *o,* preceded by any other letter than *e, i, o* or *u,* form their plural by adding *es* to the singular; as, hero, *heroes;* potato, *potatoes.*

Except junto, *juntos;* canto, *cantos;* tyro, *tyros;* grotto, *grottos;* portico, *porticos;* solo, *solos;* quarto, *quartos;* octavo, *octavos;* duodecimo, *duodecimos;* halo, *halos.*

Irregular Plurals.

28. The plural of the following nouns is irregular:—

Singular.	Plural.	Singular.	Plural.
Man	men	Tooth	teeth
Child	children	Louse	lice
Woman	women	Goose	geese
Ox	oxen	Mouse	mice

29. Words ending in *man* form their plural in *men* when they are compounds of the word *man;* as, alderman, *aldermen;* statesman, *statesmen;* boatman, *boatmen.* When they are not compounds of the word *man,* they form their plural in *mans;* as, Turcoman, *Turcomans;* Mussulman, *Mussulmans;* talisman, *talismans.*

30. The following nouns have **two** plurals, one regular and the other irregular, according to their meaning:—

Singular.	Plural.	Plural.
Brother	brothers (of one family)	brethren (of one society)
Die	dies (for coining)	dice (for gaming)
Genius	geniuses (persons of genius)	genii (spirits)
Index	indexes (tables)	indices (algebraic signs)
Pea	peas (separate seeds)	pease (a quantity of grain)
Penny	pennies (separate coins)	pence (a sum of money).

31. Some nouns are the same in the plural as in the singular; as, *deer, sheep, salmon, bellows, cannon, means, series, species.*

32. *Fish*, in the plural, makes either *fish* or *fishes*. *Summons* makes *summons* or *summonses*. *Gallows* makes *gallows*, vulgarly, *gallowses*. *Sail*, a piece of canvas, makes *sails;* *sail*, a vessel, makes *sail*,—as, "Thirty *sail* were seen in the bay, with their *sails* torn."

33. The nouns *pair, brace*, and some others, when preceded by a word expressing number, have the same form in the plural as in the singular; but when not so preceded, they form their plural by adding *s* or *es* to the singular. We say *two pair, three brace*, but *by pairs and braces.*

Plural of Foreign Words.

34. Many nouns taken from foreign languages without change, retain their former plural in English. A few general rules for these nouns follow.

I. Foreign nouns ending in *on* and *um*, in the plural change these terminations into *a*.

II. Foreign nouns ending in *a*, in the plural generally change *a* into *æ*, but sometimes into *ata*.

III. Foreign nouns ending in *us*, in the plural generally change *us* into *i*, but sometimes into *era*.

IV. Foreign nouns ending in *is*, in the plural generally change *is* into *es*, but sometimes into *ides*.

Examples of these rules will be found in the following alphabetical table.

35. When words adopted from foreign languages come into common use, they very often, besides their foreign form, take a regular English

PLURAL OF FOREIGN WORDS.

plural in *s* or *es*. Such words as do this have the letter R placed after their foreign plural in the table. When, therefore, the letter R occurs, mention both forms; as, *apex, apices,* and *apexes.*

Singular.	Plural.	Singular.	Plural.
Alumnus	alumni	Gymnasium	gymnasia, R.
Amanuensis	amanuenses	Hypothesis	hypotheses
Analysis	analyses	Ignis fatuus	ignes fatui
Animalculum	animalcula	Lamina	lamina
Antithesis	antitheses	Larva	larvæ
Apex	apices, R.	Medium	media, R.
Appendix	appendices, R.	Memorandum	memoranda, R.
Arcanum	arcana	Metamorphosis	metamorphoses
Automaton	automata, R.	Miasma	miasmata
Axis	axes	Momentum	momenta, R.
Bandit	banditti, R.	Monsieur	messieurs
Basis	bases	Nebula	nebulæ
Beau	beaux, R.	Oasis	oases
Calx	calces, R.	Parenthesis	parentheses
Cherub	cherubim, R.	Phasis	phases
Chrysalis	chrysalides	Phenomenon	phenomena
Datum	data	Radius	radii
Desideratum	desiderata	Scholium	scholia, R.
Diæresis	diæreses	Scoria	scoriæ
Effluvium	effluvia	Seraph	seraphim, R.
Ellipsis	ellipses	Speculum	specula
Emphasis	emphases	Stamen	stamina, R.
Encomium	encomia, R.	Stimulus	stimuli
Ephemeris	ephemerides	Stratum	strata
Erratum	errata	Thesis	theses
Focus	foci	Vertebra	vertebræ
Formula	formulæ, R.	Vertex	vertices, R.
Fungus	fungi, R.	Virtuoso	virtuosi
Genus	genera	Vortex	vortices, R.

Plural of Compound Nouns, Letters, &c.

36. Most compound nouns, in which the principal word stands first, vary the principal word to form their plural; as, mother-in-law, *mothers-in-law;* court-martial, *courts-martial;* commander-in-chief, *commanders-in-chief.*

37. In a few compounds, both words take the plural form; as, man-servant, *men-servants;* woman-servant, *women-servants.*

38. Nouns ending in *ful* and *full*, and compounds in which the principal word stands last, annex *s* or *es*, to form their plural; as, spoonful, *spoonfuls;* bowl-full, *bowl-fulls;* man-trap, *man-traps;* step-son, *step-sons.*

39. The names of letters, figures, &c., used merely as names, take an apostrophe (') and the letter *s*, to form their plural; as, "Your *a's* and *o's* are too small;" "the 7*'s* and 8*'s;*" "do not omit the +*'s.*"

Other parts of speech used as nouns either want the plural, or form it regularly; as, His *buts* and *ifs.*

Plural of Proper Nouns.

40. Proper nouns generally have no plural; as, *Edith, Plantagenet, London, Plato.*

41. The proper names of races, communities, and nations, and proper nouns applied to several individuals of the same family, name, or character, have a plural regularly formed; as, the *Turks*, the *Mormons*, the *Germans*, the *Plantagenets;* there are two *Londons* on the map.

42. Complex nouns, preceded by a word expressing number (such as *two, three, four*), or when the title prefixed to the name is *Mrs.*, add the plural termination to the name, and not to the title; as, "the two *Lord Coxes*," NOT "the two *Lords Cox;*" "the *Mrs. Grays.*"

43. Complex nouns that have any other title than *Mrs.* prefixed to the name, and are not preceded by a word expressing number, add the plural termination either to the title or the name, but not to both; as, "the *Misses Brush*," or "the *Miss Brushes*," — but NOT "the *Misses Brushes;*" "the *Messrs. Browning*," or "the *Mister Brownings*," — but NOT "the *Messrs. Brownings.*"

44. When the title is applied to two different names, the title alone can receive the plural termination; as, "*Lords* Cox and Shrewsbury;" "the *Misses* Brush and Forrester;" "the *Misses* Jane and Sarah Brush;' "*Messrs.* Haines and Herrick;" "*Generals* Lambert and Packenham."

Nouns found only in one Number.

45. Some nouns, from the nature of the things they denote, have no plural.

NOUNS OF ONLY ONE NUMBER. 49

These are, — 1. The names of the metals; as, *gold, lead.* 2. The names of virtues and vices; as, *prudence, indolence.* 3. The names of things weighed and measured, except when applied to different varieties of the same articles; as, *flour, wheat, molasses.* 4. The names of arts and sciences; as, *music, algebra.* 5. The names of some diseases; as, *cholera, measles.*

The word *news* is now used only in the singular. The same may be said of the names of sciences ending in *s*; as, *mathematics, optics,* &c.

46. Some nouns have no singular. A table of some of these follows: —

Annals	Calends	Hysterics	Nones
Antipodes	Clothes	Ides	Riches
Archives	Drawers (an article	Literati	Shambles
Ashes	of dress)	Lees	Thanks
Assets	Dregs	Letters (literature)	Tidings
Billiards	Entrails	Manners	Vespers
Bitters	Goods	Matins	Victuals
Bowels	Hatches	Minutiæ	Vitals
Breeches	Hose (stockings)	Morals	Wages

Add to the above the names of things consisting of two parts; as, *nippers, pincers, scissors, shears, snuffers, tongs.*

EXERCISE.

I. Spell the plural of each of the following nouns: —

Tax; brush; gas; monkey; attorney; fly; lady; liberty; city; berry; prodigy; nuncio; negro; portico; motto; punctilio; tyro; elf; wolf; leaf; half; thief; handkerchief; life; knife; staff; flagstaff; brother; foot; emphasis; handful; penny; genus; index; father-in-law; brother-in-law; genius; seaman; soliloquy; washerwoman; dormouse; talisman; sheep; ignus fatuus; bean; ox-cart; Miss Black; seraph; step-daughter; Master Vail; Henry; way; pair.

II. Analyze each of the following sentences. Select the nouns in order, state to what class they belong, and give the person and number of each.

1. Mechanics and Optics are branches of Physics.
2. The commander-in-chief of the army was a field-marshal.
3. How many sheep and oxen are killed every year!

4

4. I, Paul, have written this letter with my own hand.
5. Oats, wheat, and barley flourish in England.
6. Will you cross the ocean, O mighty queen?
7. What means have you of learning the news?

Gender.

47. Gender is the accident that distinguishes objects with respect to sex.

48. There are three genders; the Masculine, the Feminine, and the Neuter.

The Masculine Gender denotes male animals.

The Feminine Gender denotes female animals.

The Neuter Gender denotes that which is neither male nor female.

49. Some names are equally applicable to males or females; thus, *parent* may denote either *father* or *mother;* *child* may denote either *son* or *daughter.* The gender of such a noun depends on the sex of the object referred to. If applied to a male, its gender is masculine; if to a female, feminine; if it cannot be determined whether it is applied to a male or a female, it may be parsed as "masculine or feminine gender."

50. Things without life have no sex, and therefore their names are neuter gender. Sometimes, however, they are figuratively spoken of as having sex. Thus we say of a ship, "*She* [instead of *it*] sails well;" and of the sun, "*He* [instead of *it*] is rising." When objects of great power, size, or sublimity (such as *death,* the *sun, winter, war*) are thus spoken of, their names become masculine; whereas objects distinguished for beauty, pleasantness, or fruitfulness (such as the *earth,* the *moon, spring, peace*) are spoken of as feminine.

51. The names of animals, strictly speaking, are either masculine or feminine. Sometimes, however, when it is not important to regard the distinction of sex, the name of an animal is made neuter gender; as, "I raised a *goat,* and sold *it* [not *him* or *her*]." "That child knows *its* father."

52. When we use the name of an animal in a general way, to denote the whole species and not any particular individual, if the species is remarkable for boldness, strength, or ferocity, it is spoken of as masculine; but, if distinguished for gentleness, weakness, or timidity, it is made feminine. "The *lion* takes up *his* abode in deserts." "The *cat* is noted for *her* love of home."

53. Masculine nouns are used to denote persons of a certain profession

or occupation spoken of generally as a class, even though females are included in the class; as, "*Poets* are entitled to the gratitude of the world," — meaning *poetesses* as well as *poets*. But if the reference is to an individual and not to a class, when there is a distinct form for each gender, the form appropriate to the sex of the individual should be used; as, "the *poet* Homer," "the *poetess* Sappho."

54. Collective nouns, when conveying the idea of unity, or when used in the plural form, are considered as neuter; as, The *army* destroyed everything in *its* course; but when reference is made to the objects composing the collection as individuals, they take the gender of the individuals denoted.

Modes of distinguishing the Genders.

55. Some masculine nouns have corresponding feminine nouns.

The feminine nouns are distinguished from their corresponding masculine nouns in three ways.

I. They may be entirely different words, as in the following list: —

Masculine.	Feminine.	Masculine.	Feminine.	Masculine.	Feminine.
Beau	belle	Gander	goose	Man	woman
Boy	girl	Gentleman	lady	Master	mistress
Brother	sister	Hart	roe	Nephew	niece
Buck	doe	Horse	mare	Papa	mamma
Bull	cow	Husband	wife	Ram *or* buck	ewe
Drake	duck	King	queen	Son	daughter
Earl	countess	Lad	lass	Stag	hind
Father	mother	Lord	lady	Uncle	aunt
Friar *or* monk	nun	Male	female	Wizard	witch

II. They may have different terminations. The three principal feminine terminations are *ess, ine*, and *ix;* as will be seen from the list below: —

Masculine.	Feminine.	Masculine.	Feminine.
Abbott	abbess	Bridegroom	bride
Actor	actress	Count	countess
Administrator	administratrix	Czar	czarina
Ambassador	ambassadress	Dauphin	dauphiness
Author	authoress	Duke	duchess
Baron	baroness	Emperor	empress
Benefactor	benefactress	Enchanter	enchantress

CASE.

Masculine.	Feminine.	Masculine.	Feminine.
Executor	executrix	Poet	poetess
Governor	governess	Priest	priestess
Heir	heiress	Prince	princess
Hero	heroine	Prior	prioress
Host	hostess	Prophet	prophetess
Hunter	huntress	Shepherd	shepherdess
Jew	Jewess	Sultan	sultaness *or* sultana
Landgrave	landgravine	Testator	testatrix
Margrave	margravine	Tiger	tigress
Marquis	marchioness	Tutor	tutoress
Negro	negress	Widower	widow
Peer	peeress		

III. In the case of compounds, they may change one of the words compounded. Examples follow.

Landlord	landlady	Man-servant	maid-servant
Gentleman	gentlewoman	Cock-sparrow	hen-sparrow
Peacock	peahen	Father-in-law	mother-in-law
He-goat	she-goat	Step-son	step-daughter

EXERCISE.

Analyze each of the following sentences. Select the nouns; state their class, and give the person, number, and gender of each.

1. The Countess of Devonshire and her nephew, the Marquis, are noted for their amiability. 2. Are lords and ladies, peers and peeresses, any better than other men and women? 3. An earl's wife is called countess; but what is a marquis's wife called? 4. Sun, moon, and stars, comets and planets, were Herschel's constant study.

Case.

56. Case is that accident of the noun that denotes its relation to other words.

57. There are three cases; the Nominative, the Possessive, and the Objective.

58. The Nominative Case usually denotes the relation which the grammatical subject bears to a finite

verb. "Edward is reading;" *Edward* is the grammatical subject, and is in the nominative case. (See Lesson VIII.)

<small>The nominative case may also be used, —
1. As the Attribute of a sentence after the copula. Thus used it is termed the Predicate Nominative; as, Paul was an *apostle*.
2. Without dependence on any other word. Thus used it is termed the Nominative Absolute; as, "The *fathers*, — where are they?"</small>

59. The Possessive Case denotes the relation of ownership or origin; as, "The Mayor's hat;" *Mayor's* is in the possessive case.

<small>The relation of ownership may also be denoted by the verb *belong*, and by the preposition *of*; but nouns used after these words are in the objective case; as, "The hat belongs to the Mayor." "The hat of the Mayor."
A noun in the possessive case is usually joined to another denoting a different person or thing.</small>

60. The Objective Case is used, —

1. To denote the object in the predicate of a sentence that receives an action. "James struck Edward;" here *Edward* is in the predicate, and receives the action expressed by the verb *struck;* it is therefore in the objective case.

2. To denote the object of such relations as are expressed by *at, in, with, from, for,* and similar words called prepositions; as, at home, in Philadelphia, by faith, with dignity, from Europe, for my sake. The nouns *home, Philadelphia, faith, dignity, Europe,* and *sake* are all in the objective case.

3. To denote time, value, distance, and direction, without a governing word; as, "This *year* I shall go *south*."

<small>61. Nouns are used in the same case, when one noun is joined to another denoting the same person, place, or thing, in order to explain or identify it. In such constructions the explanatory noun is said to be *in apposition with* the other; as, Peter, *the hermit*, convinced Philip, *the king*.</small>

62. *Rules for forming the Cases.*

1. The objective case is like the nominative in both numbers. In the examples just given, *Edward* was found to be nominative case in one sentence, and objective in another.

II. The possessive singular is formed from the nominative singular by adding an apostrophe (') and *s ;* as, *dog, dog's ;* Charles, *Charles's.*

III. The possessive plural is formed from the nominative plural by adding an apostrophe to it if it ends in *s,* and an apostrophe and *s* if it ends in any other letter; as, boys, *boys' ;* men, *men's.*

When the last syllable of a word contains several *s* sounds, its possessive case is formed by adding an apostrophe alone; as, *Moses'* father, not *Moses's* father. So, when a word ending with an *s* sound stands before another word commencing with the same sound, the possessive case of the former takes the apostrophe alone; as, "for *conscience'* sake;" "*Charles'* sins." In both these cases, the object is to prevent the two frequent recurrence of the unpleasant hissing sound of *s.*

SECTION III.

Declension of Nouns.

63. Declension is the regular variation of the cases of nouns and pronouns in both numbers.

EXAMPLES.

	Singular.	Plural.		Singular.	Plural.
Nom.	King,	kings,		City,	cities,
Poss.	king's,	kings',		city's,	cities',
Obj.	king.	kings.		city.	cities.
Nom.	Man,	men,		Moses,	———
Poss.	man's,	men's,		Moses',	———
Obj.	man.	men.		Moses.	———
Nom.	Goose,	geese,		Gold,	———
Poss.	goose's,	geese's,		gold's,	———
Obj.	goose.	geese.		gold.	———

DECLENSION OF NOUNS.

EXERCISE.

I. Spell the objective plural of the following nouns:

Lad, key, negro, money, bamboo, knight-errant, lady, ice-house, fife, tooth, wife, ox, wolf, fisherman, Mussulman.

II. Spell the possessive singular of the following nouns:—

Desk, rat-trap, stove, Darius, cow, Barnabas, Xerxes, Thomas, city, goose, step-daughter, sister-in-law.

III. Spell the possessive plural of the following nouns:—

Woman, child, head, boatman, hero, city, goose, flag-staff, vespers, pincers, scissors, mouse, book, potato, house, step-father.

IV. Analyze the following sentences. Select the nouns, state their class, and give the person, number, gender, and case of each. Always observe the order just given.

Form for parsing. — Noun, class, person, number, gender, case; rule.

Parsing Model. — The man's dog bit James.

1. *Man's* is a common noun, third person, singular number, masculine gender, and possessive case, because it limits *dog*, according to Rule IX. *A noun or pronoun which limits the meaning of a noun denoting a different person or thing, is put in the possessive.*

2. *Dog* is a common noun, third person, singular number, masculine gender, and nominative case, because it is the subject of the verb *bit*, according to Rule II. *The subject of a finite verb is in the nominative case.*

3. *James* is a proper noun, third person, singular number, masculine gender, and objective case, because it is the object of the verb *bit*, according to Rule X. *The object of a transitive verb or a preposition is put in the objective case.*

Franklin, the philosopher, was a native of Boston.

4. *Philosopher* is a common noun, third person, singular number, masculine gender, nominative case, and is in *apposition* with *Franklin*, according to Rule I. *A noun or pronoun annexed to another noun or pronoun and denoting the same person or thing, is put by apposition in the same case.*

5. *Native* is a common noun, third person, singular number, masculine gender, and nominative case, because it is used as the attribute after

the intransitive verb *was*, according to Rule IV. *A noun or pronoun in the predicate after an intransitive verb, and the passive of certain transitive verbs, is put in the same case as the subject, when both words refer to the same person or thing.*

NOTE.—The teacher may anticipate the rules of Syntax or not, at his option. The most important rules will be given in the parsing models.

The sun's rays disperse the darkness. The youth's diligence deserves praise. They took Joseph's coat, and killed a kid of the goats, and dipped the coat in the blood. The attraction of gravitation was discovered by Sir Isaac Newton ; but how little did Newton himself realize the importance of that discovery! Where are the Platos and the Aristotles of modern times? Bonaparte swayed the destinies of Europe for a time; but was he not finally defeated? The prince obeys the king's command. Arnold's treason disgraced his name.

RECAPITULATION.

Noun.
- Proper.
  - Proper; as, *Washington.*
  - Complex; as, *Dr. Franklin.*
- Common.
  - Common; as, *tree.*
  - Collective; as, *army.*
  - Abstract; as, *vanity.*
  - Verbal; as, *singing.*

Accidents of Nouns.
- Person.
  - First.
  - Second.
  - Third.
- Number.
  - Singular.
  - Plural.
- Gender.
  - Masculine.
  - Feminine.
  - Neuter.
- Case.
  - Nominative.
  - Possessive.
  - Objective.

REVIEW QUESTIONS ON CHAPTERS I., II.

[The numbers prefixed to the following questions refer to the numbered paragraphs of Part II., from which the answers may be obtained.]

What is English Grammar? Into what four parts is it divided? To what does each relate? 1. What is a word? 2. Define Etymology. 3. What is a primitive word? What is a derivative word? What is a compound word? How may you tell whether a word is a derivative or a compound? 4. When are words said to be declinable? When are words said to be indeclinable? 5. How many words are there in the English language? 6. What are nouns? pronouns? adjectives? verbs? adverbs? prepositions? conjunctions? interjections? 7. What are parts of speech? How many parts of speech are there? 8. Which of the parts of speech are declinable? Which are indeclinable? Define Inflection. Define Accidents. 9. What is parsing? 10. What is analysis?

11. What is a noun? What is a substantive element? 12. How may we determine whether any given word is a noun or not? 14. Into how many classes are nouns divided? What is a common noun? What is a proper noun? 15, 16. In what two cases do common nouns become proper? 17. When does a proper noun become common? 18. Into what other classes are nouns divided? What is a collective noun? What is an abstract noun? What is a verbal noun? What is a complex noun?

19. How many accidents has the noun? Name them.

20. What is person? 21. How many persons are there? Name them. What does the first person denote? The second person? The third person? 22. How may you determine what person a noun is? 24. Show how the third person sometimes takes the place of the first and the second.

25. What is number? 26. How many numbers are there? Name them. What does the singular number denote? What does the plural number denote? 27. Repeat Rule I. for forming the plural of nouns. Repeat Rule II. Repeat Rule III. Mention the words in *fe* and *f* that are exceptions to this rule. What is the plural of *staff* used as a military term? What is the plural of *staff*, a cane? Repeat Rule IV. Repeat Rule V. Mention the exceptions to this rule.

28. What is the plural of *child?* Of *mouse?* What is the singular of *women?* Of *teeth?* Of *geese?*

29. How do words ending in *man* form their plural? 30. Give the two plurals of *brother*, and the meaning of each. Of *die*. Of *genius*. Of *pea*. Of *penny*.

31. What is the plural of *deer?* Of *cannon?* Of *fish?* Of *summons?* Of *gallows?* Of *sail?* Of *pair* and *brace?*

34. What is said of the plural of many nouns taken from foreign lan-

guages? How is the plural of foreign nouns ending in *on* and *um* formed? Of foreign nouns ending in *a?* Of foreign nouns ending in *us?* Of foreign nouns ending in *is?* What is the plural of *amanuensis?* Of *automaton?* Of *cherub?* Of *gymnasium?* Of *vertebra?* Of *radius?* What is the singular of *memoranda?* Of *phenomena?* Of *indices?* Of *data?* Of *oases?*

36. How do most compound words in which the principal word stands first form their plural? 37. How do a few compounds, like *man-servant*, form their plural? 38. How do compounds ending in *ful* or *full* form their plural? How do compounds in which the principal word stands last form their plural? 39. How do the names of letters, figures, &c., used merely as names, form their plural? When other parts of speech are used as nouns, how do they form their plural?

40. What nouns generally have no plural? 41. When do proper nouns have a regularly formed plural? 42. How do complex nouns form their plural, when they are preceded by a word expressing number? How when the title prefixed to the name is *Mrs.?* 43. How do complex nouns form their plural when they are not preceded by a word expressing number, and when the title prefixed to the name is not *Mrs.?* 44. What is the rule for forming the plural when the title is applied to two different names?

45. What classes of nouns have no plural? How is the word *news* now used? 46. Name some of the nouns that have no singular.

47. What is gender? 48. How many genders are there? Name them. What does the masculine gender denote? What does the feminine gender denote? What does the neuter gender denote? 49. When is a noun said to be of "masculine or feminine gender"?

50. What is the gender of things without life? When objects without life are figuratively spoken of as having sex, which are made masculine? Which, feminine? 51. What gender is the name of an animal sometimes made? 52. Give the rule that applies when we use the name of an animal in a general way. 53. What gender is used to denote persons of a certain profession, spoken of generally? What gender must be used when reference is made to an individual?

55. In how many ways are feminine nouns distinguished from the corresponding masculine nouns? Mention these three ways. What is the feminine of *hart?* Of *nephew?* Of *marquis?* Of *duke?* Of *peacock?* Of *step-son?*

56. What is case? 57. How many cases are there? Name them. 58. What does the nominative case denote? 59. What does the possessive case denote? How may the relation of ownership be denoted without the possessive case? 60. What does the objective case denote? For what purposes is the nominative case used? the possessive? the objective? When are nouns in apposition? 61. What is the objective case like? How is the possessive singular formed? How is the possessive plural formed? 62. When does the possessive case take the apostrophe alone?

63. Define Declension. Decline the noun *king*. Decline *lady; fireman, Charles; ox; silver*. Give the form for parsing a noun.

CHAPTER III.

THE PRONOUN.

64. A Pronoun is a word used instead of a noun.

"He reads." "She writes." "I study." In these sentences, *he*, *she*, and *I* stand for the names of the persons referred to, and are therefore pronouns.

"The boy who plays;" "the cat which mews;" *who*, standing for *boy*, and *which*, standing for *cat*, are pronouns.

SECTION I.

CLASSES OF PRONOUNS.

65. Pronouns are divided into four classes; Personal, Possessive, Relative, and Interrogative.

66. A Personal Pronoun is one that both represents a noun and shows by its form whether it is of the first, second, or third person; as, *I, thou, he.*

When I say, "*he* writes," instead of "*Henry* writes," *he* both stands for the noun *Henry* and shows by its form that it is of the third person.

67. A Possessive Pronoun is one that represents at the same time the possessor and the thing possessed.

"Your house is on the plain; *ours* is on the hill." Here *ours* stands for *our house,*—*our*, the possessor, and *house*, the thing possessed; therefore *ours* is a possessive pronoun.

68. A Relative Pronoun is one that relates to a preceding noun, pronoun, or equivalent expression, called its Antecedent.

69. The term *antecedent* means *going before;* and the word in question is so called because it generally goes before the pronoun.—"Napoleon, *who* had escaped from Elba, was defeated at Waterloo." *Who* is a relative pronoun, relating to the noun *Napoleon* as its antecedent.

The antecedent is sometimes omitted, in which case it is said to be *understood;* as, "Who steals my purse, steals trash." The antecedent of the relative *who* is *person* understood,— "[*The person*] who steals my purse, steals trash."

70. **An Interrogative Pronoun is one that is used for asking a question.**

"*Who* is there?" "*Which* of my sons has returned?" "*What* do I hear?" The word *who* is used for asking the first question, *which* for the second, and *what* for the third; they are therefore interrogative pronouns.

Questions are also introduced by adverbs, or are asked without introductory words; as *When did he come? Have you learned your lesson?*

The noun which the interrogative pronoun represents is always in the answer to the question, and is therefore unknown, or unmentioned. When interrogative propositions are incorporated into complex sentences, the proposition often loses much of its interrogative character; but as the noun for which the pronoun stands is unknown or unmentioned, the pronoun must still be regarded as interrogative; hence,—

The Interrogative Pronouns are also used in indirect questions, indefinite answers to direct questions, and dependent expressions of similar construction; as, "I asked *who* was there." "I do not know *which* of your sons has returned." "We all learn, sooner or later, *what* the world is."

SECTION II.
ACCIDENTS OF PRONOUNS.

71. **Pronouns have the same four accidents as nouns; Person, Number, Gender, and Case.**

72. **The person, number, and gender of a pronoun are always the same as those of its antecedent.**

Sometimes the form of a pronoun indicates its person, number, gender, and case. Thus *he* is always third person, because it denotes the person spoken of; singular number, because it refers to but one; masculine gender, because it is applied only to male animals; and nominative case, because it denotes the relation expressed by the subject of the verb. Some pronouns, however, do not change their form in the different persons and numbers, genders and cases. Thus we may say, " The man that laughs," " The woman that sings," " The fire that burns." In the first of these expressions, the pronoun *that* is *masculine*, since it relates to *man*; in the second, it is *feminine*, since it relates to *woman*; in the third, it is *neuter*, since it relates to *fire*. In such a case, the only way of determining the gender of a pronoun is to refer to its antecedent.

SECTION III.

DECLENSION OF PRONOUNS.

Personal Pronouns.

73. The Personal Pronouns are subdivided into Simple Personals and Compound Personals.

Simple Personal Pronouns.

74. There is one simple personal pronoun of the first person, — *I*. It is either masculine or feminine gender, according to the sex of the speaker.

There is one simple personal pronoun of the second person, — *thou*. It is either masculine or feminine, according to the sex of the person spoken to.

There are three simple personal pronouns of the third person, — *he*, masculine; *she*, feminine; and *it*, neuter.

75. The simple personal pronouns are declined as follows: —

	FIRST PERSON.		SECOND PERSON.	
	Singular.	*Plural.*	*Singular.*	*Plural.*
Nom.	I,	we,	Thou,	you, ye,
Poss.	my, mine,	our,	thy, thine,	your,
Obj.	me,	us.	thee,	you.

		THIRD PERSON.				
Singular.	*Plural.*	*Siugnlar.*	*Plural.*	*Singular.*	*Plural.*	
Nom.	He,	they,	She,	they,	It,	they,
Poss.	his,	their,	her,	their,	its,	their,
Obj.	him,	them.	her,	them.	it,	them.

76. *Mine* and *thine* were formerly used instead of *my* and *thy* before nouns beginning with *a, e, i, o,* and *u* not involving the sound of *y;* as, *mine* eye, *thine* urn. This usage is now retained only in solemn style.

REMARKS ON THE SIMPLE PERSONAL PRONOUNS.

77. In editorials and royal proclamations, *we* is often used instead of *I*, when but one person is referred to; as, " *We*, George III., king of Great Britain and Ireland, do hereby proclaim," &c.

78. *Thou, thy, thine*, and *thee* are seldom used, except in solemn or poetical style. *You* and *your* take their place, representing nouns in the singular as well as the plural number. We say, " How do *you* do ? " whether we refer to one person or more than one.

79. *Ye*, which is one of the forms of the nominative plural of *thou*, is very little used, except in solemn or poetical style.

80. *It* is sometimes thrown in after a word expressing action merely for the sound, without referring to any antecedent or adding anything to the sense; as, " Trip *it* in the mazy dance.

It is also used in the nominative case as the grammatical subject of a sentence, without referring to any particular antecedent; as, " *It* is he." " *It* thunders."

81. Observe that the apostrophe ('), which is the distinguishing mark of the possessive case of nouns, is not used in the possessive case of personal pronouns; we write *its*, NOT *it's*.

Compound Personal Pronouns.

82. The compound personal pronouns are formed by combining the word *self* with certain cases of the simple personals.

83. There are two compound personal pronouns of the first person, — *myself* and *ourself*. They are either masculine or feminine, according to the sex of the speaker.

Ourself corresponds with the simple personal *we*, as used in editorials and royal proclamations with reference to a singular noun.

84. There are two compound personal pronouns of the second person, — *thyself* and *yourself*. They are either masculine or feminine, according to the sex of the person spoken to.

COMPOUND PERSONAL PRONOUNS. 63

Yourself corresponds with the simple personal *you*, as used in ordinary discourse with reference to a singular noun.

85. There are three compound personal pronouns of the third person, — *himself,* masculine ; *herself,* feminine ; and *itself,* neuter.

86. The compound personals have no possessive case. They are the same in the objective as in the nominative, and are declined as follows : —

FIRST PERSON.

	Singular.		Plural.
Nom.	Myself,	*Nom.* ourselves,	
Obj.	myself,	*Obj.* ourselves.	
Nom.	Ourself,		
Obj.	ourself,		

SECOND PERSON.

	Singular.		Plural.
Nom.	Thyself,	*Nom.* yourselves,	
Obj.	thyself,	*Obj* yourselves.	
Nom.	Yourself,		
Obj.	yourself,		

THIRD PERSON.

	Singular.	Plural.	Singular.	Plural.	Singular.	Plural.
Nom.	Himself,	themselves,	Herself,	themselves,	Itself,	themselves,
Obj.	himself,	themselves.	herself,	themselves.	itself,	themselves.

87. The syntactical relations of pronouns are generally the same as those of nouns. They have the same accidents and office in the sentence.

Personal pronouns are parsed by declining them, and then stating their person, number, gender, case, and rule.

PARSING MODEL. — Parse the pronouns in the sentence, "I thought she hurt herself."

I is a simple personal pronoun, thus declined: Nom. *I*, poss. *my*, obj. *me ;* plural, nom. *we*, poss. *our*, obj. *us*. It is found in the first person, singular number, masculine or feminine gender, and is in the nominative case, because it is the subject of the verb *thought,* according to Rule I., — *The subject of a finite verb is in the nominative case.*

She is a simple personal pronoun (decline). It is found in the third person, singular number, and feminine gender, and is in the nominative case, because it is the subject of the verb *hurt,* according to Rule I., — *The subject,* &c.

Herself is a compound personal pronoun (decline). It is found in the third person, singular number, and feminine gender, and is in the objective case, because it is the object of the verb *hurt*, according to Rule X., — *The object of a transitive verb or preposition is put in the objective case.*

EXERCISE.

Analyze the following sentences. Select and parse the nouns and pronouns in order.

Did you say that they had drowned themselves, or did I misunderstand you? Diogenes lived by himself in a tub. Lend him your pen till he writes his exercise. How much we missed our brother and your sister! His mother herself wrote to me, did she not? Time itself shall be no more.

Possessive Pronouns.

88. The possessive pronouns are *mine, thine, his, its, hers, ours, yours,* and *theirs.*

Mine, thine, and *his,* as sometimes used, are personal pronouns in the possessive case. We may determine when they are personals and when they are possessives by observing whether they are joined to nouns. If so, they are personals in the possessive case; but if they represent their nouns understood, they are possessives. "It is *his* hat;" here *his* is joined to *hat,* and is therefore a personal pronoun in the possessive case. "Here is my hat, there is *his;*" in this sentence *his* represents *hat* understood, and is a possessive pronoun.

89. A possessive pronoun has the same person, number, gender, and case as the noun that it represents. To parse it, therefore, we must look at that noun. Thus: "Is that book yours?" *Yours* is here equivalent to *your book,* and is in the same person, number, gender, and case as *book,* — that is, third, singular, neuter, nominative. "Those boys are yours." *Yours* is here equivalent to *your boys,* and is in the same person, number, gender, and case as *boys,* — that is, third, plural, masculine, nominative.

90. The possessive pronouns are indeclinable, and lack the possessive case.

EXERCISE.

Analyze the following sentences. Select and parse the nouns and the personal and possessive pronouns.

That house is not ours; it is theirs. These pens are not mine; they must be his or hers. That sister of yours has not come. His coat is made of cloth, but yours is not. How natural that you should like your country better than mine! Where is that cane of yours which you showed me yesterday?

Relative Pronouns.

91. The Relative Pronouns are subdivided into Simple Relatives and Compound Relatives.

Simple Relative Pronouns.

92. There are four simple relative pronouns:—

Who, applied only to persons and things personified; as, "the man who walks;" "Peace, who smiles upon the land."

Which, applied only to irrational animals or things; as, "the horse which kicks;" "the stove which smokes."

That, applied either to persons, irrational animals, or things; as, "the man that walks;" "the horse that kicks;" "the stove that smokes."

What, which has the force of both antecedent and relative, being equivalent to *the thing which, the things which*, or *that which*. "I give *what* I can," is equivalent to "I give *that which* I can."

93. The simple relatives are the same in the plural as in the singular. They are declined as follows:—

	Sing. & Plur.	Sing. & Plur.	Sing. & Plur.	Sing. & Plur.
Nom.	Who,	Which,	That,	What,
Poss.	whose,	whose,	—	—
Obj.	whom.	which.	that.	what.

94. *That* is not a relative pronoun in every sentence. It is a relative only when *who, whom*, or *which* can be substituted for it without marring the sense. Thus: "The island *that* Columbus discovered was inhabited by savages;" here *that* is a relative, because we can substitute *which* for it, — "The island *which* Columbus discovered," &c. "I knew that he would go;" here *that* is not a relative, because we cannot say, "I knew *who* he would go," "*whom* he would go," or "*which* he would go."

95. *As* has sometimes the construction of a relative pronoun, especially after *such, many,* and *same;* as, "The Lord added to the church daily *such as* should be saved."

96. Relative pronouns always connect the clause in which they stand to the element of the sentence which contains the antecedent; as, "The man *that does his duty* will be happy." In this example, *that* introduces the clause *that does his duty,* and connects it with the leading proposition, *The man will be happy.*

97. *What* applies to things, and is used as a relative only when the antecedent is omitted; as, "I know *what* you want."

98. Changes in person, number, and gender make no difference in the form of a relative pronoun. When, therefore, we wish to determine its person, number, and gender, we must look at its antecedent. "I, who speak unto you, am he." Here the relative *who* is the same person, number, and gender as its antecedent *I,*—that is, first person, singular number, masculine gender.

99. In case, the relative is independent of its antecedent. To ascertain its case, we must look at the relation it sustains to its own clause. In the sentence, "I, who speak unto you, am he," *who* is in the nominative case, because it is the subject of the clause *who speak unto you.* "The house in which Shakespeare was born is still preserved." *House,* the antecedent, is nominative case; but the relative *which* is objective, being the object of the preposition *in.*

100. A simple relative pronoun is parsed by stating the antecedent to which it refers; declining it and stating its person, number, and gender, its relation to its antecedent, and rule; and its case (which depends on the relation it sustains to its own clause), its disposal, and rule.

What must be resolved into *the thing which* or *the things which* (whichever makes the better sense), and antecedent and relative must be parsed separately.

PARSING MODEL.—" We obey you, whom we love."

Whom is a simple relative pronoun. It has *you* for its antecedent, and is thus declined: Nom. *who,* poss. *whose,* obj. *whom*; plural the same. It is in the second person, singular number, and masculine or feminine gender, because its antecedent *you* is, according to Rule XV.,—*Pronouns must* agree with their antecedents, or with the words for which they stand, in person, number, and gender. It is in the objective case, because it is the object of the verb *love*, according to Rule X.,— *The object of a transitive verb* &c.

Let us know what we must do.

What is a simple relative pronoun, equivalent to *things which*.

Things, the antecedent part of *what*, is a common noun, third person, plural number, neuter gender, and is the object of the verb *know*, according to Rule X. (Repeat it.)

Which is a simple relative pronoun. It has *things* for its antecedent. (Decline it.) It is found in the third person, plural number, and neuter gender, because its antecedent *things* is, according to Rule XV. (repeat it), and is in the objective case after the verb *must do*, according to Rule X. (Repeat it.)

EXERCISE.

Select the relative and the antecedent in each of the following sentences.

Parse the nouns, the personal, possessive, and relative pronouns, according to the models given.

Addison, who was a fine writer, and whose " Spectator " is justly famous, lived in the days of Queen Elizabeth. Galvanism was so called from Galvani, by whom its principles were discovered. Those who are contented are happy. The first newspaper that was ever issued appeared at Venice. There is nothing that I dislike so much as those who slander their neighbors. I have some grain that I have just bought, and some horses that I would like to sell. I know what you will say. Remember what you learn. What you have said astonishes me.

Compound Relative Pronouns.

101. The Compound Relative Pronouns are formed by combining *ever* and *soever* with the simple relatives.

102. There are six compound relatives, — *whoever* and *whosoever*, *whichever* and *whichsoever*, *whatever* and *whatsoever*.

Whoso, once used as a short form for *whosoever*, has now gone out of use, except in poetry. It is found only in the nominative case.

103. The compound relatives, with the exception of *whoever* and

COMPOUND RELATIVE PRONOUNS.

whosoever, are indeclinable, and are never used in the possessive case. *whoever* and *whosoever* are the same in the plural as in the singular, and are declined like *who*, as follows: —

Singular and Plural.		*Singular and Plural.*
Nom.	Whoever,	whosoever,
Poss.	whosever,	whosesoever,
Obj.	whomever,	whomsoever.

104. The compound relatives have the force of a relative and an indefinite antecedent; as, *the person* or *persons who, the thing* or *things which.* "Whoever dreads punishment deserves it," — that is, *the person who* dreads, &c.

An antecedent must never be used before a compound relative, but is sometimes introduced after it for the sake of greater emphasis. It would be wrong to say, "*He whoever* dreads punishment deserves it;" but we read, "*Whosoever* will, let *him* take of the water of life freely."

105. In parsing, compound relatives and the simple relative *what* may be resolved into separate words, or may be considered as including the relative and the indefinite antecedent. Rules should be given for their disposal both as relatives and antecedents. Their form depends upon their use as relatives.

NOTE. Compound relatives and *what* generally introduce substantive clauses which are used as the subject or object in place of the antecedent. The substantive clause may then be parsed instead of the antecedent, and the relative parsed as depending on an omitted antecedent.

Parsing Form. — Compound relative, decline, person, number, gender, case as antecedent, rule; case as relative, rule.

PARSING MODEL. — I love whoever loves me.

Whoever is a compound relative (decline it), third person, singular number, masculine or feminine gender; as antecedent, it is in the objective case after the verb *love*, according to Rule X. (repeat it); as relative, it is in the nominative case, and is the subject of the verb *loves*, according to Rule II. (Repeat it.)

EXERCISE.

Parse the nouns and pronouns in the following sentences: —

Whatever is mine is yours. Whichever of you conducts himself the better shall receive the prize. Whosesoever sins ye remit, they are remitted. I will see whatever I can. She will reward whoever deserves it.

Interrogative Pronouns.

106. The interrogative pronouns are *who, which*, and *what*. They are declined like the relatives *who, which, what* (see § 93).

Who, which, and *what*, the interrogatives, are to be distinguished from *who, which*, and *what*, the relatives. If a question is asked with them, they are interrogatives; if they refer to an antecedent, and do not ask any question, they are relatives. " *Who* did this? " A question is asked with *who*, and it is therefore interrogative. — " Did you see the man *who* did this? " Here, though a question is asked, it is not asked with *who; who* refers to *man* for its antecedent, and is a relative.

107. Interrogative pronouns are parsed by stating their person (which is always third), number, gender, case, and rule.

PARSING MODEL. — Who knocks?

Who is an interrogative pronoun, third person, singular number, masculine or feminine gender, and nominative case, and is the subject of the verb *knocks*, according to Rule II. (Repeat it.)

I care not whose friend he is.

Whose is an interrogative pronoun, third person, singular number, masculine gender, and possessive case, and limits *friend*, according to Rule IX. (Repeat it.)

EXERCISE.

I. Analyze the following sentences, and parse the nouns and pronouns they contain.

Who doubts that the planets are inhabited? What have you learned to day? Cornwallis asked who led the van. Whose hat is this, mine or yours? Whom have we here, walking by herself? Which of the stars is nearest to us? I cannot tell which of them is nearest, but Sirius seems to me the brightest. From whom did she hear the news?

II. Compose three sentences containing a personal pronoun each, three containing possessives, three containing relatives, three containing interrogatives, three containing compound personals, three containing compound relatives.

RECAPITULATION.

Pronouns.
- Personal { Simple; as, *I.* / Compound; as, *myself.*
- Possessive . . . . . ; as, *ours.*
- Relative { Simple; as, *who.* / Compound; as, *whoever.*
- Interrogative . . . . ; as, *what?*

CHAPTER IV.

THE ADJECTIVE.

108. An Adjective is a word joined to a noun or pronoun, to qualify or limit its meaning.

"An extensive landscape:" *extensive* qualifies the noun *landscape*, and is an adjective. "Five children;" *five* limits the signification of *children*, and is an adjective.

SECTION I.
Classes of Adjectives.

109. Adjectives are divided into two general classes, Descriptive and Definitive.

110. A Descriptive Adjective is one that expresses a quality; as, *good, handsome, short.*

111. A Definitive Adjective is one that defines or limits the meaning of its noun or pronoun; as, *two, the, these.*

THE ADJECTIVE.

If we say "good men," *good* tells what kind of men are meant; it expresses a quality, and is therefore a descriptive adjective. If, on the other hand, we say "two men," *two* tells how many men are meant; it defines or limits the number of men, and is therefore a definitive adjective.

112. Among the most common definitive adjectives are *an* or *a*, *the one, two, three*, &c., *first, second, third*, &c., *this, that, these, those, both, each, every, either, neither, some, other, any, one, all, such, much, many, no*, or *none, same, few*.

113. Descriptive adjectives and some of the definitives, preceded by *the*, are often used without a noun; as, the *rich*, the *wicked*, "the *last* shall be *first*, and the *first* shall be *last*." Here *rich, poor, last*, and *first* have the force of plural nouns. They should be parsed as *adjectives used as nouns, third, plural, masculine* or *feminine*, &c.

On the contrary, nouns placed before other nouns to express a quality, or the material of which a thing is made, are used as adjectives, and should be parsed as such; as, *gold* pens, *brick* houses, *land* breezes.

EXERCISE.

I. Join the descriptive adjective *bad* to such nouns as you can recollect; also the descriptive adjectives *sweet, hard, bitter, small, idle, selfish, round, hungry*.

EXAMPLE.— Bad boys, bad bread, bad lessons, &c.

II. Join the definitive adjective *those* to such nouns as you can recollect; also the definitive adjectives *the, this, each, several, fifteen, tenth, any, that*.

EXAMPLE.— Those women, those apples, those stones, &c.

III. Join first a descriptive and then a definitive adjective to each of the following nouns:—

— moon   — parents   — tree   — grass
— home   — rose   — house   — mouse

EXAMPLE. — *Silvery* moon; *the* moon.

IV. Pick out the descriptive and the definitive adjectives in the following expressions:—

The lofty sky. That silent orb. This shaggy brow. Auburn locks. The impetuous tempers of these passionate men. A gentle moon. Many dark clouds. The same turbid stream. One of those dashing waves. The first gleam of rosy morn. He is short, she is shorter, you are shortest.

Descriptive Adjectives.

114. Besides the common adjectives expressing quality, as *good, bad, happy,* we have two classes of descriptive adjectives.

I. Proper Adjectives, or such as are derived from proper nouns; as, *American, Alpine, Newtonian.*

II. Verbal Adjectives, or such as are derived from verbs (or words that assert) and end in *ing* or *ed;* as, *enduring* from the verb *endure, bereaved* from the verb *bereave.* "Enduring friendship." "A bereaved parent."

Definitive Adjectives.

115. Definitive adjectives include,—

I. *The,* and *an* or *a,* two words constantly occurring, by some grammarians made a distinct part of speech called Articles.

II. Numeral Adjectives, or such as denote number; as, *one, two,* &c.; *first, second,* &c.

III. Pronominal Adjectives, or such as are sometimes used with nouns as adjectives, and sometimes in their place as pronouns.

"This course is wrong;" here *this* is used with the noun *course,* and is a pronominal adjective. "This is wrong;" here *this* takes the place of its noun, and is to be parsed as a *pronominal adjective used as a pronoun.*

The.—An or A.

116. *The* and *an* or *a* are used only with nouns. They always stand before the nouns whose meaning they limit, either immediately, or with some other modifying word or words between them; as, *the* bird, *the* little bird, *an* owl, *an* ugly and ill-tempered owl. *a* bird, *a* very lively bird.

USE OF *AN* AND *A*.

117. *The* is used with both singular and plural nouns; as, *the* arm, *the* arms. *An* or *a* (denoting but one) is used only with a singular noun; as, *an* arm, *a* foot (not *an* arms, *a* feet).

A has been formed from *an* by dropping *n*. *An* and *one* have a common origin, — the Saxon word *an*, *ane*. By custom *one* is used in numbering, while *an* is employed as a definitive adjective to denote an individual, either definitely or indefinitely.

118. The definitive *the* is used before specific individuals or classes of objects, as distinguished from others of the same kind; as, "*the* laws of morality;" "*the* hope of the Christian;" "*the* sun;" "*the* earth."

It is also used with singular nouns to denote the whole species, or an indefinite number; as, "*The* almond-tree shall flourish."

119. *An* or *a* is used definitely to designate an individual object as known, certain, or specified; as, "I hear *a* sound;" "I see *an* elephant;" "it weighs *an* ounce."

An or *a* is used indefinitely to denote some individual of a class or species, without specifying any particular one; as, "*A* kingdom for *a* horse." Here, *a* specifies no particular kingdom or horse, but merely denotes one of each.

120. In such expressions as *to go a riding, a fishing, a swimming*, &c., *a* appears to have been formed from *at*, to which it is equivalent in meaning. In such a connection, it is to be parsed, not as a definitive adjective, but as a preposition.

USE OF *AN* AND *A*.

121. *An* and *a* are the same word, and convey exactly the same idea, but a distinction is to be observed in their use.

An is to be used

1. Before all words commencing with *a*, *i*, and *o* (except *one* and its compounds, and *once*).
- 2. Before words commencing with *e* not followed by *u* or *w*.
3. Before words commencing with *u*, when its sound does not involve that of *y*.
4. Before words commencing with silent *h*, — that is, *h* not sounded; as, *hour* (pronounced *our*).

5. Before words commencing with *h* sounded, if the accent is on the second syllable; as, *an* hero'ic action.

A is used in all other cases.

EXAMPLES.— An apple, an inkstand, an orange, an eel, an urn, an hour, an histo'rian, an Hero'dian.

BUT,— A bee, a comb, a pin, a year, a wind, a one-sided story, a ewer, a eulogist, a he'ro, a his'tory, a hippopot'amus.

EXERCISE.

I. Correct the following sentences, and give the reason for making the correction. — Select the adjectives, and tell whether they are descriptive or definitive.

The clock is a hour and an half too fast. A honest man sold me a ox. A Indian is a hard master. Such an one can be a upright judge. A early pear will keep but an short time. A old coat is an useless garment. A idle man stole an horse from a honest one. A ounce of prevention is worth an hundred pounds of cure. In an once lordly house lives a one-eyed woman. She has an handsome goat and an ewe. A European war calls out many an hero and exhibits many an heroic act.

II. Insert *an* or *a* (as may be required) before each of the following words:—

youth	head	errand	hand'kerchief
castle	herb	eulogy	harp'sichord
onion	eye	wonder	harmon'ica

Numeral Adjectives.

122. Numeral Adjectives are subdivided into Cardinals, Ordinals, and Multiplicatives.

The Cardinals denote *how many;* as, *one, two, three, ten, ninety-nine,* &c.

The Ordinals denote *which in order;* as, *first, second, third, tenth, ninety-ninth,* &c.

The *Multiplicatives* denote *how many fold;* as, single, double, triple.

Both cardinals and ordinals must be distinguished from nouns identical with them in form. "*Twenty* can be divided by *two.*" "*Four* is an even number." "Three times *six* is *eighteen.*" "Give me a *third.*" "One *tenth* of the army." Here, *twenty, two, four,* &c., are the names of numbers, and therefore *nouns.*

Pronominal Adjectives.

123. Pronominal Adjectives are subdivided into Distributives, Demonstratives, and Indefinites.

124. The Distributives represent the individual objects composing a certain number as taken separately. There are four distributives; *each, every, either,* and *neither.*

125. The Demonstratives clearly point out individual objects. The demonstratives are *this,* plural *these;* and *that,* plural *those.*

This and *these* refer to what is near or present; *that* and *those,* to what is remote or absent. *This* man means the man who is near or present; *that* man, the man who is at a distance or absent. "The path of pleasure and the path of duty lie before us; that leads to ruin, this to happiness." *That* refers to the first-mentioned object as the more distant, *the path of pleasure; this,* to the last-mentioned, *the path of duty.*

126. The Indefinites designate objects in a general way, without pointing out any in particular.

The principal indefinites are *some, any, all, such, same, former, latter, own, little, much, both, several, many, few, no* or *none, one, other, another, which, whichever, whichsoever, what, whatever, whatsoever.*

127. The indefinites, with the exception of *one, other,* and *another,* used as pronouns, are indeclinable, and are not found in the possessive case. *Another* has no plural; *one* and *other* are found in both numbers. Their declension is as follows:—

	Sing.	*Plur.*	*Sing.*	*Plur.*	*Sing.*
Nom.	One,	ones,	Other,	others,	Another,
Poss.	one's,	ones',	other's,	others',	another's,
Obj.	one,	ones.	other,	others.	another.

RECAPITULATION.

Remarks on the Indefinites.

128. *Some, any, all, such, same, former, latter,* and *own* are used with or in place of either singular or plural nouns; as, *some* bread, *some* men. "*Some* is good, the rest is bad." "*Some* are good, others bad."

129. *Little* and *much* are used with or in place of singular nouns only; as, *little* wealth, man needs but *little*.

130. *Both, several, many,* and *few* are used with or in place of plural nouns only; as, *both* sentences, *both* are happy.

131. *No* or *none* are different forms of the same word. *No* is the adjective form — that is, the form used with a noun (either singular or plural); as, *no* man, *no* men. *None* is the pronoun form, — that is, the form used instead of a noun (either singular or plural); as, *none* is happy, *none* are happy.

132. *Which, whichever, whichsoever, what, whatever, whatsoever,* have been already mentioned among pronouns. They are indefinite pronominal adjectives (indeclinable and not found in the possessive case), when used with nouns; as, "Which way did he go?" "Whichever way he goes." "Whatsoever course he pursues."

133. It may seem strange that *one* can have a plural. But it must be remembered that it is not the number *one*, the cardinal adjective, that is declined above, but the pronominal adjective. "The world runs after great men, neglects good *ones.*" Here *ones* is a pronominal adjective used instead of *men,* and is in the plural number.

134. *Own* is used after possessive pronouns and the possessive case of nouns and pronouns with or without its noun, to bring out the idea of possession more emphatically; as, Mine *own* heart. Napoleon's *own* guard. Napoleon's *own.* "He came to his *own,* and his *own* received him not."

EXERCISE.

I. Analyze the following sentences. Pick out the pronouns and adjectives, and state to what class they belong.

How long this will be remembered! That event has been recorded. One is apt to love one's self. Some were wise, others were foolish. Much labor has been bestowed on both subjects. Many hours have been wasted. A few days will determine his destiny. Let others boast; I will be silent. All must die; none can escape. A thousand soldiers were encamped. What can be thought of those that forsake their own? I will give to this object the tenth part of whatsoever I possess.

II. Complete the following sentences by inserting adjectives of the classes specified: —

Dogs are (descriptive adjective). (Proper adj.) horses are strong. Music is a (verbal adj.) accompaniment to the voice. America has been called (definitive adj.) land of (definitive adj.) free. There are (cardinal) days in (cardinal) week. Sunday is the (ordinal) day of (definitive) week. Let (distributive) passenger hold his (indefinite) ticket. The joys of (demonstrative) world are fleeting. Men praise (demonstrative) who succeed. (Indefinite) must die. There are (indefinite) men that are really happy. (Indefinite) eyes can look upon (demonstrative) mourners without compassion !

SECTION II.

COMPARISON OF ADJECTIVES.

135. A quality belonging to an object may be compared with the same quality in some other object, or in the same object under different circumstances.

Examples. — The same quality in three different objects may be compared as follows: —

Iron is *hard;* hardness is a quality of iron.

Steel is *harder* than iron; hardness is a quality of steel, and belongs to it in a higher degree than to iron.

Diamond is the *hardest* of the three; hardness is a quality of diamond, and belongs to it in a higher degree than to either iron or steel.

The same quality in three different persons may be compared as follows: —

A *wise* man; a *wiser* man than he; the *wisest* man of the three, or of all.

The same quality as exhibited in the same object under different circumstances may be compared as follows: —

The boy was *mischievous* at home, *more mischievous* at school, but *most mischievous* at church.

136. Comparison is the variation of an adjective to denote the same quality in different degrees.

137. There are three degrees of comparison; the Positive, the Comparative, and the Superlative.

The Positive expresses the simple quality; as, *mild*, *great*.

The Comparative expresses a higher or lower degree of the quality than that expressed by the positive; as, *milder, less mild.*

The Superlative expresses the highest or lowest degree of the quality; as, *mildest, least mild.*

138. The superlative does not always imply comparison. When formed with *most* and not preceded by *the*, it implies merely a very high degree of the quality; as, a *most beautiful* landscape, — that is, an *exceedingly beautiful* landscape. So used, it is called the Superlative of Excellence.

139. Without comparing an adjective, an inferior degree of the quality denoted by it may in some cases be expressed by appending *ish* to the positive; as, *sweetish, darkish,* — equivalent to *slightly sweet, somewhat dark.*

Rules for Forming the Degrees.

140. RULE I. — Adjectives of one syllable are compared by annexing to the positive *er* for the *comparative*, and *est* for the *superlative;* as, *warm, warmer, warmest.*

Adjectives ending in silent *e* drop this letter before *er* and *est;* as,

wise	wiser	wisest	tame	tamer	tamest
NOT	wiseer	wiseest	NOT	tameer	tameest

The final letter of certain adjectives is doubled before *er* and *est:* as, *fit, fitter, fittest; hot, hotter, hottest.*

RULE II. Adjectives of two or more syllables form their *comparative* degree by prefixing the adverb *more* to the positive, and their *superlative* by prefixing the adverb *most;* as, *skilful, more skilful, most skilful; enterprising, more enterprising, most enterprising.*

Some adjectives of two syllables are compared with *er* and *est* when they can be easily pronounced; as, *lofty, loftier, loftiest; handsome, handsomer, handsomest.*

In this case, if the adjective ends in *y*, it changes *y* to *i* before *er* and *est;* as, *noisy, noisier, noisiest.*

Rule III. — To express a lower degree of the quality denoted, a *comparative* is formed with *less ;* and to express the lowest degree, a *superlative* with *least ;* as,

Positive.	Comparative.	Superlative.
Warm,	less warm,	least warm.
Skilful,	less skilful,	least skilful.
Enterprising,	less enterprising,	least enterprising.

Irregular Comparison.

141. The following adjectives are irregular in their comparison: —

Pos.	Comp.	Sup.	Pos.	Comp.	Sup.
Good	better,	best.	Near,	nearer,	nearest, next.
Bad, or ill,	worse,	worst.	Fore,	former,	foremost, first.
Little,	less,	least.	Old,	{ older,	oldest.
Much,	more,	most.		{ elder,	eldest.
Many,	more,	most.	Far,	{ farther,	farthest.
Late,	later,	latest, last.		{ further,	furthest.

142. *Lesser* is sometimes used instead of *less;* as, *Lesser* Asia, the *lesser* faults.

143. *Late*, when it refers to time, makes *later, latest;* as, *late* news, *later* news, the *latest* news. When it refers to order, it makes *latter, last;* as, the *latter* of two clauses, the *last* of his race.

144. *Old* has two forms: *older, oldest*, equally applicable to persons and things; *elder, eldest*, applicable only to persons of the same family. We say, the *oldest* man, the *oldest* city; but, an *elder* sister, the *eldest* of the family.

145. Of the two comparatives of *far, farther* implies distance, *further* quantity. " Troy is farther than Albany," — that is, *at a greater distance.* " Have you anything further to suggest? " — that is, *anything more.*

146. Some adjectives form their superlative in *most:* —

Pos.	Comp.	Sup.
Hind,	hinder,	hindmost *or* hindermost.
Low,	lower,	lowest *or* lowermost.

147. Some adjectives have no positive degree, forming their comparative and superlative from adverbs: —

PARSING OF ADJECTIVES.

Pos.	Comp.	Sup.
(In)	inner,	inmost *or* innermost.
(Out)	{ outer,	outmost *or* outermost.
	utter,	utmost *or* uttermost.
(Up)	upper,	upmost *or* uppermost.

148. Some adjectives have no comparative degree.

Pos.	Sup.	Pos.	Sup.
Front,	frontmost.	Rear,	rearmost.
Northern,	northernmost.	Southern,	southernmost.
Eastern,	easternmost.	Western,	westernmost.

149. Adjectives that express qualities which do not exist in different degrees cannot be compared. Among these are,—

    1. All definitives except *little, much, many, few, former, latter.*
    2. All proper adjectives; as, *Russian.*
    3. All adjectives expressing *figure,* and generally those implying *matter, time,* and *place;* as, *square, golden, daily.*
    4. All adjectives denoting the highest or lowest degree of the quality; as, *infinite, empty.*

Some adjectives have the force of the comparative or the superlative without its form; as, *preferable, superior, extreme, chief.* Such adjectives are to be regarded as in the positive degree, and cannot be compared; though sometimes, to strengthen their meaning, we find some of them used in the superlative degree in poetry; as, *extremest, chiefest.*

EXERCISE.

Compare the following adjectives:—

High	Grateful	Good	Never-ending	Wooden
Low	Unmindful	Little	Generous	Inferior
Small	Cheerful	Happy	Penurious	Round
Great	Attractive	Lofty	Extravagant	English

SECTION III.
Parsing of Adjectives.

150. Adjectives have no accidents except comparison. To parse them, state the class to which they belong; if they admit of comparison, compare them and mention their degree; if not, state the fact; tell to

what noun they belong, — that is, what noun they describe or limit.

Pronominal adjectives *used as pronouns* are to be parsed like pronouns. Tell their person, number, gender, case.

To find the noun or pronoun to which an adjective belongs, ask a question with *what*, as shown below. Whatever answers the question is the word required. "Wicked men are abundant." *Wicked what?* Answer, *wicked* MEN: *wicked* belongs to *men.*— *What are abundant?* Answer, MEN: *abundant* belongs to *men*.

Form for Parsing.

Adjective. — Class, compare, degree, modifies, rule.

Pronominal Adj. { Used as adjective, limits, rule.
{ Used as pronoun, person, number, gender, disposal, rule.

PARSING MODEL — The Swiss hunters of this mountain region are the most enduring of all.

The is a definitive adjective, cannot be compared, and belongs to *hunters*, according to Rule XIV., — *An adjective belongs to the noun or pronoun whose meaning it qualifies or limits.*

Swiss is a proper adjective, cannot be compared, and belongs to *hunters*, according to Rule XVI. (Repeat it.)

This is a demonstrative pronominal adjective, used as an adjective, cannot be compared, and belongs to *region*, according to Rule XVII., — *Pronominal adjectives belong to the nouns which they limit, or are used alone as pronouns.*

Mountain is a noun used as an adjective, cannot be compared, and belongs to *region*, according to Rule XVI. (Repeat it.)

Most enduring is a verbal adjective; compared, *enduring, more enduring, most enduring*; superlative degree; and belongs to *hunters*, according to Rule XVI. (Repeat it.)

All is an indefinite pronominal adjective used as a pronoun, third, plural, masculine, objective, and is the object of the preposition *of*, according to Rule X. (Repeat it.)

I bought some handsome books yesterday: they are superior to these in every point of view.

Some is a pronominal adjective, cannot be compared, and belongs to *books*, according to Rule XVI. (Repeat it.)

PARSING OF ADJECTIVES.

Handsome is a descriptive adjective; compared, *handsome, handsomer, handsomest*; positive degree; and belongs to *books*, according to Rule XVI. (Repeat it.)

Superior is a descriptive adjective, cannot be compared, and belongs to *they*, according to Rule XVI. (Repeat it.)

These is a demonstrative pronominal adjective used as a pronoun; third, plural, neuter, objective, and is the object of the preposition *to*, according to Rule X. (Repeat it.)

Every is a distributive pronominal adjective, cannot be compared, and belongs to *point*, according to Rule XVII. (Repeat it.)

EXERCISE.

Analyze the following sentences. Parse the nouns, pronouns, and adjectives they contain.

Whichever way I turn, I see no practicable means of escape. Let none be banished except the thirty tyrants. What could have induced the French and Austrians to engage in this most bloody war? There are twenty-four stars of the first magnitude, each of which you have seen. How many comets, from the most distant regions of space, have visited the solar system! The Western continent is colder than the Eastern at corresponding latitudes. The flame burns bright and clear. Keen blows the wind, and piercing is the cold. A light shineth in the path of the upright. The young blood of modern literature has put new life into the literature of the dead languages. All the features of a great heroic age, from which European civilization dates, and political and domestic order takes its rise, stand forth in living reality. He is happier than thou.

  The encumbered oar scarce leaves the hostile coast,
  Through purple billows and a floating host.

RECAPITULATION.

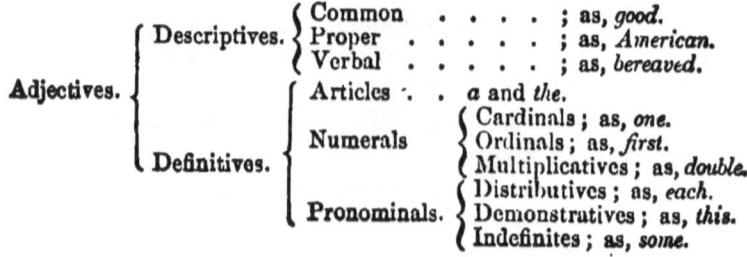

REVIEW QUESTIONS ON CHAPTERS III., IV.

64. What is a pronoun? 65. How are pronouns divided? 66. What is a personal pronoun? 67. What is a possessive pronoun? 68. What is a relative pronoun? 69. What does the term *antecedent* mean? Why is it so called? When it is said to be *understood?* 70. What is an interrogative pronoun? In what besides direct questions are interrogative pronouns used? How may questions be asked without interrogative pronouns?

71. What accidents have pronouns? 72. How can the person, number, gender, and case of a pronoun be told when they are not indicated by its form?

73. How are the personal pronouns subdivided? 74. Name the simple personal of the first person. Of the second. Name those of the third person. 75. Decline *I; thou; he; she; it.* 76. Where were *mine* and *thine* formerly used? 77. In what is *we* often used instead of *I?* 78. To what style is *thou* appropriate? What takes its place in ordinary language? 79. In what style is *ye* used? 80. Show how *it* is sometimes used without referring to any antecedent. 81. Is the apostrophe used or omitted in the possessive case of nouns? Of personal pronouns? 82. How are the compound personal pronouns formed? 83. Name the compound personals of the first person. 84. Of the second. 85. Of the third. Give the gender of each. 86. Decline *myself; ourself; thyself; yourself; himself; herself; itself.* 87. How are personal pronouns parsed?

88. Name the possessive pronouns. How are we to determine when *mine, thine, his,* and *its* are personals, and when possessives? 89. What person, number, gender, and case has a possessive pronoun? 90. What case do the possessive pronouns lack?

91. How are the relative pronouns subdivided? 92. Name the simple relatives, and tell to which each is applied. 93. Decline *who; which; what.* 94. When is *that* a relative pronoun? 95. When has *as* the construction of a relative pronoun? 96. What office do relative pronouns have? 97. When is *what* used as a relative? 98. How are we to determine the person, number, and gender of a relative? 99. How are we to ascertain the case of a relative? 100. How is a simple relative parsed? How is *what* parsed? 101. How are the compound relative pronouns formed? 102. Name the compound relatives. 103. Which of them are indeclinable? Decline *whoever; whosoever.* 104. What is the force of the compound relatives? How may an antecedent be used with a compound relative? 105. How are compound relatives parsed?

106. Mention the interrogative pronouns. How are they declined? How can *who, which* and *what*, as interrogatives, be distinguished from

REVIEW QUESTIONS.

the same words as relatives? 107. How are interrogative pronouns parsed?

108. What is an adjective? 109. How are adjectives divided? 110. What is a descriptive adjective? 111. What is a definitive adjective? 112. Mention some of the most common definitive adjectives. 113. Under what circumstances are adjectives used as nouns? How should they then be parsed? How are nouns sometimes used as adjectives?

114. What two classes are embraced under the head of descriptive adjectives? Define each. 115. What are included among definitive adjectives? What are *the* and *an* or *a* sometimes called? What are numeral adjectives? Pronominal adjectives?

116. With what are *the* and *an* or *a* used? How do they stand? 117. With nouns of what number is *the* used? *An* or *a?* What is the origin of *an* or *one*, and the difference in their use? 118. What is the force of *the?* 119. What is the force of *an* or *a* used definitely? Used indefinitely? 120. How is *a* to be parsed in the expression *to go a riding?* 121. Before what words is *an* to be used? Before what words must *a* be used?

122. How are numeral adjectives subdivided? What do cardinals denote? Ordinals? From what must cardinals and ordinals be distinguished? What do multiplicatives denote?

123. Into what classes are pronominal adjectives subdivided? 124. How do the distributives represent objects? 125. The demonstratives? What is the difference between *this, these,* and *that, those?* 126. How do the indefinites designate objects? Mention the principal indefinites. 127. Which of the indefinites are declined? Decline *one; other; another.* 128. Which of the indefinites are used with either singular or plural nouns? 129. Which are used with singular nouns only? 130. Which with plural nouns only? 131. What is the difference in use between *no* and *none?* 132. When are *which, whichever,* &c., pronominal adjectives? 133. How can *one* have a plural? 134. How is *own* used?

135. With what may a quality belonging to an object be compared? Give examples. 136. What is comparison? 137. How many degrees of comparison are there? What does the positive degree express? The comparative? The superlative? 138. Define the superlative of excellence. 139. How may an inferior degree of a quality be expressed?

140. What is Rule I. for forming the degrees? What changes are made in certain adjectives before *er* and *est* are appended? Repeat Rule II. How are some adjectives of two syllables compared? In this case, if the adjective ends in *y*, what change is made? Repeat Rule III. 141. Give one or two examples of adjectives irregularly compared. 142. What is sometimes used instead of *less?* 143. What is the difference between *later, latest,* and *latter, last?* 144. Between *older, oldest,* and *elder, eldest?* 145. Between the two comparatives of *far?*

146. In what do some adjectives form their superlative? 147. Give an example of adjectives that form their comparative and superlative from adverbs. 148. Give an example of those that have no comparative degree. 149. What adjectives cannot be compared? What degree is *preferable?* *Extreme?* Name the classes of adjectives that are not compared. 150. How are adjectives to be parsed? How are pronominal adjectives used as pronouns to be parsed? How can you find the noun or pronoun to which an adjective belongs?

CHAPTER V.

THE VERB.

151. **A Verb is a word by means of which something is affirmed.**

NOTE.— The word *affirm* is here applied to the office of the verb in direct and indirect assertions, commands, entreaties, and inquiries.

Birds sing. Sing, pretty birds.
Let the birds sing. Do the birds sing?

In each of the above sentences, *sing* is a verb, because with it something is affirmed.

Is Italy free? — *Is* is a verb, because it affirms respecting the state of Italy.

Go thy way. — *Go* is a verb, because it is the word that affirms in the command given.

EXERCISE.

I. Point out the verbs in the following sentence:—

The moon rises. The sun sets. The child reads his book. The sword kills. The loud thunder peals. The waves dash violently. Have you no conscience? Rest, sleep, dream, if you can forget the past.

II. Make sentences with the following subjects by inserting verbs in place of the dashes:—

The waves —	The sun —	The dog —	The rain —
The day —	Camels —	The lion —	The ships —
Wild flowers —	The stars —	My head —	The wind —
Heavy showers —	School —	Bad men —	The teacher —

SECTION I.
General Classes of Verbs.

152. Verbs are divided into two general classes, Transitive and Intransitive.

Transitive Verbs.

153. A Transitive Verb is one that requires an object to complete the sense; as, " Fire *consumes* " (what?); an object is required to complete the sense, and therefore *consumes* is a transitive verb.

The *object* of a transitive verb is generally a noun or pronoun in the objective case, used immediately after the verb, without a preposition expressed or understood.

The object of a transitive word is sometimes omitted, when it is suggested by the connection; as, " The husbandman *ploughs, sows,* and *reaps.* The object of each of these verbs is naturally suggested," — " ploughs *the ground,* sows *the seed,* and reaps *the grain.*"

EXERCISE.

Complete the following sentences by inserting transitive verbs in place of the dashes: —

Subjects.	Objects.	Subjects.	Objects.	Subjects.	Objects.
George ——	play.	Trees ——	fruit.	Children ——	books.
Water ——	thirst.	Food ——	hunger.	Eyes ——	light.
Teeth ——	food.	Diamond ——	glass.	Water ——	fire.
They ——	him.	Richard ——	me.	We ——	ourselves.

Intransitive Verbs.

154. An Intransitive Verb is one that does not require an object to complete the sense; as, I *stand;* he *sits.*

Intransitive verbs often express an action in the strongest manner; but the application of the action to an object is denoted, not by the verb, but by *of, at, on, upon,* or some other preposition, introduced after the verb. as, " He *stamped* on the ground " " They *fell* upon the enemy." " She

INTRANSITIVE VERBS.

laughs AT her friends." Here the preposition and the verb taken together form a compound expression equivalent to a transitive verb; but the verb, taken separately, is intransitive.

The verb *to be* generally expresses no attribute of the subject, but serves as a *copula* to connect subject and attribute. The verbs *to seem, to become, to appear, to feel* (*strong*), and some others denoting condition, sometimes have the same office, and are termed *copula verbs*.

The copula and attribute taken together form the predicate of a sentence. Most verbs combine the copula and attribute in themselves; as, *he runs*, i. e. *he is running*. When the copula verbs denote *existence* they also combine in themselves copula and attribute; as, *it appears so*. This is likewise the case with the simple copula *be*, when it is introduced by the adverb *there;* as, There was a man.

155. Some intransitive verbs may be followed by an object that has a meaning akin to their own; as, "to *dream* a dream;" "to *run* a race;" "to *live* a life," &c. Here, *dream, run, live*, may be parsed as *intransitive verbs used transitively*.

Again, transitive verbs may be used intransitively.

TRANSITIVE. { Ellen *reads* her lesson well.
{ Ellen *writes* her exercise neatly.
INTRANSITIVE. Ellen *reads* and *writes*.

The last sentence is equivalent to "Ellen is able to read and write." No object is here required to complete the sense; and *read* and *write* may be parsed as *transitive verbs used intransitively*.

Some verbs have two significations, in one of which they are transitive and in the other intransitive; as, "He acts his part well." (Trans.) "The mind acts upon the body." (Intrans.)

156. It is important to be able to distinguish between transitive and intransitive verbs. The following rules will be found useful:—

1. A verb followed by an object, unless it is one of kindred signification, as in § 155, is transitive.

2. When a verb is not followed by an object, if it takes *me, him*, or *it* after it without injuring the sense, it is transitive; if not, intransitive. "Fire consumes me;" this makes sense, and *consumes* is transitive. "He sits me;" "he sits him;" "he sits it;"—none of these sentences makes sense, and *sits* is intransitive.

EXERCISE.

Point out the verbs in the following sentences, and tell whether they are transitive or intransitive:—

Children play. Foxes bark. Masters teach. Cæsar conquered Britain. Pompey fled. Water runs. Air invigorates the body.

Ice melts.   Gold glitters.   Kings rule their subjects.   I teach. They learn rapidly.   The Chinese eat rats and puppies.   Palmyra stood in a wilderness.   Many a brave soldier slept the sleep of death.

SECTION II.

Voice.

157. Voice is that accident of the verb which shows the relation of the subject to the action expressed by the verb.

Transitive verbs have two forms, called the Active and the Passive Voice.

In the Active Voice the subject of the verb is represented as acting; as, "The sun *warms* the earth."

In the Passive Voice the subject of the verb is represented as being acted upon; as, "The earth *is warmed* by the sun."

In these examples the sense is the same, but the form of expression is different. *Earth*, the object in the active form, becomes the subject in the passive; while the subject *sun* appears in the passive form as the object of the preposition *by*.

158. Most intransitive verbs are found only in the active voice.

Intransitive verbs, as a general rule, have a passive form only when they are used transitively. We can say, "the race *is run*," but not "he *is run*." A few, however, among which are, *come, go, arrive, become, rise,* and *fall*, have a passive form, authorized by good writers. "*Is* Hector *arrived* and *gone?*"—*Shakespeare.* "My lord, your loving nephew now *is come.*" —*Ibid.* "The Lord *is risen.*"

When an intransitive verb becomes transitive by the addition of a preposition, the compound term may be used in the passive form; as, "Her friends *were laughed at.*"

Intransitive verbs denoting existence merely have no voice. To this class belong the copula verbs *to be, to become,* &c.

EXERCISE.

Preserve the sense of the following sentences, but change their form by putting the verb in the passive voice, making the object the subject, and introducing the subject after the preposition *by* as its object.

MODEL.— *Verb, active.* Farmers raise grain.
　　　　　Verb, passive. Grain is raised by farmers.

The hunter kills the fox.　　　　The wind shakes the tree.
The farmer tills the ground.　　The sun melts the snow.
The waves toss the ship.　　　　Grocers sell sugar.
Sailors navigate the sea.　　　　All love the good man.

SECTION III.
MODE.

159. Mode is that accident of the verb which distinguishes the manner of the action or state affirmed.

160. Examples of the different modes in which the verb is used follow.

1. We say of a flower, *it blooms, it bloomed, it has bloomed, it will bloom;* or, *did it bloom? has it bloomed?* &c. This manner of asserting or inquiring is called the INDICATIVE mode.

NOTE. — *Indicative* means "showing" or "declaring."

2. We say, the child *may learn, can learn, must learn, could learn, should learn;* or, *may he learn? can he learn? must he learn?* &c. This manner of asserting or inquiring is called the POTENTIAL mode.

NOTE. — *Potential* means "having power or ability."

3. We say, *if it rain, lest it rain, unless it rain,* &c. This manner of representing an action or state is called the SUBJUNCTIVE mode.

NOTE. — *Subjunctive* means "subjoined to;" and the mode in question is so called, because the clause in which it occurs must be "subjoined to" or connected with some other clause, to make complete sense. *If it rain* expresses only a supposition; but when subjoined to *I will not work,* the sense is complete, — "If it rain, I will not work."

4. We say, *learn thou, obey ye, do go,* &c. This manner of speaking is called the IMPERATIVE mode.

NOTE. — *Imperative* means "commanding."

THE MODES DEFINED.

5. We say, *to read, to have read,* &c. This manner of speaking is called the INFINITIVE mode.

NOTE. — *Infinitive* means "unlimited."

EXERCISE.

I. Point out the verbs in the following expressions, and tell their mode: —

I love. I have loved. I will love. I loved. — To do. To learn. To speak. To have seen. — I may move. I might move. I can move. I must move. — If I like. Unless you hear. Though he slay me. Lest he be angry. — Shun thou. Shun. Shun ye. Obey your rulers.

II. Give an example of each of the five modes with each of the following verbs: —

| command | deny | praise | turn |
| obey | forgive | blame | walk |

The Modes Defined.

161. There are five Modes; the Indicitive, the Potential, the Subjunctive, the Imperative, and the Infinitive.

162. The Indicative Mode is used simply to declare something; as, "*He writes.*"

163. The Potential Mode is used to affirm something as permitted, possible, necessary, or obligatory; as, "He *may write;*" "he *can write;*" "he *must write;*" "he *should write.*"

The potential mode is indicated by the sign *may, can, must, might, could, would,* or *should.*

164. Both the indicative and the potential mode are used in asking questions; as, "*Does* he *write?*" [indicative]. "*May* he *write?*" "*Can* he *write?*" "*Must* he *write?*" "*Should* he *write?*" [potential].

165. The Subjunctive Mode is used to affirm something as uncertain, conditional, or contingent; as, If I *were* he, I would not go."

The subjunctive mode may generally be known by the sign *if, though, unless, whether, lest*, or some word that implies uncertainty or supposition; but this word is a conjunction, and forms no part of the verb.

This sign, however, is often omitted, especially before *were, had, could*, and *should*; as, "*Were* I," "*Had* I the wings of a dove," for "*If* I were," "*If* I had the wings of a dove."

166. The indicative and the potential are often used instead of the subjunctive mode, after the conjunctions above mentioned, to affirm something conditionally; as, "If I *am* not there, wait for me." "If she *could go*, she would be happy." In such a case, the verb may be parsed as in *the indicative mode used contingently*, or *the potential mode used contingently*.

167. The Imperative Mode is used to command, entreat, exhort, or permit; as, "*Obey* at once." "O *come*." "*Do* your duty." "*Go*, this time."

The imperative mode may generally be known by having its subject understood; as in all the above examples, where *thou* or *you* is understood for the subject. If the subject is expressed, it always stands after the verb, if the latter consists of but a single word; as, *Go thou, obey ye.*

168. The Infinitive Mode is used to express an action, or state, in an unlimited manner; as, *to live, to know, to have known.*

The infinitive mode may be known by the sign *to*, which is generally used to introduce it.

169. The infinitive may generally be considered as a verbal noun in the nominative or the objective case; as, "*To travel* [that is, *travelling*] is pleasant." " Boys should love *to read* [that is, should love *reading*]."

170. A verb in any other mode than the Infinitive is said to be Finite.

EXERCISE.

Point out the verbs in the following sentences; state whether they are transitive or intransitive; mention their voice and mode.

The sun warms the earth. James should love his book. I will walk in the field. You must not kill the bird. If sinners entice thee, consent thou not. Love justice. Speak the truth. He wished he could learn. He might learn if he would. I must go. Suppose it should rain. If it should rain, I shall not go. He should strive to improve. Go and do likewise. Seek peace and enjoy it. Does he believe the rumor? Must I go? How could Cain kill Abel?

SECTION IV.

TENSE.

171. Tense is that accident of the verb which distinguishes the time of the action or state affirmed.

172. Examples of the different tenses in which the verb is used follow.

1. We say, The flowers *bloom*. Here, the act of blooming is represented as going on at the present time, and the verb is said to be in the PRESENT tense.

2. We say, The flowers *were blooming*. Here, the blooming is represented as going on at some past time, and not completed; the verb *were blooming* is said to be in the IMPERFECT tense.

3. We say, The flowers *have bloomed*. Here, the blooming is represented as completed at the present time, and the verb *have bloomed* is said to be in the PERFECT tense.

4. We say, The flowers *had bloomed* before I arrived. Here, the blooming is represented as having been completed in past time before some other act which is itself past. The verb *had bloomed* is said to be in the PLUPERFECT tense.

5. We say, The flowers *will bloom*. Here, the blooming is represented as about to take place at some future time, and the verb is said to be in the FIRST FUTURE tense.

6. We say, The flowers *will have bloomed* before I arrive. Here, the blooming is represented as about to be completed before some other future act, and the verb is said to be in the SECOND FUTURE tense.

173. There are six Tenses: the Present, which denotes present time; the Imperfect, Perfect, and Pluperfect, which denote past time; and the First and Second Future, which denote future time.

174. Verbs have two forms in each tense of the active voice, the Simple and the Progressive. The Simple form is the shorter of the two, and is the one more frequently used. The Progressive form denotes an action in progress at the time indicated.

	Simple.	Progressive.
Present.	I write.	I am writing.
Imperfect.	I wrote.	I was writing.
Perfect.	I have written.	I have been writing.

TENSES OF THE INDICATIVE MODE. 93

EXERCISE.

I. Point out the verbs in the following expressions, and tell their tense:—

I will speak. I am walking. You screamed. Did you scream? Have you screamed? They had gone. They will have arrived. They were riding. They rode. I have finished. Thou hast erred. How she blushed! What a sight it was! Men and women stare, cry out, and run.

II. Give an example of each of the six tenses with each of the following verbs:—

kill	move	destroy	scold
heat	burn	permit	enter
spell	mend	depart	paint

Tenses of the Indicative Mode.

THE PRESENT TENSE.

175. The Present Tense denotes present time; as, "I *write*." "I *am writing*."

The *simple form* expresses what is customary or always true; as, "The sun *rises* and *sets*." "God *is* eternal."

It embraces any extent of time, a portion of which is included in the present; as, Caligula *is* justly *abhorred* for his cruelty,"— that is, *was* and still *is abhorred*.

The simple form of the present tense is sometimes used in the narration of past events to impart vivacity to the style; as, "He *fights, conquers*, and *takes* an immense booty, which he *divides* among his soldiers, and *returns* home."

This form sometimes refers to future time also, especially when preceded by the words *when, before, after, as soon as*, &c.; as, "When he *arrives*, he will hear the news." "Mr. Colman *goes* to Boston to-morrow."

THE IMPERFECT TENSE.

176. The Imperfect Tense denotes past time simply; as, "I *wrote*." "I *was writing*."

The *simple form* of the imperfect expresses an action or state as completed in past time; as, "The ship *sailed* yesterday."

It also expresses what was habitual in past times; as, "Humboldt *rose* at four in the morning [that is, *was in the habit of rising*]."

THE PERFECT TENSE.

177. The Perfect Tense denotes past time with some reference to the present; as, "I *have written.*" "I *have been writing.*"

The signs of this tense are *have, hast, has.*

The *simple form* of this tense expresses an action or state that took place at any period of past time, together with the idea of continuance to the present; as, "Philosophers *have made* great discoveries in the present century." Here, the action spoken of is past, but the idea of continuance to the present time is implied.

If there is no reference to present time, either in the act itself or its consequences, the perfect should not be used. It would be wrong to say, "Philosophers *have made* great discoveries in the seventeenth century."

This form expresses also an action or event as just finished; as, "I *have spoken* freely what I had to say."

The simple form of the perfect, preceded by *when, before, as soon as,* &c., sometimes denotes future time; as, "We will go as soon as we *have completed* our work."

THE PLUPERFECT TENSE.

178. The Pluperfect Tense denotes time past at or before some other specified past time; as, "I *had written.*" "I *had been writing.*" "I *had finished* my letter before he arrived."

The signs of this tense are *had, hadst.*

The pluperfect bears the same relation to the imperfect that the perfect does to the present.

THE FIRST FUTURE TENSE.

179. The First Future Tense denotes future time simply; as, "I *shall write.*" "I *shall be writing.*"

The signs of this tense are *shall, shalt, will, wilt.*

THE SECOND FUTURE TENSE.

180. The Second Future Tense denotes time that will be past at or before some future time specified; as, "I *shall have written.*" "I *shall have been writing.*" "They *will have finished* their work by the appointed time."

The signs of this tense are *shall have, shalt have, will have, wilt have.*

Tenses of the Potential Mode.

181. Only four of the six tenses appear in the Potential Mode; the Present, Imperfect, Perfect, and Pluperfect.

SIGNS. — The signs of the Present Potential are *may, can, must.*
Imperfect Potential, *might, could, would, should.*
Perfect Potential, *may have, can have, must have.*
Pluperfect Potential, *might have, could have, would have, should have.*

182. The tenses of the Potential Mode do not denote the same distinctions of time as the corresponding tenses of the Indicative.

183. The Present Potential implies permission, ability, or necessity. It refers to either present or future time, according to the modifying words with which it is accompanied; as,

	Present.	*Future.*
Permission.	You *may go* now.	You *may go* to-morrow.
Ability.	I *can go* now.	I *can go* to-morrow.
Necessity.	He *must go* now.	He *must go* to-morrow.

184. The Imperfect Potential implies permission, ability, determination, or obligation, with reference either to past, present, or future time; as,

Permission — past. Last week he said I *might go* yesterday.
Ability — past. I *could* not *go* last year.
Determination — present. I *would go* now, if it were possible.
Obligation — future. You *should* by all means *return* next week.

185. The Perfect Potential implies the present possibility or necessity of an action or state's having taken place at some past time; as,

She *may have returned;* MEANING, It is possible that she has returned.
She *can* not *have returned;* " It is not possible that she has returned.
She *must have returned;* " It must be that she has returned.

186. The Pluperfect Potential implies past possibility, determination, or obligation, with respect to an action or state's having taken place at some past time; as,

She *might have returned;* MEANING, It was possible for her to have returned.
She *could have returned;* " It was possible for her to have returned.
She *would have returned;* " It was her determination to have returned.
She *should have returned;* " It was her duty to have returned.

Tenses of the Subjunctive Mode.

187. Only two of the six tenses appear in the Subjunctive Mode ; the Present and the Imperfect.

As before remarked, the various tenses of the Indicative and the Potential are often used subjunctively.

188. The Present Subjunctive generally expresses a condition on which something future depends ; as, " If I *justify* myself, mine own mouth shall condemn me." "If I *be* wicked, woe unto me!"

The Imperfect Subjunctive expresses a present supposition in connection with which something present or future is asserted; as, "If I *were* he, I would return [either immediately or at some future time]."

This tense also implies that the opposite of the supposition is the case. If used in an affirmative clause, it implies a negation; as, "If he *were* industrious, he would succeed [implying that he is not industrious]." If used in a negative clause, it implies an affirmation; as, "If he *were* not industrious, he would not succeed [implying that he is industrious]."

Tense of the Imperative Mode.

189. A command can be given only at the present time, and therefore the Imperative Mode has but one tense, the Present.

Tenses of the Infinitive Mode.

190. The Infinitive Mode has two tenses, the Present and the Perfect; as, *to write, to have written.*

191. The Present Infinitive expresses an uncompleted action or state in an unlimited manner, with reference either to past, present, or future time; as,

Past.—I wished *to write* last week.
Present.—I wish *to write* now.
Future.—I intend *to write* next week.

The Perfect Infinitive expresses a completed action or state in an unlimited manner; as, "Metius is thought *to have invented* the telescope."

EXERCISE.

Point out the verbs in the following sentences; state whether they are transitive or intransitive; mention their voice, mode, and tense.

Venus is a planet. I am reading history. Cortez invaded Mexico before Pizarro had overrun Peru. Many have tried in vain to discover the philosopher's stone. If it is I you mean, produce your proof. When the sky falls, we shall catch larks. Napoleon would have given much to have been on the field himself. If I were sure he would come, I would remain. He will have failed before the steamer can arrive. You may have heard this. We have been trying to catch fish.

SECTION V.

PARTICIPLES.

192. A Participle is a word that partakes of the properties of a verb and an adjective; as, "*Hearing* the music, he returned."

Hearing is a participle. It partakes of the properties of the verb *hear*, in that it implies action. It partakes of the properties of an adjective, in that it is joined to the pronoun *he* to qualify it.

193. An intransitive verb has three participles, known as the Present, the Perfect, and the Compound. The three participles of the verb *rove* are *roving, roved, having roved.*

PARTICIPLES.

194. The Present Participle ends in *ing*, and implies an action or state going on and not completed; as, *roving, turning, being*.

The present participle implies time present, in relation to the action or state denoted by the leading verb of the sentence. Thus, absolutely, it may imply either past, present, or future time. *Seeing me, you trembled; Seeing me, you tremble; Seeing me, you will tremble.* Here the *seeing* is present relatively to the *trembling;* but, absolutely, it is past, present, or future, according to the tense of the verb *tremble.*

195. The present participle of a transitive verb, though generally active in its signification, is sometimes used passively; as, "The book is *printing* [equivalent to *the book is* being printed]."

196. The present participle must be distinguished from a verbal noun having the same form. "While *reading*, he fainted." "I am fond of *reading*." In the former sentence, *reading* is a present participle, because it implies an action, and describes the pronoun *he*. In the latter sentence, it is the name of something, and is a noun.

197. The Perfect Participle generally (though not always) ends in *ed*, and implies an action or state completed; as, *roved, turned, been*.

This participle is never used by itself, but enters into many compound forms of the verb; as, *have loved, had loved.*

198. The Compound Participle is formed by combining the participle *having* with the perfect participle, and implies an action or state completed before the commencement of some other action or state; as, *having roved, having turned, having been.*

199. A transitive verb has six participles: the three mentioned above, which are then distinguished as the Present Participle Active, the Perfect Participle Active, and the Compound Participle Active; and three corresponding to them in the passive voice.

The Present Participle Passive of the verb *loved* is *being loved.* The Perfect Participle Passive is *loved;* as, "*Loved* by his friends, he lived happily." The Compound Participle Passive is *having been loved.*

EXERCISE.

Analyze the following sentences. Parse the nouns, pronouns, and adjectives they contain. Point out the participles, and give the name of each.

Drawing a line on the sand, and eying the men arrayed before him, Pizarro thus addressed them. Expelled by the Greeks, I came to Italy, believing I should there find safety. Being thus led on, Hastings joined the conspiracy. Having once been deceived, the king was exceedingly cautious. The horse, having fallen in leaping the ditch, was afraid to approach the place again.

Trembling, hoping, lingering, flying,—
O the pain, the bliss of dying!

SECTION VI.
REGULAR AND IRREGULAR VERBS.

200. A Regular Verb is one that forms its imperfect indicative and perfect participle by adding *ed* to the present, or *d* when the present ends in silent *e*; as,

Indic. Present.	Indic. Imperfect.	Perfect Participle.
Arrive,	arrived,	arrived.
Conceal,	concealed,	concealed.
Perform,	performed,	performed.

201. Regular verbs ending in *y* preceded by any other letter than *a*, *e*, or *o*, change *y* into *i* before *ed*; as,

	Cry,	cried,	cried.	Deny,	denied	denied.
But	Pray,	prayed,	prayed.	Prey,	preyed,	preyed.
	Toy,	toyed,	toyed.	Enjoy,	enjoyed,	enjoyed.

202. Certain regular verbs double their final letter before the termination *ed*; as, fit, fitted; plan, planned; regret, regretted; drop, dropped.

203. An Irregular Verb is one that does not form its imperfect indicative and perfect participle by adding *ed* to the present, or *d* when the present ends in silent *e*; as,

Indic. Present.	Indic. Imperfect.	Perfect Participle.
Know,	knew,	known.
Stand,	stood,	stood.
Go,	went,	gone.

204. To find whether a verb is regular or irregular, add *d* or *ed* to the present, and see whether that forms the imperfect tense and perfect participle. If it does, the verb is regular; if not, irregular. — Is the verb *bring* regular or irregular? Add *ed*, — *bringed.* There is no such word; therefore *bring* is irregular. — Is *move* regular or irregular? Add *d*, — *moved.* This is both the imperfect tense and the perfect participle; therefore *move* is regular.

Are the following verbs regular or irregular? — *Open; fatigue; set; prove; have; regret; transfer; plan; lend; sit; create; command; come; complain; relate; rest; lose; deceive; improve; make.*

SECTION VII.

PERSON AND NUMBER OF THE VERB.

205. Besides voice, mood, and tense, the verb has two other accidents, — Person and Number.

206. Verbs, like nouns and pronouns, have three persons and two numbers. The 1st person singular affirms something of one person speaking; the 2d, of one person spoken to; the 3d, of one person or thing spoken of. The 1st person plural affirms something of more than one person speaking; the 2d, of more than one person spoken to; the 3d, of more than one person or thing spoken of.

207. A verb has the same person and number as its subject; and sometimes, in undergoing a change in person and number, it also undergoes a change of form; as,

	1st Person.	2d Person.	3d Person.
Sing.	I love,	Thou lovest,	He loves;
Plur.	We love,	You love,	They love.

It will be seen that *st* is added to form the second person; and *s*, to form the third.

208. *I*, the pronoun of the first person (or a relative referring to it), is the only word that can be the subject of a verb in the first, singular; *thou*, of a verb in the second, singular. *We* (or a relative standing for it) is always the subject of the first, plural, and *you* or *ye* of the second, plural. A verb in the third person may have any noun or any pronoun of the third person for its subject. In going over the parts of a verb, the pronouns

are given with them to distinguish the different persons and numbers; but it must be remembered that they form no part of the verb.

209. The second person singular of the verb (as, *thou lovest*) is not much used except in solemn style. The second plural (*you love*) takes its place, being used both when one person and more than one are spoken to.

210. The imperative mode is commonly used only in the second person; as, *come thou ; go ye.*

In poetry, however, and in certain forms, we sometimes find both the first and the third person used in the imperative mode; as,

1*st person.* — Well, *march we* on.
          Meet we the medicine of the sickly weal. — *Shakespeare.*
3*d person.* — *Be it enacted.*
Blessed *be he* that cometh. *Fall he* that must.

211. The infinitive mode and the participles have no person or number.

EXERCISE.

Point out the verbs; tell whether they are regular or irregular, transitive or intransitive; state the voice, mode, tense, person, and number of each.

They labor. They labored. I have labored. I shall labor. He will labor. It moves. It moved. It will move. We know. We knew. We shall know. We have known. The bees sting. The bees stung. The bees will sting. The bees may sting. They can sting. They might sting. You have. You had. You have had. You will have. You might have. You may have. To sting. To ave. To have had. To have stung.

SECTION VIII.

Auxiliary Verbs.

212. Conjugation is the inflection of a verb in its different voices, modes, tenses, numbers, and persons.

213. A verb is conjugated briefly by mentioning its three principal parts, the Present Indicative, Imperfect Indicative, and Perfect Participle; as,

Present Indicative, *love;* Imperfect Indicative, *loved;* Perfect Participle, *loved.*
Present Indicative, *draw;* Imperfect Indicative, *drew ;* Perfect Participle *drawn.*

214. From the parts of the verb that have been given as illustrations, it must have been observed that some of the tenses consist of but a single word, and others of several words. The former are called Simple tenses, the latter Compound. "I *love*," the present indicative, is simple; "I *may love*," the present potential, is compound.

The compound tenses are formed by combining with the principal verb certain short words called **Auxiliary Verbs.** *Auxiliary* means *helping*.

The auxiliary is often separated from the principal verb by one or more intervening words; as, "The accused *will* certainly *be convicted*."

215. Auxiliary verbs are such as help to form the modes and tenses of other verbs.

The auxiliaries are *do, be, have, will, shall, may, can,* and *must.*

216. *Do, be, have,* and *will* are also principal verbs, and, used as such, must be distinguished from the auxiliaries. "Do this for my sake;" *do* is a principal verb. "Do come;" *do* helps to form a compound tense of the verb *come*, and is an auxiliary.

217. Instead of the compound tense of a verb, its auxiliary alone is sometimes used, to avoid repetition; as, "I shall come; but, if I *do* not, remember me [that is, if I *do* not *come*]."—"'Will you come?' 'I *will* [*come*.]'"

218. *Be* is used as an auxiliary in all its parts; the other auxiliaries are for the most part used in the present and imperfect, and those tenses only. *Be* and *have* are conjugated at length hereafter; the parts of the remaining auxiliaries are given below.

219. Conjugation of the Auxiliaries.

	Singular.			Plural.		
	1st per.	2d per.	3d per.	1st per.	2d per.	3d per.
	I	*Thou*	*He*	*We*	*You*	*They*
Pres.—Do	dost	dost	does	do	do	do
Imp.—Did	didst	didst	did	did	did	did
Pres.—Will	will	will	will	will	will	will
Imp.—Would	wouldst	wouldst	would	would	would	would
Pres.—Shall	shalt	shalt	shall	shall	shall	shall
Imp.—Should	shouldst	shouldst	should	should	should	should
Pres.—May	mayst	mayst	may	may	may	may
Imp.—Might	mightst	mightst	might	might	might	might
Pres.—Can	canst	canst	can	can	can	can
Imp.—Could	couldst	couldst	could	could	could	could
Pres.—Must	must	must	must	must	must	must

Remarks on the Auxiliaries.

DO, DID.

220. *Do* is a sign of the present indicative or the present imperative; *did*, of the imperfect indicative. They are used, —

1. In negative and interrogative sentences; as, "I *do* not see." "I *did* not see." "*Do* you see?" "*Did* you see?"
2. In emphatic expressions; as, "'You *do* not love me.' 'I *do* love you with all my heart.'" — "'You *did* not smile.' 'I *did*.'"
3. Expletively; that is, without any special force; as, "Expletives their feeble aid *do* join."

In the imperative mode, *do* is used to express an urgent command, entreaty, or exhortation; as, "*Do* help me." "Make haste, *do*."

SHALL, WILL, SHOULD, WOULD.

221. *Shall* and *will* are signs of the first future tense. In the different persons they express different shades of meaning, as set forth below.

SHALL in the first person, in declarative sentences, announces or declares what will take-place, or expresses the decision of the speaker in reference to some future action or state; as, "I *shall* go to-morrow." Sometimes it is used in these senses contingently; as, "I *shall* go to-morrow, if the weather permit."

Shall in the second and the third person generally expresses the will, decision, promise, or command of the speaker in reference to some other person or thing; as, "He *shall* go [it is my *will* that he go]." "Then *shall* ye return, saith the Lord of hosts [*promise*]." "Thou *shalt* not kill [*command*]."

Shall in all the persons denotes futurity simply after *if* and some other words that express a condition; as, "If I, we, you, or he *shall* go."

In questions, *shall* in the first person implies simple futurity; as, "*Shall* I reach the boat in season?" It also asks the advice or direction of the person addressed; as, "*Shall* I go?" "*Shall* I suffer such injustice?" "What *shall* I do?" "Whither *shall* I fly?"

WILL in the first person, in declarative sentences, expresses the determination of the speaker with respect to his own action or state; as, "I *will* go." "I *will* be [that is, it is my *determination* to be] happy."

Will in the second and third person generally denotes futurity simply; as, "He *will* not go to-morrow." Sometimes, however, it implies strong determination on the part of the subject; as, "Why *will* ye die?" "He *will* not listen [that is, he is *determined* not to listen]."

The difference between *shall* and *will* in declarative sentences may be summed up as follows: —

Shall in the first person, and *will* in the second and third, imply simple futurity.

Will in the first person, and *shall* in the second and third, imply determination.

Simple Future.

| I shall, | thou wilt, | he will |
| We shall, | ye will, | they will. |

Future of Determination.

| I will, | thou shalt, | he shall; |
| We will, | ye shall, | they shall. |

Will is also used without any reference to future time, to express what is customary; as, "She *will* lie beneath the trees for hours at a time."

222. *Should* and *would* are signs of the imperfect potential.

SHOULD in all the persons commonly expresses obligation; as, "We [you or they] *should* do right."

After *if, though, unless,* and some other conjunctions, *should* expresses future contingency; as, "If it *should* happen." "Though all *should* deny thee."

WOULD implies will, desire, or determination, under a *condition* or *supposition;* as, "I *would* if I could." "I could if I *would.*"

It is also used to express simply a future event or state under a condition or supposition; as, "He *would* be censured, if he should remain longer."

Would sometimes expresses what was customary in past time; as, "She *would* talk of these scenes by the hour."

MAY, CAN, MUST, MIGHT, COULD.

223. *May, can,* and *must* are the signs of the present potential.

224. MAY implies, —
1. *Possibility;* as, "Something *may* happen to defeat our plans."
2. *Liberty,* or *permission;* as, "A man *may* do what the laws permit." "Thou *mayst* be no longer steward." "He *may* go, if he wishes."
3. *Wish,* when placed before the subject; as, "*May* prosperity attend you."

The expressions *may be, it may be,* are equivalent to *perhaps*, or *by chance;* as, "*May be* I will go [that is, *perhaps* I will go]."

225. CAN implies ability. "*Can* faith save him [*is* it *able* to save him]?" "An astronomer *can* [*is able* to] calculate an eclipse."

226. MUST implies necessity, certainty, or obligation, and undergoes no variation to express time, person, or number.

227. *Might* and *could* are signs of the imperfect potential.

MIGHT is the imperfect of *may;* like *may*, it implies possibility, liberty, or wish, and is sometimes used in place of it; as, "O that Ishmael *might* live before thee!"

COULD is the imperfect of *can*, and like it implies ability, particularly with reference to past time; as, "He *could* not come."

EXERCISE.

Select the auxiliaries. Parse the verbs as before directed, being careful in parsing never to separate an auxiliary from the rest of the verbal form.

I have moved. They had called. We shall move. I will write. They have elected. He has read. They will come. They will have learned. I may go. May he go? Can he go? He must go. They cannot go. They might go. They could succeed. They would learn, if they would try. They must have been informed. I did not know. You might have known.

SECTION IX.

CONJUGATION OF THE VERB *HAVE*

228. HAVE is an irregular transitive verb. As a principal verb, it is complete. As an auxiliary, it is used only in certain parts. It is conjugated as follows:—

When a tense has more than one sign, it should be inflected with each.

PRINCIPAL PARTS.

Present Ind.	Imperf. Ind.	Perfect Part.
Have,	Had,	Had.

CONJUGATION OF THE VERB *HAVE*.

INDICATIVE MODE.
Present Tense.

Singular.	Plural.
1. I have,	1. We have,
2. Thou hast,	2. You * have,
3. He has,	3. They have.

Imperfect Tense.

1. I had,	1. We had,
2. Thou hadst,	2. You had,
3. He had,	3. They had.

Perfect Tense.
SIGN,—*have*.

1. I have had,	1. We have had,
2. Thou hast had,	2. You have had,
3. He has had,	3. They have had.

Pluperfect Tense.
SIGN,—*had*.

1. I had had,	1. We had had,
2. Thou hadst had,	2. You had had,
3. He had had,	3. They had had.

First Future Tense.
SIGNS,—*shall, will*.

1. I shall or will have,	1. We shall or will have,
2. Thou shalt or wilt have,	2. You shall or will have,
3. He shall or will have,	3. They shall or will have.

Second Future Tense.
SIGNS,—*shall have, will have*.

1. I shall or will have had,	1. We shall or will have had,
2. Thou shalt or wilt have had,	2. You shall or will have had,
3. He shall or will have had,	3. They shall or will have had.

POTENTIAL MODE.
Present Tense.
SIGNS,—*may, can, must*.

1. I may have,	1. We may have,
2. Thou mayst have,	2. You may have,
3. He may have,	3. They may have.

---

* *Ye* and *you* require the same form of the verb. As *you* is the common form, *ye* is not used in the conjugation.

CONJUGATION OF THE VERB *HAVE.*

Imperfect Tense.

SIGNS,— *might, could, would, should.*

Singular.	*Plural.*
1. I might have,	1. We might have,
2. Thou mightst have,	2. You might have,
3. He might have,	3. They might have.

Perfect Tense.

SIGNS,— *may have, can have, must have.*

1. I may have had, 1. We may have had,
2. Thou mayst have had, 2. You may have had,
3. He may have had, 3. They may have had.

Pluperfect Tense.

SIGNS,— *might, could, would,* or *should have.*

1. I might have had, 1. We might have had,
2. Thou mightst have had, 2. You might have had,
3 He might have had, 3. They might have had.

SUBJUNCTIVE MODE.

Present Tense.

1. If I have, 1. If we have,
2. If thou have, 2. If you have,
3. If he have, 3. If they have.

Imperfect Tense.

1. If I had, 1. If we had,
2. If thou had, 2. If you had,
3. If he had, 3. If they had.

IMPERATIVE MODE.

2. Have thou, 2. Have you.

INFINITIVE MODE.

Present, To have. *Perfect,* To have had.

PARTICIPLES.

Present, Having. *Perfect,* Had. *Compound,* Having had.

SECTION X.

Conjugation of the Verb Be.

229. *Be* is an irregular intransitive verb. It is conjugated as follows: —

PRINCIPAL PARTS.

Present Ind.	*Imperf. Ind.*	*Perfect Participle.*
Am,	Was,	Been.

INDICATIVE MODE.
Present Tense.

	Singular.	*Plural.*
PERSON.	1. I am,	1. We are,
	2. Thou art,	2. You are,
	3. He is,	3. They are.

Imperfect Tense.

1. I was,   1. We were,
2. Thou wast,   2. You were,
3. He was,   3. They were.

Perfect Tense.

1. I have been,   1. We have been,
2. Thou hast been,   2. You have been,
3. He has been,   3. They have been.

Pluperfect Tense

1. I had been,   1. We had been,
2. Thou hadst been,   2. You had been,
3. He had been,   3. They had been.

First Future Tense.

1. I shall or will be,   1. We shall or will be,
2. Thou shalt or wilt be,   2. You shall or will be,
3. He shall or will be,   3. They shall or will be.

Second Future Tense.

1. I shall or will have been,   1. We shall or will have been,
2. Thou shalt or wilt have been,   2. You shall or will have been,
3. He shall or will have been,   3. They shall or will have been.

CONJUGATION OF THE VERB *BE*.

POTENTIAL MODE.

Present Tense

SIGNS,—*may, can, must.*

Singular.
1. I may be,
2. Thou mayst be,
3. He may be,

Plural.
1. We may be,
2. You may be,
3. They may be.

Imperfect Tense.

SIGNS,—*might, could, would, should.*

1. I might be,
2. Thou mightst be,
3. He might be,

1. We might be,
2. You might be,
3. They might be.

Perfect Tense.

SIGNS,—*may have, can have, must have.*

1. I may have been,
2. Thou mayst have been,
3. He may have been,

1. We may have been,
2. You may have been,
3. They may have been.

Pluperfect Tense.

SIGNS,—*might, could, would, should have.*

1. I might have been,
2. Thou mightst have been,
3. He might have been,

1. We might have been,
2. You might have been,
3. They might have been.

SUBJUNCTIVE MODE.

Present Tense.

1. If I be,
2. If thou be,
3. If he be,

1. If we be,
2. If you be,
3. If they be.

Imperfect Tense.

1. If I were or were I,
2. If thou wert or wert thou,*
3. If he were or were he,

1. If we were or were we,
2. If you were or were you,
3. If they were or were they.

IMPERATIVE MODE.

2. Be thou,
2. Be you.

---

* *If thou were* or *were thou* is also used.

EXERCISE ON THE VERBS *BE* AND *HAVE*.

INFINITIVE MODE.

Present, To be.   *Perfect*, To have been.

PARTICIPLES.

Present, Being.   *Perfect*, Been.   *Compound*, Having been.

EXERCISE.

I. Give the first person singular of each tense of the verb *have*, in order, naming the tense with each; as,

INDICATIVE MODE. — *Present*, I have; *Imperfect*, I had; *Perfect*, I have had; *Pluperfect*, I had had, &c.

Give the first plural of each tense in the same way.
Give the second singular of each tense of the verb *be*.
Give the second plural of each tense.

II. Parse the following words: —

I have had. I had been. I shall be. I shall have been. I can be. He may have. He may be. May he be? May he have? We must have. We must be. We may have been. We must have been. I might be. I might have. They could have. They should have. He would have been. He might have been. You were. You have been. You might be. You could be. You should be. They were. He was. We are. We have. We have been. They have been. If I be. If thou wert. To have. To have had. To have been. Having had. Been. Having.

III. Correct the following sentences: —

You was. They has been. When was you there? There has been men without a single honorable feeling. There is some sweet flowers. We was ten days on our journey. There was men, women, and children in the assembly. I be contented. They be robbers. We be true men. Was you there?

IV. Compose a sentence to contain each of the following words: —

Have. Has. Am. Was. Were. Has been. Have been. Would be. Shall be. Be. Wert. Might have. Could have. To have. To have been.

SECTION XI.
CONJUGATION OF THE VERB *Love*.

230. As an example of the conjugation of a transitive verb in the active and the passive voice, we may take the regular transitive verb *love*.

Active Voice.

PRINCIPAL PARTS.

Present Ind.	*Imperf. Ind.*	*Perfect Participle.*
Love,	Loved,	Loved.

INDICATIVE MODE.

Present Tense, simple form.

Singular.	Plural.
1. I love,	1. We love,
2. Thou lovest,	2. You love,
3. He loves.	3. They love.

Present Tense, emphatic form.

1. I do love,	1. We do love,
2. Thou dost love,	2. You do love,
3. He does love,	3. They do love.

Imperfect Tense, simple form.

1. I loved,	1. We loved,
2. Thou lovedst,	2. You loved,
3. He loved,	3. They loved.

Imperfect Tense, emphatic form.

1. I did love,	1. We did love,
2. Thou didst love,	2. You did love,
3. He did love,	3. They did love.

Perfect Tense.

1. I have loved,	1. We have loved,
2. Thou hast loved,	2. You have loved,
3. He has loved,	3. They have loved

CONJUGATION OF THE VERB *LOVE*.

Pluperfect Tense.

Singular.
1. I had loved,
2. Thou hadst loved,
3. He had loved,

Plural.
1. We had loved,
2. You had loved,
3. They had loved.

First Future Tense.

1. I shall or will love,
2. Thou shalt or wilt love,
3. He shall or will love,

1. We shall or will love,
2. You shall or will love,
3. They shall or will love.

Second Future Tense.

1. I shall or will have loved,
2. Thou shalt or wilt have loved,
3. He shall or will have loved,

1. We shall or will have loved,
2. You shall or will have loved,
3. They shall or will have loved.

POTENTIAL MODE.

Present Tense.

SIGNS,— *may, can, must.*

1. I may love,
2. Thou mayst love,
3. He may love,

1. We may love,
2. You may love,
3. They may love.

Imperfect Tense.

SIGNS,— *might, could, would, should.*

1. I might love,
2. Thou mightst love,
3. He might love,

1. We might love,
2. You might love,
3. They might love.

Perfect Tense.

SIGNS,— *may have, can have, must have.*

1. I may have loved,
2. Thou mayst have loved,
3. He may have loved,

1. We may have loved,
2. You may have loved,
3. They may have loved.

Pluperfect Tense.

SIGNS,— *might, could, would,* or *should have.*

1. I might have loved,
2. Thou mightst have loved,
3. He might have loved,

1. We might have loved,
2. You might have loved,
3. They might have loved.

PROGRESSIVE FORM.

SUBJUNCTIVE MODE.

Present Tense.

Singular.
1. If I love,
2. If thou love,
3. If he love,

Plural.
1. If we love,
2. If you love,
3. If they love.

Imperfect Tense.

1. If I loved,
2. If thou loved,
3. If he loved,

1. If we loved,
2. If you loved,
3. If they loved.

IMPERATIVE MODE.

2. Love thou,   2. Love you.

INFINITIVE MODE.

Present, To love.   *Perfect,* To have loved.

PARTICIPLES.

Present, Loving.   *Perfect,* Loved.   *Compound,* Having loved.

Progressive Form.

231. The Progressive Form of the verb denotes an action as begun and in progress, but not completed.

A verb is conjugated in the progressive form by annexing the present participle active to the different parts of the verb *to be.* This form appears in all the active tenses. The first persons are given below; in reciting, give all the persons, — *I am loving, thou art loving,* &c.

Indicative Mode.

Present. I am loving.   *Pluperfect.* I had been loving.
Imperfect. I was loving.   *1st. Future.* I shall be loving.
Perfect. I have been loving.   *2d. Future.* I shall have been loving.

Potential Mode.

Present. I may, can, or must be loving.
Imperfect. I might, could, would, or should be loving.
Perfect. I may, can, or must have been loving.
Pluperfect. I might, could, would, or should have been loving.

Subjunctive Mode.

Present. If I be loving.   *Imperfect.* If I were loving.

Imperative Mode.
2. Be thou loving.   Be you loving.

Infinitive Mode.
Present. To be loving.   *Perfect.* To have been loving.

Negative Form.

232. A verb is conjugated negatively by introducing the adverb *not*, after the verb in the simple tenses, after the first auxiliary in the compound tenses, before *to* in the infinitive mode, and before the participles; as,—

IND. MODE.—I love not, do not love, am not loving; I loved not, did not love, was not loving; I have not loved; I had not loved; I shall or will not love; I shall or will not have loved.

POT. MODE.—I may, can, or must not love; I might, could, would, or should not love; I may, can, or must not have loved; I might, could, would, or should not have loved.

SUB. MODE.—If I love not, if I do not love; if I loved not, if I did not love.

IMP. MODE.—Love not, do not love.

INF. MODE.—Not to love; not to have loved.

PARTICIPLES.—Not loving; not loved; not having loved.

Interrogative Form.

233. A verb is conjugated interrogatively in the indicative and the potential mode by placing the subject after the verb in the simple tenses, and in the compound tenses after the first auxiliary.

IND. MODE.—Love I, do I love, am I loving? Loved I, did I love, was I loving? Have I loved? Had I loved? Shall or will I love? Shall or will I have loved?

POT. MODE.—May, can, or must I love? Might, could, would, or should I love? May, can, or must I have loved? Might, could, would, or should I have loved?

PASSIVE VOICE. **115**

Negative Interrogative Form.

234. A verb is conjugated negatively and interrogatively by introducing the adverb *not* immediately after the subject in each tense of the interrogative form.

IND. MODE.— Love I not, do I not love, am I not loving? Loved I not, did I not love, was I not loving? Have I not loved? Had I not loved? Shall or will I not love? Shall or will I not have loved?

POT. MODE. — May, can, or must I not love? Might, could, would, or should I not love? May, can, or must I not have loved? Might, could, would, or should I not have loved?

Passive Voice.

235. A verb is conjugated in the passive voice by placing its perfect participle after the various parts of the verb *to be*.

A progressive form is sometimes used in the present and imperfect passive; as, "The house *is being built*." "The picture *was being painted*." Instead of these constructions, most grammarians and good writers prefer the progressive form of the active voice, assigning it a passive signification; as, "The house *is building*." "The picture *was painting*."

INDICATIVE MODE.
Present Tense, simple form.

Singular.
1. I am loved,
2. Thou art loved,
3. He is loved,

Plural.
1. We are loved,
2. You are loved,
3. They are loved.

Present Tense, progressive form.

1. I am being loved,
2. Thou art being loved,
3. He is being loved,

1. We are being loved,
2. You are being loved,
3. They are being loved.

Imperfect Tense, simple form.

1. I was loved,
2. Thou wast loved,
3. He was loved,

1. We were loved,
2. You were loved,
3. They were loved.

Imperfect Tense, progressive form.

1. I was being loved,
2. Thou wast being loved,
3. He was being loved,

1. We were being loved,
2. You were being loved,
3. They were being loved.

PASSIVE VOICE OF THE VERB *LOVE.*

Perfect Tense.

Singular.   Plural.
1. I have been loved,   1. We have been loved,
2. Thou hast been loved,   2. You have been loved,
3. He has been loved,   3. They have been loved.

Pluperfect Tense.

1. I had been loved,   1. We had been loved,
2. Thou hadst been loved,   2. You had been loved,
3. He had been loved,   3. They had been loved.

First Future Tense.

1. I shall or will be loved,   1. We shall or will be loved,
2. Thou shalt or wilt be loved,   2. You shall or will be loved,
3. He shall or will be loved,   3. They shall or will be loved.

Second Future Tense.

SIGNS,— *shall have, will have.*

1. I shall have been loved,   1. We shall have been loved,
2. Thou shalt have been loved,   2. You shall have been loved,
3. He shall have been loved,   3. They shall have been loved.

POTENTIAL MODE.

Present Tense.

SIGNS, — *may, can, must.*

1. I may be loved,   1. We may be loved,
2. Thou mayst be loved,   2. You may be loved,
3. He may be loved,   3. They may be loved.

Imperfect Tense.

SIGNS, —*might, could, would, should.*

1. I might be loved,   1. We might be loved,
2. Thou mightst be loved,   2. You might be loved,
3. He might be loved,   3. They might be loved.

Perfect Tense.

SIGNS, — *may have, can have, must have.*

1. I may have been loved,   1. We may have been loved,
2. Thou mayst have been loved,   2. You may have been loved,
3. He may have been loved,   3. They may have been loved.

PASSIVE VOICE OF THE VERB *LOVE*.

Pluperfect Tense.

SIGN, — *might, could, would,* or *should have.*

Singular.
1. I might have been loved,
2. Thou mightst have been loved,
3. He might have been loved,

Plural.
1. We might have been loved,
2. You might have been loved,
3. They might have been loved.

SUBJUNCTIVE MODE.

Present Tense.

1. If I be loved,
2. If thou be loved,
3. If he be loved,

1. If we be loved,
2. If you be loved,
3. If they be loved.

Imperfect Tense.

1. If I were loved,
2. If thou wert loved,
3. If he were loved,

1. If we were loved,
2. If you were loved,
3. If they were loved.

IMPERATIVE MODE.

2. Be thou loved,

2. Be you loved.

INFINITIVE MODE.

Present, To be loved.   *Perfect,* To have been loved.

PARTICIPLES.

Pres. Being loved.   *Perf.* Loved.   *Comp.* Having been loved.

EXERCISE.

1. Give the third person singular of each tense of the passive voice of the verb *love*, in order.

Give the third person plural of each tense of the passive voice.

Conjugate the verb *love* negatively in the passive voice, giving the first person singular of each tense; as, *I am not loved, I was not loved,* &c.

Conjugate *love* interrogatively in the passive voice, giving the second person singular of each tense; as, *Art thou loved? Wast thou loved?* &c.

Conjugate *love* negatively and interrogatively in the passive voice, giving the second person singular of each tense; as, *Art thou not loved? Wast thou not loved?* &c.

Syntactical Relations.

A finite verb is said to agree with its subject when it has the same person and number; as, He *lives*.

A verb in the infinitive is used, —
1. As a verbal noun in the nominative and objective cases; as, " *To study* is hard work."
2. To limit the meaning of the word on which it depends; as, " He desires to *learn*."
3. With a subject in the objective case; as, " I believe *him to be* an honest man."

A partciple is used, —
1. As an adjective to modify nouns and pronouns; as, " The birds, *singing* sweetly."
2. As a noun in the nominative and objective cases; as, " *Cultivating* the ground is hard work."

Any form of the verb may be modified by an adverbial element, and, if transitive, may be followed by an object.

When the object completes the meaning of a verb without the aid of any preposition expressed or understood, it is called the *direct object;* as, " I gave the *book* to him." When the prepositions *to, for,* or *from* may be supplied without injury to the sense, it is called the *indirect object;* as, " I gave (to) *him* the book."

II. Parse the following words. When a verb is in the progressive, emphatic, or interrogative form, mention it after the voice.

Form for Parsing.

Verb. — Transitive or intransitive, principal parts, regular or irregular, voice, mode, tense, person, number, agreement, rule.

PARSING MODEL. — Those men have been selling pigeons.

Those is a demonstrative pronominal adjective, cannot be compared, and belongs to *men*, according to Rule XVII. (Repeat it.)

Men is a common noun, third person, plural number, masculine gender, and nominative case. It is the subject of the verb *have been selling*, according to Rule II. (Repeat it.)

Have been selling is a transitive verb. The principal parts are, present *sell*, imperfect *sold*, perfect participle *sold*, irregular; active voice, progressive form, indicative mode, perfect tense, third person, plural number, to agree with its subject *men*, according to Rule V., — *A verb agrees with its subject nominative in person and number.*

Pigeons is a common noun, third, plural, masculine or feminine, objective, and is the object of the verb *have been selling*, according to Rule X. (Repeat it.)

Would Sir Isaac Newton have doubted this?

Would have doubted is a transitive verb. The principal parts are, present *doubt*, imperfect *doubted*, perfect participle *doubted*, regular; active voice, interrogative form, potential mode, pluperfect tense, third person, singular number, to agree with its subject *Sir Isaac Newton*, according to Rule V. (Repeat it.)

Sir Isaac Newton is a complex proper noun, third person, singular number, masculine gender, nominative case, and is the subject of the verb *would have doubted*, according to Rule II. (Repeat it.)

This is a demonstrative pronominal adjective used as a pronoun, third, singular, neuter, objective, and is the object of the verb *would have doubted*, according to Rule X. (Repeat it.)

I love to study my lesson.

To study is a transitive verb from the verb *to study:* principal parts, present *study*, imperfect *studied*, perfect participle *studied*. It is a regular verb, active voice, infinitive mode, and limits *love*, according to Rule XIX., — *A verb in the infinitive generally limits the meaning of a verb, noun, or adjective.*

I hear the birds singing.

Singing is a participle from the verb *to sing*. The participles are, present *singing*, perfect *sung*, compound participle *having sung*. It is a present participle used as an adjective, and belongs to *birds*, according to Rule XXI., — *Participles belong to nouns which they limit or modify.*

Writing letters is a profitable exercise.

Writing is a participle from the verb *to write*. The participles are, present *writing*, perfect *written*, compound *having written*. It is a present participle used as a noun, and is the subject of the verb *is*, according to Rule XXII., — *Participles used as nouns have the construction of nouns, while they are modified in the same way, and govern the same case, as the verbs from which they are formed.*

I have labored. He has proved. He created. They commanded. We have commanded. It will rain. It has rained. The children mocked. The soldiers were marching. It was raining. We were hoping. The time is approaching. I have been listening. Were you listening? Was he learning? Did he learn? Do you believe? Can you walk? We shall be walking. Shall we walk? The world was created. The world has been created. The soldiers were commanded. They will be commanded. The work will be accomplished. The work might be accomplished. They might accomplish the work. I do believe. We do affirm. They did maintain.

I am anxious to go. Hearing him speak, I changed my opinion regarding his merits. He is a man to be loved. I saw him writing a letter. He wishes to write a letter. To write letters is profitable.

SECTION XII.

Irregular Verbs.

236. Irregular verbs are easily conjugated when their imperfect tense and perfect participle are known, the auxiliaries used in the respective tenses being the same as in regular verbs. *Have* (§ 228) is an example.

Some of the most common verbs are irregular. It is important, therefore, to learn the following list:—

The letter R denotes that, besides the irregular form given, there is a regular form in *d* or *ed*. In reciting, both forms should be given; as, *gild, gilt* or *gilded, gilt* or *gilded.*

List of Irregular Verbs.

[Compounds enclosed within parentheses go like the primitives after which they are placed. Forms once authorized, but now no longer in good use, are put in italics.]

Present.	*Imperfect.*	*Perf. Part.*
Abide	abode	abode
Am	was	been
Arise	arose	arisen
Awake	awoke, R.	awoke, R.

LIST OF IRREGULAR VERBS.

Present.	Imperfect.	Per. Part.
Bear, *to bring forth*	bore, *bare*	born
Bear, *to carry*	bore, bare	borne
Beat	beat	beat, beaten
Begin	began	begun
Behold	beheld	beheld
Bend	bent, R.	bent, R.
Bereave	bereft, R.	bereft, R.
Beseech	besought	besought
Bet	bet, R.	bet, R.
Bid	bid, bade	bid, bidden
Bind (*unbind*)	bound	bound
Bite	bit	bitten, bit
Bleed	bled	bled
Blow	blew	blown
Break	broke, *brake*	broken, *broke*
Breed	bred	bred
Bring	brought	brought
Build (*rebuild*)	built, R.	built, R.
Burst	burst	burst
Buy	bought	bought
Cast	cast	cast
Catch	caught, R.	caught, R.
Chide	chid	chidden, chid
Choose	chose	chosen
Cleave, *to adhere*	clove, *clave*, R.	cleaved
Cleave, *to split*	cleft, clove	cleft, cloven, R.
Cling	clung	clung
Clothe (*unclothe*)	clad, R.	clad, R.
Come (*become*)	came	come
Cost	cost	cost
Creep	crept	crept
Crow	crew, R.	crowed
Cut	cut	cut
Dare, *to venture* *	durst	dared
Deal	dealt, R.	dealt, R.
Dig	dug, R.	dug, R.
Dive	dove, R.	dived
Do (*outdo, undo*)	did	done
Draw	drew	drawn
Drink	drank	drunk, drank

* Dare, *to challenge*, is regular.

LIST OF IRREGULAR VERBS.

Present.	*Imperfect.*	*Perf. Part.*
Drive	drove	driven
Drell	dwelt, R.	dwelt, R.
Eat	ate, eat [pron. *et*]	eaten, eat
Fall (*befall*)	fell	fallen
Feed	fed	fed
Feel	felt	felt
Fight	fought	fought
Find	found	found
Flee	fled	fled
Fling	flung	flung
Fly	flew	flown
Forbear	forbore	forborne
Forget	forgot	forgotten, forgot
Forsake	forsook	forsaken
Freeze	froze	frozen
Get (*beget*)	got, *gat*	got, *gotten*
Gild	gilt, R.	gilt, R.
Gird (*begird*)	girt, R.	girt, R.
Give (*forgive*)	gave	given
Go (*undergo*)	went	gone
Grave	graved	graven, R.
Grind	ground	ground
Grow	grew	grown
Hang	hung, R.	hung, R.
Have	had	had
Hear	heard	heard
Heave	hove, R.	hoven, R.
Hew	hewed	hewn, R.
Hide	hid	hidden, hid
Hit	hit	hit
Hold (*withhold*)	held	held, *holden*
Hurt	hurt	hurt
Keep	kept	kept
Kneel	knelt, R.	knelt, R.
Knit	knit, R.	knit, R.
Know	knew	known
Lade	laded	laden
Lay	laid	laid
Lead (*mislead*)	led	led
Leave	left	left
Lend	lent	lent
Let	let	let

LIST OF IRREGULAR VERBS.

Present.	*Imperfect.*	*Perf. Part.*
Lie, *to recline* *	lay	lain
Light	lit, R.	lit, R.
Lose	lost	lost
Make (*unmake*)	made	made
Mean	meant	meant
Meet	met	met
Mow	mowed	mown, R.
Pay (*repay*)	paid	paid
Prove	proved	proven, R.
Put	put	put
Quit	quit, R.	quit, R.
Read	read [pron. *red*]	read [*red*]
Rend	rent	rent
Rid	rid	rid
Ride (*outride*)	rode	ridden, rode
Ring	rung, rang	rung
Rise	rose	risen
Rive	rived	riven, R.
Run (*outrun*)	ran, run	run
Saw	sawed	sawn, R.
Say	said	said
See	saw	seen
Seek	sought	sought
Seethe	sod, R.	sodden, R.
Sell (*resell*)	sold	sold
Send	sent	sent
Set (*beset*)	set	set
Shake	shook	shaken
Shape	shaped	shapen, R.
Shave	shaved	shaven, R.
Shear	sheared	shorn
Shed	shed	shed
Shine	shone, R.	shone, R.
Shoe	shod	shod
Shoot	shot	shot
Show †	showed	shown, R.
Shred	shred	shred
Shrink	shrunk, *shrank*	shrunk, *shrunken*
Shut	shut	shut

* Lie, *to utter falsehood*, is regular.
† By old writers sometimes spelled *shew, shewed, shewn*, R.

LIST OF IRREGULAR VERBS.

Present.	Imperfect.	Perf. Part.
Sing	sung, sang	sung
Sink	sunk, sank	sunk
Sit	sat	sat
Slay	slew	slain
Sleep	slept	slept
Slide	slid	slidden, slid
Sling	slung	slung
Slink	slunk	slunk
Slit	slit, R.	slit, R.
Smite	smote	smitten
Sow	sowed	sown, R.
Speak (*bespeak*)	spoke, *spake*	spoken
Speed	sped, R.	sped, R.
Spend (*mis-spend*)	spent	spent
Spin	spun, *span*	spun
Spit	spit, *spat*	spit
Split	split	split
Spread	spread	spread
Spring	sprung, *sprang*	sprung
Stand (*withstand*)	stood	stood
Stave	stove, R.	stove, R.
Steal	stole	stolen
Stick	stuck	stuck
Sting	stung	stung
Stink	stunk, *stank*	stunk
Stride (*bestride*)	strode, strid	stridden, strid
Strike	struck	struck, *stricken*
String	strung	strung
Strive	strove	striven
Strow *	strowed	strown
Swear	swore, *sware*	sworn
Sweat	sweat, R.	sweat, R.
Sweep	swept	swept
Swell	swelled	swollen, R.
Swim	swam, *swum*	swum
Swing	swung	swung
Take (*be-, re-, under-*)	took	taken
Teach	taught	taught
Tear	tore	torn
Tell	told	told

* By old writers sometimes spelled *strew, strewed, strewn*, R.

EXERCISE ON IRREGULAR VERBS. 125

Present.	*Imperfect.*	*Perfect Part.*
Think	thought	thought
Thrive	throve, R.	thriven, R.
Throw	threw	thrown
Thrust	thrust	thrust
Tread	trod	trod, trodden
Understand (*mis-*)	understood	understood
Wax	waxed	waxen, R.
Wear (*outwear*)	wore	worn
Weave	wove, R.	woven, R.
Weep	wept	wept
Wed	wed, R.	wed, R.
Wet	wet, R.	wet, R.
Whet	whet, R.	whet, R.
Win	won	won
Wind	wound, R.	wound, R.
Work	wrought, R.	wrought, R.
Wring	wrung, R.	wrung, R.
Write	wrote	written

NOTE. — Some regular verbs in familiar discourse have their imperfect indicative and perfect participle pronounced as if they ended in *t* instead of *ed*, and we sometimes find them so written; as, *burnt* for *burned*, *past* for *passed*. As the regular form is much to be preferred, these verbs are not inserted in the above list of irregular verbs.

237. In parsing, irregular verbs, whenever they occur, should be conjugated briefly — that is, their three principal parts should be mentioned — immediately after their class is stated. Thus, "*We grind;*" — *grind* is an irregular transitive verb; *grind, ground, ground;* active voice, indicative, present, first, plural.

EXERCISE.

Correct the irregular verbs in the following sentences. When the sentences are corrected, analyze them, and parse the nouns, pronouns, adjectives, and verbs they contain.

The horses drawed the carriage. The timber was drawed a great distance. The horses were drove too fast. Does a glutton know when he has ate enough? The birds have flew away. The stream has froze over. A stone laid in the street. It has laid there a month. The old man has lain down his burden. He lay down his book and walked to the door.

They have wrote to-day. The bell has just rang. The meeting has began. I begun my work yesterday. She has sang a song. They have set there until they are weary. I sat the instrument down at your door. The sun sat in a cloud last evening. I saw him setting by the wayside. A tree was laying across the street. They done their work faithfully. He has mistook the way. His garments are nearly wore out. My watch was stole last night. The tempest blowed the ship ashore.

The chaff has blowed away. The building was blowed up. The rioters throwed stones. The ball was throwed dexterously. The sailor throwed away his money. The leaves were shook from the tree. The blossoms have fell to the ground. The leaves are tore out. Have you tore your book? The letter was so badly wrote that I read it with difficulty. We rid a mile. How is the room het? We dared not go. How many things your father has gave you! I have forborn as long as possible.

SECTION XIII.

Defective Verbs.

238. A Defective Verb is one that wants some of its parts. The defectives include, —

1. All the auxiliaries except *be*.

2. *Ought*, found only in the present and the imperfect. When used with the present infinitive of another verb, it is present; as, "You *ought* to go." When used with the perfect infinitive, it is imperfect; as, "You *ought* to have gone." *Had ought* or *could ought* is improper.

3. *Quoth*, formerly used as equivalent to *say*, now obsolete except in comic style. It is used only in the present and the imperfect, and does not vary in form. *Quoth* always stands before its subject; as, *quoth I*, *quoth he*.

4. *Beware* (derived from *be wary*), used chiefly in the imperative and the infinitive mode, but occasionally in the first future indicative and the imperfect potential.

5. *To wit*, "to know," is now used only in the infinitive, in the sense of *namely, that is to say*.

6. *Wot* (meaning *know*), formerly used in the present and the imperfect, is now obsolete.

239. Among the defectives is a class of verbs known as Impersonals.

Impersonal Verbs.

240. An Impersonal Verb is one that is used only in the third person singular, and has *it* for its subject; as, *it rains, it hails, it snows.*

Transitive verbs identical in form with the impersonals, but not to be confounded with them, have all their parts complete; as, "I *will rain* fire on them."

Among impersonals are generally classed the anomalous forms *methinks, methought,* — equivalent to *I think, I thought.*

EXERCISE.

Analyze the following sentences. Parse the nouns, pronouns, adjectives, and verbs.

INDICATIVE MODE.

Victory perched upon our banner; our arms triumphed, and the enemy suffered severely. We have compared the vast relics of decayed and mouldering literature to animal and vegetable remains. He has been diligent. He will have gone. It rained hard. Did you see the beautiful rainbow after the shower? They have resolved, examined their hearts, and made new plans. His words of this day are planted in my memory, and will there remain till my heart shall beat no more. I shall see his face and hear his voice no more. "You surprise me," quoth my friend.

POTENTIAL MODE.

It may be expected that I should accompany the resolution with some suitable remarks. His intercourse with the living world is ended; and those who would hereafter find him, must seek him in his grave. Thou canst do every thing. No thought can be withheld from thee. To meet death as becomes a man, is a privilege bestowed on few. I would endeavor to make it mine. We might have succeeded in our undertaking.

IMPERATIVE MODE.

Incline my heart unto thy testimonies. Keep my commandments and live. Bind them upon thy fingers, write them upon the table of thy heart. Hear instruction; be wise and refuse it not. And Reuben said unto them, Shed no blood, but cast him into this pit and lay no hand on him. Beware of mischief-makers.

INFINITIVE MODE.

Birds love to sing. The youth tries to learn. The man has a desire to hear. Learn to obey. He may hope to succeed. It is kind to forbear. Methinks it is pleasant to hear the sweet music of birds. Ask the hero, ask the statesman whose wisdom you have been accustomed to revere, and he will tell you. The rain began to patter down in broad and scattered drops. Influenced by a desire to stamp on these expressions their merited disgrace, and to preserve dignity in our deliberations, I felt it my duty to call the gentleman to order. We ought to avoid temptation. Cæsar ought not to have crossed the Rubicon.

RECAPITULATION.

Verbs.
- Forms.
  - Regular . . . . ; as, *Love.*
  - Irregular.
    - Principal; as, *Run.*
    - Auxiliary; as, *Be.*
    - Defective; as, *Ought.*
    - Impersonal; as, *It rains.*
- Uses.
  - Transitive . . . . ; as, *Write.*
  - Intransitive . . . ; as, *Run.*

Accidents of Verbs.
- Voice.
  - Active; as, *He loves.*
  - Passive; as, *He is loved.*
- Mode.
  - Indicative; as, *He loves.*
  - Potential; as, *He may love.*
  - Subjunctive; as, *If he love.*
  - Imperative; as, *Love thou.*
  - Infinitive; as, *To love.*
- Tense.
  - Present; as, *He loves.*
  - Imperfect; as, *He loved.*
  - Perfect; as, *He has loved.*
  - Pluperfect; as, *He had loved.*
  - First Future; as, *He will love.*
  - Second Future; as, *He will have [loved.*
- Person.
  - First; as, *I love.*
  - Second; as, *Thou lovest.*
  - Third; as, *He loves.*
- Number.
  - Singular; as, *He loves.*
  - Plural; as, *They love.*

REVIEW QUESTIONS ON CHAPTER V.

151. What is a verb? What does the word *affirm* mean in this definition? Give examples. 152. Into what classes are verbs divided? 153. What is a transitive verb? What is generally the object of a transitive verb? When is it omitted? 154. What is an intransitive verb? What part of speech used with an intransitive verb sometimes makes it transitive? Name the copula verbs. · Of what does the predicate consist? When do the copula verbs form the predicate of a sentence? 155. What may follow an intransitive verb as its object? When may a verb be either transitive or intransitive? 156. How can transitive and intransitive verbs be distinguished?

157. How many forms have transitive verbs? What are they called? How is the subject of a verb represented in the active voice? In the passive? What is voice? 158. In what case alone do intransitive verbs have a passive form? What voice have intransitive verbs? What verbs have no voice?

159. What is mode? 160. Give examples of the different modes in which the verb is used. What does the word *indicative* mean? *Potential? Subjunctive? Imperative? Infinitive?* 161. How many modes are there? Name them. 162. For what is the indicative mode used? 163. The potential? What are the signs of the potential? 164. For what are both the indicative and the potential used? 165. For what is the subjunctive mode used? How may it be known? Before what is the sign *if* often omitted? 166. What modes are often used instead of the subjunctive? 167. For what is the imperative mode used? How may it generally be known? 168. For what is the infinitive mode used? How may it be known? 169. What is sometimes the force of the infinitive mode? 170. When is a verb said to be finite?

171. What is tense? 172. Give an example of the present tense. The imperfect. The perfect. The pluperfect. The first future. The second future. 173. How many tenses are there? Name them. 174. How many forms are there in each tense? Name and define them.

175. What does the present tense denote? What does its simple form express? Its progressive form? 176. What does the imperfect tense denote? What does its simple form express? Its progressive form? 177. What does the perfect tense denote? What are its signs? What does the simple form of the perfect express? What force has it, when preceded by *when, before,* &c.? What does the progressive form of the perfect express? 178. What does the pluperfect tense denote? What are its signs? 179. What does the first future tense denote? What are its signs? 180. What does the second future tense denote? What are its signs?

181. Name the tenses that appear in the potential mode, and give their signs. 182. What is said of the tenses of the potential mode, as

compared with those of the indicative? 183. What does the present potential imply? Give examples. 184. What does the imperfect potential imply? Give examples. 185. What does the perfect potential imply? Give examples. 186. What does the pluperfect potential imply? Give examples. 187. How many tenses has the subjunctive mode? 188. What does the present subjunctive express? The imperfect? What does the imperfect also imply? 189. How many tenses has the imperative mode? 190. How many has the infinitive mode? 191. What does the present infinitive express? The perfect infinitive?

192. What is a participle? 193. How many participles has an intransitive verb? Name them. 194. What does the present participle end in and imply? 195. How is the present participle sometimes used? 196. From what must it be distinguished? 197. What does the perfect participle end in and imply? How is it used? 198. How is the compound participle formed? 199. How many participles has a transitive verb? Name them. Give examples.

200. What is a regular verb? 201. What change is made in regular verbs ending in *y*, before adding *ed?* 202. What other change is made in certain regular verbs? 203. What is an irregular verb? Give examples. 204. How do you find whether a verb is regular or irregular?

205. Besides voice, mode, and tense, what other accidents has the verb? 206. How many persons and numbers have verbs? What is the force of each? 207. What person and number has a verb? What change does the verb sometimes undergo? 208. What must a verb in the first person have for its subject? In the second? What may a verb in the third person have for its subject? 209. What generally takes the place of the second person singular of the verb? 210. What person alone is found in the imperative mode? What exceptions are noted? 211. What parts of the verb have no person or number?

212. What is conjugation? 213. How is a verb conjugated briefly? 214. What are simple tenses? Compound tenses? How are the compound tenses formed? 215. What are auxiliary verbs? Name the auxiliaries. 216. Which of these are also principal verbs? 217. What is sometimes used instead of the compound tense of a verb? 218. In what parts is *be* used as an auxiliary? In what tenses are the other auxiliaries used? 219. Go through the present and imperfect of *do; will; shall; may; can.*

220. Of what are *do* and *did* the signs? Give the three cases in which they are used. What is the force of *do* in the imperative mode? 221. Of what are *shall* and *will* the signs? What does *shall* denote in declarative sentences in the first person? In the second and the third person? What does *shall* denote after *if?* In questions? What does *will* denote

THE ADVERB. 131

In declarative sentences in the first person? In the second and the third person? Inflect the simple future. Inflect the future of determination. What else does *will* express? 222. Of what are *should* and *would* the signs? What does *should* express? What does *would* express? 223. Of what are *may, can,* and *must* the signs? 224. What does *may* imply? 225. *Can?* 226. *Must?* 227. Of what are *might* and *could* signs? What does *might* imply? *Could?*
228. What kind of a verb is *have?* Conjugate *have.* 229. What kind of a verb is *be?* Conjugate *be.* 230. What kind of a verb is *love?* Conjugate the active voice. 231. How is a verb conjugated in the progressive form? Carry the verb *love* through the various tenses in the progressive form. 232. How is a verb conjugated negatively? Conjugate *love* negatively. 233. How is a verb conjugated interrogatively? Conjugate *love* interrogatively. 234. How is a verb conjugated negatively and interrogatively? Conjugate *love* negatively and interrogatively. 235. How is a verb conjugated in the passive voice? In what tenses of the passive voice is a progressive form sometimes used? Go through the passive voice of the verb *love.* When is a verb said to agree with its subject? How is a verb in the infinitive used? A participle? How may a verb be modified? What is the direct object? The indirect object?
238. What is a defective verb? What whole class of verbs are defective? In what parts is *ought* found? How are the two tenses of *ought* distinguished from each other? In what tenses is *quoth* used? How does it stand as regards its subject? In what parts is *beware* used? In what part is *to wit* used? What is said of *wot?* 239. What class of verbs are included among defectives? 240. What is an impersonal verb? What must not be confounded with impersonal verbs? What anomalous forms are generally classed among the impersonals?

CHAPTER VI.

THE ADVERB.

241. An Adverb is a word joined to a verb, an adjective, or another adverb, to modify its meaning.

"The youth studies diligently;" *diligently* is joined to the verb *studies*, to tell *how* he studies, — that is, to modify its meaning, — and is an adverb.

"A very handsome flower;" *very* is joined to the adjective *handsome*, to tell *how* handsome the flower is, and is an adverb.

"He galloped quite fast;" *quite* is joined to the adverb *fast*, to tell how fast he galloped, and is an adverb.

242. Adverbs are apt to be confounded with adjectives, inasmuch as they are both modifying words. There is this difference between them: adjectives modify the meaning of nouns or pronouns; adverbs, that of verbs, adjectives, or other adverbs. "The sun shines pleasantly;" *pleasantly* modifies the verb *shines*, and is an adverb. "The sun is pleasant;" *pleasant* modifies the noun *sun*, and is an adjective.

243. The meaning of most adverbs can be expressed by a combination of other words; as, "He acted *wisely* [*with wisdom*]." "She walked *rapidly* [*in a rapid manner*]." "He stopped *here* [*in this place*]." "*When* [*at what time*] shall I see you?" "They visited me *often* [*many times*]." "*Whence* [*from what place*] art thou?"

244. A combination of words which taken separately are unconnected in construction and sense with the rest of the sentence, but taken together convey a single idea, and modify the meaning of a verb, adjective, or adverb, is called an Adverbial Phrase; as, *by and by*, *in vain*, *by far*.

EXERCISE.

Analyze the following sentences. Pick out the adverbs and adverbial phrases, and tell what words they modify.

The storm rages violently. The sluggard sleeps soundly. The birds were singing sweetly. At least, the time was passing pleasantly. The hour will soon arrive. The ship did not sail at all. The news came to-day. In short, Themistocles could not rest. Friends will certainly part. The man will never listen. Perhaps the child will recover. Roots grow downward. He lives in vain. We walked to and fro.

SECTION I.

CLASSES OF ADVERBS.

245. Adverbs are divided, according to their meaning, into various classes. The principal of these are Adverbs of Manner, Time, Place, Direction, Degree,

Quantity, Inference, Affirmation, Negation, Order, Numeral Adverbs, and Interrogative Adverbs.

246. Adverbs of Manner answer the question *how*.

How did he conduct himself? *Answer*, bravely, gallantly, ably, prudently, wisely, badly, well, ill, thus, &c. These words are all adverbs of manner.

247. Adverbs of manner are more numerous than those of any other class. Most of them end in *ly*, and are formed from adjectives. They can be recognized by their being convertible into the adverbial expression, *in a —— manner*: *wisely*, in a wise manner; *ill*, in a bad manner; *thus*, in this manner; *how*, in what manner.

248. Adverbs of Time answer the question *when*.

When will he come? *Answer*, to-day, to-night, to-morrow, soon, hereafter, often, seldom, never, now, &c. These are all adverbs of time.

249. *Now* frequently stands at the beginning of paragraphs, in argumentative and familiar discourse, as a general connective, without meaning *at this time* or modifying any particular word; as, "*Now*, it is evident," &c. In this case it is not an adverb, but a conjunction.

250. *Then* belongs to this class of adverbs, being generally equivalent to *at that time*. Sometimes, however, it is used with a meaning *to sum up the matter;* as, "You think, then, you will not go." In this case it is an adverb of inference.

251. Adverbs of Place answer the question *where*.

Where is he? *Answer*, here, there, everywhere, somewhere, &c.

252. The adverb *there* is often used expletively to introduce a sentence, not having its usual meaning *in that place* or modifying any particular word, as, "*There* were many who believed."

253. To this class of adverbs belong a number of words commencing with *a;* as, *abed, ashore, aground*, &c. — probably contracted for *at bed, at shore, at ground*, &c.

254. Adverbs of Direction answer the question *whither*.

Whither did he go? *Answer*, thither, hither, up, down, forward, backward, eastward, &c. These are all adverbs of direction.

In familiar language, *where, there*, and *here* are used instead of *whither, thither*, and *hither;* as, "*Where* [whither] did he go?" "Come *here* [hither]."

255. Adverbs of Degree modify other adverbs and adjectives.

Very short; *exceedingly* well done; *quite* pretty; *as* tall as I; not *so* tall as I. *Very, exceedingly, quite, as,* and *so,* expressing the degree of the quality denoted by the words they modify, are called adverbs of degree.

256. *So* is sometimes used to express the idea of some previous word or words, the repetition of which would be awkward; as, " You deserve to be miserable, and you are *so* [that is, *miserable*]." " I feared he was aiming too high, and I told him *so* [that is, *that I feared he was aiming too high*]."

257. Adverbs of Quantity include such words as *much, little, greatly, somewhat, enough, sufficiently,* **&c.**

We have already had *much* and *little* mentioned as pronominal adjectives. In the following expressions, they modify, not nouns or pronouns, but verbs or adjectives, and are therefore adverbs:—I *much* prefer; I *little* thought; *much* more learned; a *little* sour.

258. Adverbs of Inference imply a conclusion drawn from some previous statement or argument. *Therefore, wherefore, consequently,* **&c., are adverbs of this class.**

Adverbs of Inference are used, either alone or with other connectives, to join co-ordinate propositions; as, "*He is honest, therefore he is respected.*"

259. Adverbs of Affirmation answer a question affirmatively, or strengthen an assertion; as, *yes, surely, certainly, verily, undoubtedly.* **Of course is an adverbial phrase of similar import.**

260. Adverbs of Negation answer a question negatively, or deny an assertion; as, *no, nay, not,* **&c.**

261. Adverbs of Order answer the question *in what rank, or order;* **as,** *first, secondly, thirdly,* **&c.**

Avoid the use of *firstly* for *first.*

262. Numeral Adverbs answer the question *how many times;* **as,** *once, twice, thrice.*

263. Interrogative Adverbs are used in asking questions; as, *how, when, where, why.*

Conjunctive Adverbs.

264. Some adverbs of manner, time, and place, besides modifying verbs, connect parts of sentences. This *connecting* is an office usually performed by conjunctions; and the words in question are therefore called Conjunctive Adverbs.

"Can you tell *how* he manages to recite so well?" *How* modifies the verb *manages*, and at the same time connects the clause before it with that which follows; it is therefore in this sentence a conjunctive adverb of manner. — "No one knows *when* the world will end." *When* modifies the verb *will end*, and also connects the two clauses into which the sentence is divided; it is therefore a conjunctive adverb of time. — "I know *where* Patagonia is." *Where* modifies the verb *is*, and connects the two clauses of the sentence; it is therefore a conjunctive adverb of place.

Such expressions as *the more, the less, the better*, introducing correlative parts of sentences, may be parsed as compound conjunctive adverbs; as, "*The more* he labored, *the more* he was laughed at." "*The less* you drink, *the better*."

EXERCISE.

I. Analyze the following sentences. Parse the nouns, pronouns, adjectives, and verbs. Pick out the adverbs, tell their class, and state what words they modify.

"A generous man bestows his favors seasonably. The old ship Constitution arrived yesterday while I was away. A large army formerly encamped here. Each member performed his part willingly. Where is my friend? Quite small children sometimes read very well. Study diligently. Always labor patiently. How often is he absent? He gives twice who gives cheerfully. I do not know where they are now, but they have gone afoot and cannot be far off.

II. Insert adverbs of manner in place of dashes in the following sentences: —

The pupil writes —	The fire burns —	The child talks —
The sun shines —	The lion roars —	The bird sings —
The waves dash —	The flags wave —	The girl coughs —
The corn grows —	Henrietta reads —	The horse runs —

III. Compose sentences each of which shall contain one of the following adverbs:—

Diligently	Rapidly	Assuredly	Pleasantly
Undoubtedly	Possibly	Probably	Cheerfully
Truly	To-day	To-morrow	Often
Yes	Not	More	Most

SECTION II.
COMPARISON OF ADVERBS.

265. Some adverbs, particularly those of manner, admit of comparison; as, "She drives *well;* he drives *better;* you drive *best* of all."

266. Most adverbs form their comparative by prefixing *more* or *less* to the positive, and their superlative by prefixing *most* or *least;* as,

Positive.	Comparative.	Superlative.
Wisely,	more wisely, less wisely;	most wisely, least wisely.
Sadly,	more sadly, less sadly;	most sadly, least sadly.

267. A few add *er* for the comparative, and *est* for the superlative; as,

Pos.	Comp.	Sup.
Soon,	sooner,	soonest.
Often,	oftener,	oftenest.

268. Some adverbs are compared irregularly; as,

Pos.	Comp.	Sup.	Pos.	Comp.	Sup.
Well,	better,	best.	Much,	more,	most.
Badly, ill,	worse,	worst.	Far,	{ farther,	farthest.
Little,	less,	least.		{ further,	furthest.

269. In parsing an adverb, state to what class it belongs; if it can be compared, compare it, and tell what degree it is; if not, state the fact; mention what it modifies.

PARSING MODEL.— Here we can live more happily.

Here is an adverb of place, cannot be compared, and modifies the verb *can live*, according to Rule XXV., — *Adverbs generally modify verbs, participles, and other adverbs.*

More happily is an adverb of manner; compared, *happily, more happily, most happily;* comparative degree; and modifies the verb *can live*, according to Rule XXV. (Repeat it.)

EXERCISE.

Analyze the following sentences. Parse the nouns, pronouns, adjectives, verbs, and adverbs.

Even when asleep, the tyrant never rests. Certainly no one can be more pleasantly situated. We went farther and fared worse. Act well your part; there all the honor lies. How calmly nature sleeps when the din of day is o'er! Those who labor the most assiduously will certainly meet with the greatest success. Thrice the British charged gallantly up the hill. I strove less than he, yet succeeded better. Were we not slaves yesterday? To-day we are freemen. To-morrow let us be conquerors. First, let us consider his labors; secondly, his trials; thirdly, his dangers.

CHAPTER VII.

THE PREPOSITION.

270. A Preposition is a word used before a noun or pronoun, to show the relation between it and some other word.

"He went — England." This expression is not a complete sentence, because there is no word to indicate the relation between the *going* and *England*. *To* inserted before *England* would indicate this relation, and would consequently be a preposition. — "It lies — the chair." Here again the preposition is left out, and we cannot tell the relation between the *lying* and the *chair*, — whether it is *on* the chair, *under* the chair, *behind* the chair, or *before* the chair. Any one of these words would indicate the relation, and would be a preposition.

NOTE. — *Preposition* means *a placing before*, and the words in question are so called because they generally stand *before* the noun or pronoun which is their object.

271. List of the Principal Prepositions.

About	athwart	concerning	on	touching
above	before	down	over	toward
across	behind	during	past	towards
after	below	ere	regarding	under
against	beneath	except	respecting	underneath
along	beside	for	round	until
amid	besides	from	save	unto
amidst	between	in	since	up
among	betwixt	into	through	upon
amongst	beyond	notwithstanding	throughout	with
around	but	of	till	within
at	by	off	to	without

As already remarked, *a* in such expressions as *a fishing, a hunting*, &c., has the force of a preposition, and should be parsed as such.

To, the sign of the infinitive, must not be parsed independently as a preposition, but must be taken in with the verbal form; as, *to go* is an irregular, intransitive verb; *go, went, gone;* infinitive mode, present tense.

272. Two or more words combined are sometimes used as a compound preposition, and may be parsed as such; as, *according to, as to, with respect to, in regard to, from above, from below, from among, from within, as for, over against, instead of, out of,* &c.

273. The object of a preposition generally stands immediately after it; as, *at home, without doubt.* Sometimes, however, in poetry, and also in familiar discourse, the object precedes the preposition; as, "the *woods among;*" "*What* is he aiming *at?*"

The object of a preposition may be, —
1. A noun in the objective case; as, in *Portland*, for my *sake.*
2. A pronoun in the objective case; as, with *me*, by *ourselves.*
3. A verb in the infinitive mode; as, about *to commence.*
4. A clause, or part of a sentence; as, without *mentioning the particulars.*

274. A preposition and its object taken together constitute what is called an Adjunct.

275. Adjuncts are used as Adjectives to modify nouns, and as adverbs to modify verbs. They are termed adjective adjuncts or adverbial adjuncts according to their use.

An adjunct may denote various relations. Among these are,—

1. *Quality*, in which case it is equivalent to an adjective: as, a man *of piety*,—that is, a *pious* man; a state of bliss,—that is, a *blissful* state; habits *of industry*,—that is, *industrious* habits.

2. *State:* as, a nation *in debt;* a person *in distress;* a ship *under sail.*

3. *Place:* as, plants in *a garden;* waters *under the earth;* he walks *in the grove.*

4. *Possession*, in which case it is equivalent to a noun in the possessive case: as, the trials *of life*,—that is, *life's* trials; the sons *of Aaron*,—that is, *Aaron's* sons.

5. Time, in which case it is equivalent to an adverb: as, he sailed *in the night.*

276. Some of the prepositions are apt to be confounded with adverbs or conjunctions identical with them in form. The word in question is a preposition when followed by an object, and not otherwise. " He rode past the house;" *past*, being followed by the object *house*, is a preposition: but if we say, " He rode past," *past* has no object, and is an adverb of direction. —" He has gone for the doctor;" *for*, being followed by *doctor* as its object, is a preposition: but if we say, " He has gone, for the doctor advised him to take a voyage," *for* is not a preposition, since it is not followed by any object, but simply connects the two members of the sentence.

277. A preposition (without an object) is sometimes connected with a verbal adjective, forming one compound term: as, " The event was *unlooked for.*" " The measure was *uncalled for.*" In parsing such an expression, the words should be taken together; as, *unlooked for* is a verbal adjective; compared, *unlooked for, more unlooked for, most unlooked for;* positive degree, and belongs to *event.*

In like manner, a preposition is sometimes joined to an intransitive verb, forming one compound term and rendering the verb transitive: as, " He *disposed of* his property." " His property *has been disposed of.*" In such expressions, the preposition should be regarded as forming part of the verb (which is thus rendered transitive), and should be parsed with it; as, *has been disposed of* is a regular transitive verb, passive voice, indicative, perfect, third, singular.

278. In parsing a preposition, state the words between which it shows the relation.

PARSING MODEL. — He walked with me the hills among.

With is a preposition, and shows the relation between its object *me* and the verb *walked.*

Among is a preposition, and shows the relation between its object *hills* and the verb *walked.*

EXERCISE.

Analyze the following sentences. Pick out the adjuncts and tell what words they modify. Parse the parts of speech that have been considered.

The sun sank below the western horizon, among clouds of foreboding darkness. I heard the crashing of the pointed rocks through the bottom of the ship. Around and above us, before us and behind us, blazed the fearful artillery of heaven. Notwithstanding his great wealth, accumulated during a life of hardships, he died uncared for. From my youth up I have noticed that without industry we cannot hope to succeed. As to John, at my suggestion he has gone a swimming. Tenedos lay over against Troy, and within a few miles of it. He sincerely repented of his sins. His sins were sincerely repented of. Over hill and dale they marched, across streams, through marshes, up mountains, amid obstacles of every kind. What was referred to in Sir Robert Peel's remarks? According to orders, they journeyed from dawn till sunset. No one but Alexander would have ventured on such an undertaking.

CHAPTER VIII.

THE CONJUNCTION.

279. A Conjunction is a word used to connect two or more single words, adjuncts, phrases, clauses, members, or sentences.

SINGLE WORDS. — *Tigers* AND *elephants* abound in India.

ADJUNCTS. — Penn met the Indians *with kindness* AND *in the spirit of love*.

PHRASES. — *The war having ended*, AND *peace being established*, we returned home.

CLAUSES. — Milton, *whose genius was transcendent* AND *whose poetry will live forever*, was blind.

MEMBERS. — *Achilles was a great warrior*, BUT *Homer was a great poet*.

SENTENCES. — *The day passeth; the night cometh.* NEVERTHELESS, *there is yet an opportunity to redeem the time.*

THE CONJUNCTION. 141

The several classes of connectives should be carefully distinguished.

1. Prepositions connect only words, and require the subsequent substantive to be in the objective case.
2. Relative pronouns connect the clauses in which they stand to their antecedents.
3. Connective adverbs, besides their connecting power, express the relations of time, place, and manner.
4. Conjugations, in general, have no modifying power, and merely serve to connect the elements of a sentence.

280. There are two classes of Conjugations, Co-ordinate and Subordinate.

Co-ordinate Conjunctions connect elements of the same construction.

Subordinate Conjunctions introduce clauses and phrases as elements of another proposition.

Conjugative adverbs and relative pronouns have the connecting power of subordinate conjugations.

LIST OF THE PRINCIPAL CONJUNCTIONS.

Co-ordinate Conjunctions. — And, also, besides, both — and, nor, neither — nor, moreover, but also, first — secondly — again — lastly; but, yet, nevertheless, however, or, either — or, else; for, therefore, accordingly, hence, wherefore.

Subordinate Conjunctions. — That, whether, if; as, before, since; because, unless, except, provided, though, although, lest, in order that, than.

281. Two or more words combined are sometimes used as a compound conjunction, and may be parsed as such; as, *in order that, inasmuch as, as well as, as if, as though,* &c.

282. We have already had *as* mentioned as an adverb of degree, — *as tall, as good.* It is a conjunction in the following cases: —

1. When used after a preceding *as* or *so*, to connect clauses containing the names of two objects compared; as, " She is as tall *as* I." " She is not so tall *as* her brother is."
2. When it connects words in apposition, — that is, words referring to the same object and in the same case; as, " The government sent Clay *as* commissioner." *Commissioner* refers to the same person as *Clay*, and is put in the same case; *as* connects the two words, and is a conjunction.
3. When it connects clauses containing adjectives and participles with the words which they qualify; as, " I regard him *as* almost ruined."
4. When it is used to introduce examples, as in the line above.

THE CONJUNCTION.

283. *Both*, already mentioned as a pronominal adjective, is a conjunction when with *and* it connects two words that are in the same construction; as, "She was *both* graceful *and* witty." *Both* and *and*, connecting the two adjectives *graceful* and *witty*, are conjunctions. — Observe that *both* must not be used in this way if more than two words are connected. It would be improper to say, "She is both handsome, graceful, and witty."

284. *But* is an adverb when equivalent to *only*, and a preposition when equivalent to *except*. In all other cases it is a conjunction.

ADVERB. — There were *but* [*only*] twelve Cæsars.
PREPOSITION. — All *but* [*except*] him were drowned.
CONJUNCTION. — Were there not ten cleansed, *but* where are the nine?

285. *Than* is a conjunction, but with the relative *who* it is used by some good writers with the force of a preposition governing the objective; as, "Nero, than *whom* no other was more cruel." This is contrary to all analogy; we would say, "more cruel than *I*," not *than me*.

286. In parsing conjunctions, state what they connect.

PARSING MODEL. — Queen Elizabeth, although discreet and energetic in public matters, was arbitrary and disagreeable in private life.

Although is a conjunction, and connects the clause *discreet and energetic in public matters* with *Queen Elizabeth was arbitrary and disagreeable in private life*.

And is a conjunction, and connects the words *arbitrary* and *disagreeable*.

EXERCISE.

I. Compose twelve sentences, each of which shall contain in order one of the first twelve conjunctions in the above list (§ 280).

II. Parse the following sentences: —

Horses, though now found wild in great numbers in Mexico and South America, are not natives of this continent, but have sprung from those introduced by the Spaniards. Both New York and Albany were founded by the Dutch. If I mistake not, I have read that labor conquers all things. Whether we shall go or not is uncertain; for our letters have not arrived. Beavers can live either on land or in the water. Neither cotton nor sugar will grow in England, because the climate is too cold. A sailor has a harder life than most men, unless he has very kind officers. I would like to be silent; but, since duty requires it, I must speak. Galileo, than whom no greater philosopher lived, died the same year in which Newton was born.

CHAPTER IX.

THE INTERJECTION.

287. An Interjection is a word used to express some strong or sudden emotion; as, *oh! alas!*

NOTE. — *Interjection* means a *throwing among;* and the words in question are so called because they are generally thrown in among other words with which they have no grammatical connection. They may, however, commence a sentence, or be used alone.

Every interjection except *O* should be immediately followed by an exclamation point (!) unless it is very closely connected with other words.

288. Interjections express,— 1. Sorrow; as, *oh! ah! alas!* 2. Exultation; as, *hurrah! huzza! aha! bravo!* 3. Disgust; as, *fie! fudge! tush! pshaw!* 4. Wonder; as, *indeed! strange! what!* 5. A sudden call; as, *ho! hallo!* 6. Salutation; as, *O, welcome! hail!* 7. Taking leave: as, *good-by, farewell, adieu.* 8. A demand for attention or silence; as, *hark! hush! hist! lo! behold!*

289. Adjectives, verbs, and other parts of speech, when thrown into a sentence without any grammatical connection with its other words, are used as interjections, and may be parsed as such; as, *wonderful! horrible! see! listen! away!*

290. *Oh* must be distinguished from *O.* The former may be used by itself, may commence with a small letter, and implies sorrow or surprise; the latter is used only with the name of some object addressed, or pronoun standing for it, and is always a capital. " *Oh!* what a fall was there!" " *O* Sleep, why hast thou fled my pillow?"

PARSING MODEL. — Fie upon thee, knave!

Fie is an interjection, expressing disgust.

PARSING EXERCISE.

Behold! how good and how pleasant it is for brethren to dwell together in unity! What! could ye not watch with me one hour! What ho! stranger, whence come you? Oh for a lodge in some vast wilderness! Ah! woe is me. Bravo! he answers like a lad of spirit. Adieu forever, home of my infancy! Enough! you have shown me the fallacy of all human pretensions. Hark! some one comes. Indeed! has he started? Pshaw! the harder I work, the less I seem to succeed.

REVIEW QUESTIONS ON CHAPTERS VII., VIII., IX.

241. What is an adverb? Give examples. 242. With what are adverbs apt to be confounded? How may adjectives and adverbs be distinguished? 243. How can the meaning of most adverbs be expressed? 244. What is an adverbial phrase?

245. How are adverbs divided? 246. What question do adverbs of manner answer? Give examples. 247. In what do most of them end? How can they be recognized? 248. What question do adverbs of time answer? Give examples. 249. What force has *now* in some sentences? 250. What is *then* sometimes equivalent to? 251. What question do adverbs of place answer? 252. How is *there* often used? 253. What words belong to this class of adverbs? 254. What question do adverbs of direction answer? Give examples. 255. In familiar language, what are used instead of *whither, thither,* and *hither?* 256. What do adverbs of degree modify? Give examples. 257. How is *so* sometimes used? 258. What words are included among adverbs of quantity? Give examples of the use of *much* and *little* as adverbs. 259. What do adverbs of inference imply? Give examples. What use have adverbs of inference? 260. What is the office of adverbs of affirmation? 261. What is the office of adverbs of negation? 262. What question do adverbs of order answer? 263. What question do numeral adverbs answer? For what are interrogative adverbs used?

264. What is meant by conjunctive adverbs? Give examples. How may such expressions as *the more, the less,* &c., be parsed?

265. Of what are some adverbs susceptible? 266. How do most adverbs form their comparative and superlative? 267. What terminations do some annex? Give examples. 268. Compare *well; badly; little; much; far.* 269. How is an adverb parsed?

270. What is a preposition? Give examples. What does the word *preposition* mean? 271. Recite the list of prepositions. How is *a* to be parsed in such expressions as *a fishing,* &c.? How is *to,* the sign of the infinitive, to be parsed? 272. What is meant by compound prepositions? Give examples. 273. How does the preposition stand, as regards its object? What may the object of a preposition be? 274. What is an adjunct? 275. To what are adjuncts joined? What may an adjunct denote? For what are adjuncts used? 276. With what are prepositions apt to be confounded? How can they be distinguished? 277. How are such expressions as *unlooked for* to be parsed? What is sometimes the force of a preposition joined to an intransitive verb? 278. In parsing prepositions, what must be stated?

279. What is a conjunction? Give examples. Name the different classes

of connectives, and their uses. 280. What are co-ordinate conjunctions? What are subordinate conjunctions? What words are used as subordinates? Name the co-ordinate conjunctions. Name the subordinate conjunctions. 281. What is a compound conjunction? 282. What part of speech is *as?* In what cases is *as* a conjunction? 283. In what case is *both* a conjunction? When is it improper to use the conjunction *both?* 284. When is *but* an adverb, when a preposition, and when a conjunction? 285. What part of speech is *than?* What is said of the construction *than whom?* 286. In parsing conjunctions what must be stated?

287. What is an interjection? What does the word *interjection* mean? By what should interjections be followed? 288. What do interjections express? 289. What may be used as interjections? 290. What distinction must be observed in the use of *oh* and *O?*

PART III.

COMBINATION OF WORDS IN SENTENCES.

CHAPTER X.

SECTION I.

THE ELEMENTS OF SENTENCES.

291. Words are either signs of ideas, or signs denoting the relation between ideas.

Idea words are nouns, pronouns, adjectives, verbs (except the copula *be*), and adverbs of time, manner, and place.

Relational words are the copula *be*, prepositions, interjections, most adverbs, and conjunctions. Relations are also expressed by the inflectional terminations of words; as, King's, whom, horses.

In the forms, *Man is mortal, Summer is pleasant,* the words *man, mortal, summer, pleasant,* express ideas; while the copula shows the relation of the ideas. The whole expresses a thought.

A thought is two or more ideas, bearing a given relation to each other and the speaker; as, *The summer is pleasant. The summer has been pleasant. The summer will be pleasant.*

A Sentence is a thought expressed in words. Every sentence consists of at least three *essential elements;* the Subject, the Copula, and the Attribute.

The Subject is that of which something is asserted, and is either a substantive, or a word, phrase, or clause used substantively.

The Copula is generally some form of the verb *to be*, and is used to show the relation between the subject and attribute.

The Attribute is that which expresses the state, quality, condition, &c. of the subject, and may be any idea, word, phrase, or clause.

The Predicate is that which is asserted of the subject, and consists of the copula and attribute taken together, or a verb embracing both.

EXAMPLES.

SUBJECT.	PREDICATE.	
	Copula.	Attribute.
Paul	was	an apostle.
Singing	is	delightful.
To lie	is	to deceive.
That I have succeeded	is	beyond question.
My motto	shall be	Let truth prevail.
The fire	is (burns)	burning.
He	is (walks)	walking.

The Subject without any modifiers is termed the Grammatical Subject; the Predicate without any modifiers is termed the Grammatical Predicate.

The subject may be modified by a noun in apposition; an adjective; a preposition with its object (adjunct); a participle; a verb in the infinitive; a clause; a phrase; and sometimes an adverb.

The Subject modified by one or more words is called the Logical Subject.

The grammatical predicate may be modified by a noun in the objective case (if the verb is transitive); a verb in the infinitive; an adverb; a preposition with its object (adjunct); a clause; an adjective; a phrase; and a quoted sentence.

The Predicate modified by one or more words is called the Logical Predicate.

A Proposition is an assertion containing one subject and one predicate; as, *Birds fly.*

A Simple Sentence consists of but one proposition; as, *Summer is pleasant.*

292. A Leading Proposition is the principal assertion of a sentence; as, *Solomon,* who was the son of David, *built the temple.*

A **Clause** is a dependent proposition, used to introduce an additional fact or circumstance into a sentence; as, Elijah, *when he challenged the priests of Baal*, mocked them.

A **Complex Sentence** consists of a leading proposition and one or more clauses; as, *Make hay, while the sun shines.*

293. A **Member** of a sentence is such a part as expresses an independent thought, and has a distinct subject and predicate of its own; as, *The wind blows* (1), and *the rain falls* (2).

A **Compound Sentence** consists of two or more members; as, *God spake, and it was done.*

Sometimes, to prevent repetition, the grammatical predicate is omitted in the last member of a compound sentence; as, "Dryden believed in astrology, Hobbes [*believed*] in ghosts."

The members of a compound sentence are connected by co-ordinate conjunctions.

Clauses, leading propositions, and members must not be confounded. A clause is always dependent in sense, and generally in construction; a leading proposition is independent in construction, and, while it makes complete sense when separated from the other words in the sentence, may be modified in meaning by phrases, adjuncts, or clauses, introducing additional facts or circumstances; a member is independent both in construction and sense, and may contain the leading proposition and its modifying clauses, or may be limited to a single proposition.

Columbus, who discovered America, was born in Italy; but his great enterprise was fostered by Spain. The two portions of this sentence separated by the semicolon are members, each being complete in itself as regards both construction and sense. The first member is a complex element; consisting of the leading proposition, *Columbus was born in Italy*, which is complete in construction and also in sense; and the clause, *who discovered America*, which merely introduces another fact concerning Columbus, does not make complete sense by itself, and is dependent in construction through the relation existing between the relative, *who*, and its antecedent *Columbus*. The second member of the sentence, *his great enterprise was fostered by Spain*, is a single and independent proposition.

294. A Phrase is two or more words which express some relation of ideas, but do not contain an entire proposition; as, *Being a young man, To live soberly, In fine.*

An Adjunct consists of a preposition and its object; as, *In Boston, Over the hills.*

295. The term Element is conveniently applied to the different parts of a sentence, whether members, leading propositions, clauses, phrases, adjuncts, or words. Elements are simple, complex, or compound, according to the number of similar or dissimilar parts they contain. They may be classified as *essential, accessory,* or *independent,* according to their use in the structure of a sentence.

The essential elements of a sentence are three; Subject, Copula, and Attribute. The accessory elements are also three, and are termed Substantive, Adjective, and Adverbial, according to their office. An independent element has no grammatical dependence on other words.

EXAMPLES. — *The wind drives the stubble over the fields.* This is a simple declarative sentence. *The wind drives the stubble* is the leading proposition; *over the fields* is an adverbial adjunct, modifying *drives.*

In vain Wellington tried to overtake the enemy fleeing before him. This is a simple declarative sentence. *Wellington tried to overtake the enemy* is the leading proposition, modified by the adverbial phrase *in vain.* *Fleeing before him* is an adjective phrase modifying *enemy* and containing the adjunct *before him.*

Solomon, who built the temple, was the son of David. This is a complex declarative sentence. *Solomon was the son of David* is the leading proposition, containing the adjunct *of David.* *Who built the temple* is a clause used to introduce an additional fact respecting *Solomon.*

Cicero, while in the enjoyment of youth, was covered with glory; but when old age came upon him, he was disturbed by the misfortunes of the republic. This is a compound declarative sentence, consisting of two members connected by *but.* *Cicero was covered with glory* is the leading proposition of the first member, containing the adjunct *with glory*. *While in the enjoyment of youth* is an adverbial phrase expressing time, containing the adjunct *in the enjoyment*, which is modified by the adjunct *of youth*. *He was disturbed by the misfortunes of the republic* is the leading proposition of the second member. *By the misfortunes* is an adjunct modifying the grammatical predicate *was disturbed*, and itself modified by the adjunct *of the republic*. *When old age came upon him* is a clause expressing time, and containing the adjunct *upon him*.

EXERCISE.

According to the examples just given, point out the members, leading propositions, clauses, phrases, and adjuncts, in the following sentences. Parse each word.

God, who made all things, is acquainted with our most secret thoughts.

The drum and fife can sometimes drown the battle's noise, when there is no way to escape it. In general, great talkers are not fluent writers.

In the beginning of this address I said, and I have endeavored to keep my word so far, that I would plead only for intellectual interests.

> The curfew tolls the knell of parting day;
> The lowing herd winds slowly o'er the lea;
> The plowman homeward plods his weary way,
> And leaves the world to darkness and to me.

SECTION II.

CLASSIFICATION OF CLAUSES.

Clauses are distinguished as Substantive, Adjective, and Adverbial.

296. A Substantive Clause is one that performs the office of a noun in the nominative or objective case.

A substantive clause may be used, —

1. In apposition with a noun; as, "The question *whether we shall go* is yet undecided."

CLASSIFICATION OF CLAUSES. 151

2. As the subject-nominative of a verb; as, "*Whether we shall go* is yet undecided."

3. As the predicate-nominative; as, "The question is *whether we shall go.*"

4. As the object of a transitive verb or preposition; as, "We have not yet said *whether we shall go.*"

297. Quotations, though constituting complete propositions in themselves, generally form part of the logical predicate of a complex sentence, modifying the grammatical predicate as the object of a verb, and hence belong to this class of clauses.

A quotation is direct when the words of a person are given unaltered in the form in which they were stated; as, " Socrates said, '*All are sufficiently eloquent in that which they understand.*' " A quotation is indirect when the words of a person are given in the form of a narration; as, " Socrates said *that all were sufficiently eloquent in that which they understood.*" Direct quotations are introduced by incorporation, that is, without introductory words; indirect quotations, by the conjunction *that.* A quoted question is introduced by *if, whether*, or some interrogative word.

Substantive clauses are also introduced by the conjunction *that*, and by the relative pronouns *that, what, whoso, whosoever, whatever, whatsoever;* as, " He rejoices *that we are free.*" "*What is right for one* is right for another."

298. An Adjective Clause is one that has the force of an adjective, generally implying some quality or attribute; as, Cabot, *who discovered Newfoundland*, was a native of Bristol.

Adjective clauses frequently serve to define the state, quality, or condition of an object more exactly than a single adjective, participle, or adjunct could do; as, Peter, *having a sword*, drew it. Peter, *who had a sword*, drew it.

Adjective clauses are introduced by the relative pronouns *who, which, that*, and *as*, or by the adverbs *where, whither, whence, when;* as, The place *where I was born.*

299. An Adverbial Clause is one that performs the office of an adverb, denoting manner, time, place, &c.; as,

Manner. — He walked *better than I ever saw him walk before.*

Time. — *When centuries shall have rolled away,* our institutions will still survive.

Place. — *Where the rapids commence,* a small point of land juts out.

Adverbial clauses are very numerous and important. They are developed from adverbs and adverbial phrases, and form six classes: —

1. Adverbial clauses of Place, introduced by *where, whither, whence;* as, I reap *where I sowed not.*

2. Adverbial clauses of Time, introduced by *as, when, while, before, till, after, since;* as, He trembled *as he spoke.*

3. Adverbial clauses of Manner, introduced by *as, so that, than,* &c.; as, He did *as he was directed.*

4. Adverbial clauses of Cause, introduced by *because, since, that, in order that, lest;* as, *Because he is good,* he is loved.

The relation of cause is generally expressed by co-ordinate propositions. This is always the case when the cause is prominent.

5. Adverbial clauses of Condition, introduced by *if, unless, except, provided, though, although,* &c.; as, *If he is in health,* I am content.

6. Adverbial clauses of Intensity, introduced by *as, than,* and the compound conjunctive adverbs *the more, the better,* &c.; as, *The more you study,* the more you will learn.

EXERCISE.

Parse and analyze the following sentences. Point out the leading propositions, clauses, and adjuncts. When a clause is mentioned state its class.

He studies that he may learn. The jailor asked, What shall I do? Although the fig-tree shall not blossom, yet will I rejoice. That you have wronged me, doth appear in this. Knowest thou the land where the citron blooms? The arrow has gone where no one can find it. He has worked harder than James has. The land that we love is our country. Whoso is wise, let him learn of me. He writes as fast as the orator speaks. In order that he might escape, he changed his dress. Unless you study more diligently, you will fail. He died before I was born. Ye know not whence it comes. Whither I go, ye know. Whatsoever I have, I will give you. While I live, I will praise him. I do not know where he is. I know when he died. I saw him when he was dying. He is richer than his brother Handsome is that handsome does.

SECTION III.

CLASSIFICATION OF PHRASES.

800. Phrases may be divided into three classes, Substantive, Adjective, and Adverbial.

A substantive phrase is one that performs the office of a noun in the nominative or objective case.

A substantive phrase may be used, —
1. In apposition with a noun or pronoun; as, It is a difficult thing *to become a poet.*
2. As the subject or predicate nominative; as, *To steal* is *to break the law.*
3. As the object of a transitive verb or preposition; as, Most men love *to be called great.*

An Adjective Phrase is one that has the force of an adjective, generally implying some quality or attribute; as, *Like all the other works of the Almighty,* the eye is wonderfully adapted to the purposes for which it is designed.

An Adverbial Phrase is one that performs the office of an adverb, denoting time, place, manner, &c.; as, *The war having ended,* we returned.

Adjuncts are frequently termed phrases; but it is better to consider them as adjective or adverbial adjuncts, according to their office in the sentence.

Other combinations frequently occur having no modifying power, which might be termed conjunctive or prepositional phrases, according to their office in the sentence; as, *as well as, on account of.*

Nouns and pronouns, denoting objects addressed, or used in exclamations, or without grammatical dependence on other words, constitute what are called independent expressions; as, Welcome, *stranger. The fathers* — where are they?

Adverbs and interjections are frequently used independently; as, *alas! hush! amen, verily.*

SECTION IV
CONTRACTED ELEMENTS.

301. Sometimes a sentence is so constructed as to have two or more subjects and but one predicate, or two or more predicates and but one subject. These abridged forms may be termed Contracted Sentences, and analyzed as such, by stating the number of subjects and predicates, and then giving their various modifications, or they may be expanded by supplying the omissions, and then treated as compound sentences.

Contracted sentences may form the principal elements of complex and compound sentences.

It is well to make three classes of contracted sentences, viz.: —

1. One subject and two or more predicates; as, " John reads and writes."
2. Two or more subjects and one predicate; as, " James and John read."
3. Two subjects and two predicates; as, " James and John read and write."

In like manner, clauses may be so changed or abridged as to form phrases of equivalent meaning; as, *while Tarquin was reigning* = *Tarquin reigning*. I hope *that I may see you there* = I hope *to see you there.*

EXERCISE.

I. Parse and analyze the following sentences. Point out the members, the leading propositions, the clauses, phrases, and adjuncts. State the class of the clauses and phrases.

He drew up a petition in which he too freely represented his own merits. In conversing on grave subjects, we should not use lively and familiar forms of expression. Some, presuming on the good-nature of their friends, write their letters in a hasty and unconnected manner. Rich gifts wax poor when givers prove unkind. Let the doors be shut upon him, that he may play the fool nowhere but in his own house. His predictions were only too true, as the event proved. His constant request was that I would permit him to sit by me in my saloon. The crime of being a young man I shall neither palliate nor deny. To plow is hard work. His attempt to rescue his friend was, alas! fatal to himself. This having failed, he gave up in despair. I have learned to live soberly; but he cannot restrain his appetites. Scipio was valiant; Cæsar, victorious; Fabricius prudent; but Hannibal was all these. The judge that sat on the bench was convinced, long before the cause was finished, that the prisoner was guilty of the crime with which he was charged.

II. Complete each of the following sentences, by inserting either a substantive, adjective, or adverbial clause, in place of the dash. State what kind of a clause you insert.

The teachers —— will be gratefully remembered. The trees —— grow thriftily. —— is hard to decide. I will not do it ——. That Great Being —— is eternal. The cars ran over a man ——. He has sent his son to Germany ——. Those —— will be respected. The letter —— contains good news. He has built a fine house ——.

SECTION V.

MODIFICATION OF WORDS.

302. Conjunctions and interjections, from their very nature, are not susceptible of modification by other words. The remaining parts of speech are modified in various ways, the principal of which are as follows.

303. A noun may be modified, —

1. By a noun in apposition; as, George, the *king*.
2. By an adjective; as, A *tall* mast.
3. By an adjunct; as, A life *of toil*.
4. By a participle; as, The sun *rising*.
5. By a clause; as, The land *that we love*.
6. By a phrase; as, Man, *made in the image of his Creator*.
7. By an adverb; as, Not my feet *only*.
8. By a verb in the infinitive; as, A time *to die*.
9. By a noun in the possessive case; as, *Lot's* wife.

A pronoun may be modified by all the above except the last two.

304. A verb or participle may be modified,—
1. By a noun in the objective case, if the verb is transitive; as, The sun gives *light*.
2. By a verb in the infinitive; as, He hopes *to return*.
3. By an adjunct; as, I walk *in the grove*.
4. By a clause; as, I hope *that you are well*.
5. By an adverb; as, The wind blows *violently*.
6. By a phrase; as, *In vain* he labors.
7. By a quoted sentence; as, Bion said, " *Know thyself.*"

305. An adjective may be modified,—
1. By an adverb; as, *Very* rich.
2. By a verb in the infinitive; as, Pleasant *to behold*.
3. By an adjunct; as, True *to nature*.
4. By another adjective; as, *Bright* red.
5. By a phrase; as, *in general* successful.

306. An adverb may be modified,—
1. By another adverb; as, *Most* assuredly.
2. By an adjunct; as, Agreeably *to nature*, most *of all*.

307. A preposition may be modified,—
1. By an adverb; as, *Far* beyond.
2. By a noun in the objective case; as, Over *the hills*.
3. By a verb in the infinitive; as, About *to depart*.

308. Modifying words may themselves be modified in various ways; as, " Alexander marched very rapidly." The adverb *rapidly*, which modifies the verb *marched*, is itself modified by the adverb *very*.

EXERCISE.

Write twelve sentences which shall contain in order,—
1. A noun modified by another noun in apposition with it.
2. A noun modified by a verb in the infinitive.
3. A noun modified by another noun in the possessive case.
4. A pronoun modified by a clause.
5. A pronoun modified by an adverb.
6. A verb modified by a noun in the objective case.
7. A participle modified by a verb in the infinitive.
8. An adjective modified by an adverb.
9. An adjective modified by an adjunct.
10. An adverb modified by another adverb.
11. A preposition modified by a noun in the objective.
'2 A preposition modified by a verb in the infinitive.

FORMS FOR PARSING AND ANALYSIS. 157

RECAPITULATION.

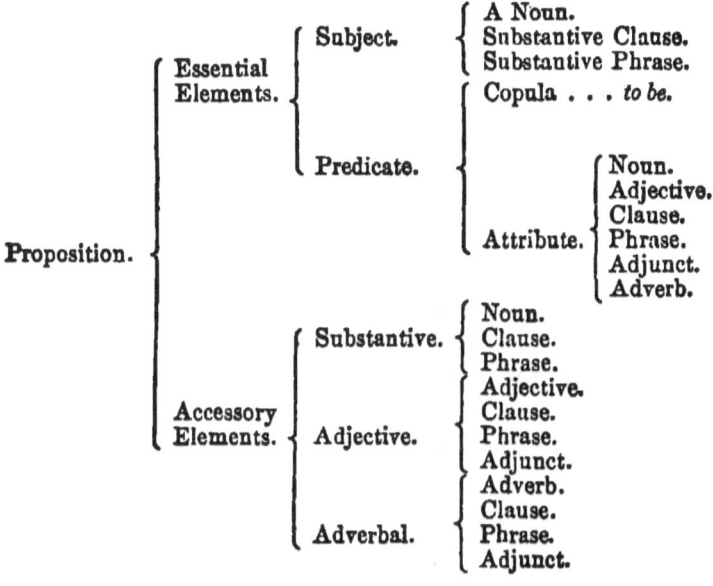

SECTION VI.

FORMS FOR PARSING AND ANALYSIS.

I. Forms for Parsing.

Noun. — Class, person, number, gender, case, disposal, rule.

Pronoun. — Class, decline, person, number, gender, case, disposal, rule.

Relative Pronoun. — Class, antecedent, decline, person, number, gender, relation, case, disposal, rule.

Adjective. — Class, compare, degree, modifies, rule.

Pronominal Adj. { Used as adjective, limits, rule.
{ Used as pronoun, person, number, gender, case, disposal, rule.

Verb. — Transitive or intransitive, principal parts, regular or irregular, voice, mode, tense, person, number, agreement, rule.

Participle.— Kind, name them, how used, government, rule.

Adverb. — Class, disposal, rule.

Preposition. — Office, rule.

Conjunction. — Office, rule.

Interjection. — Use, rule.

II. Rules for Analysis.

1. *Never supply words unless necessary to the construction.*

2. *Restore the omitted words before commencing to analyze.*

III. Forms for Analysis.

I. Classify the sentence as { simple, complex, compound, } and as { declarative, interrogative, imperative, exclamatory, } or mixed.

II. If simple, state the kind:
1. Name the grammatical subject, the modifiers in order, the logical subject;
2. Name the grammatical predicate, copula, attribute, the modifiers in order, the logical predicate.

III. If complex, state the kind:
1. Name the leading proposition;
2. Name the clauses and give the office of each:
3. Analyze the leading proposition as in II.;
4. Analyze each clause as in II.

IV. If compound, state the kind:
1. Name the members composing it;
2. Analyze each member in order.
   a. The simple members as in II.
   b. The complex members as in III.

FORMS FOR PARSING AND ANALYSIS. 159

MODEL I.— Large trees of the forest grow very rapidly in summer.

This is a simple declarative sentence.

The grammatical subject is *trees*, which is modified by the adjective *large*, and the adjunct *of the forest*.

The adjunct *of the forest* is composed of the preposition *of*, and its object, *forest*, which is modified by the adjective *the*.

The logical subject is *large trees of the forest*.

The grammatical predicate is *grow*, which embraces copula and attribute, and is modified by the adverb *rapidly*, and this is modified by the adverb *very;* the grammatical predicate is also modified by the adjunct *in summer*, which consists of the preposition *in*, and its object, *summer*.

The logical predicate is *grow very rapidly in summer*.

MODEL II.— You will depart with but a small retinue, said the baronet.

This is a complex declarative sentence.

The leading proposition is *the baronet said*.

The direct quotation, *You will depart with but a small retinue*, is a substantive clause, modifying the predicate of the leading proposition.

The grammatical subject of the leading proposition is *baronet;* it is modified by the adjective *the*.

The logical subject is *the baronet*.

The grammatical predicate of the leading proposition is *said*, which embraces copula and attribute, and is modified by its object, the substantive clause, *You will depart*, &c.

The logical predicate of the sentence is *said you will depart with but a small retinue*.

The substantive clause, *You will depart with but a small retinue*, is a simple proposition, introduced by incorporation.

You is the grammatical and logical subject.

The grammatical predicate is *will depart*, which embraces copula and attribute, and is modified by the adjunct *with but a small retinue*.

The adjunct *with but a small retinue* consists of the preposition *with*, and its object, *retinue*, which is modified by the adjectives *a* and *small*. The adjective *small* is modified by the adverb *but*. The logical predicate is *will depart with but a small retinue*.

MODEL III. — I thought that Titus was your friend.

This is a complex declarative sentence, consisting of the leading proposition *I thought*, and the substative clause *Titus was your friend*, which is connected to the leading proposition by the conjunction *that*.

I is the simple and logical subject of the leading proposition.

Thought is the grammatical predicate, embracing copula and attribute, and is modified by the substantive clause *Titus was your friend.*

Thought that Titus was your friend is the logical predicate of the sentence.

The substantive clause, *Titus was your friend*, is a simple proposition.

Titus is the grammatical and logical subject; *was friend* is the grammatical predicate, consisting of the copula *was* and the attribute *friend*, which here serves as the predicate-nominative to the substantive verb *was*, and is modified by the pronoun *your.*

Was your friend is the logical predicate.

MODEL IV. — A soft answer turneth away wrath; but grievous words stir up anger.

This is a compound declarative sentence, consisting of two members connected by the conjunction *but.*

The first member is *A soft answer turneth away wrath;* the second member is *grievous words stir up anger.* Each member is a simple proposition.

The grammatical subject of the first member is *answer*, which is modified by the adjectives *a* and *soft.* The logical subject is *a soft answer.*

The grammatical predicate is *turneth*, which embraces copula and attribute, and is modified by its object, *wrath*, and the adverb *away.*

The logical predicate is *turneth away wrath.*

The grammatical subject of the second member is *words*, which is modified by the adjective *grievous.*

The logical subject is *grievous words.*

The grammatical predicate is *stir*, which embraces copula and attribute, and is modified by its object, *anger*, and the adverb *up.*

The logical predicate is *stir up anger.*

EXERCISE.

Give a full analysis of the following sentences on the plan of the models just given. Parse them.

I recollect hearing a traveller, of poetical temperament, expressing the kind of horror which he felt at beholding, on the banks of the Missouri, an oak of prodigious size, which had been in a manner overpowered by an enormous wild grape-vine. The vine had clasped its huge folds round the trunk, and thence had wound about every branch and twig, until the mighty tree had withered in its embrace. It seemed like Laocoön struggling ineffectually in the hideous coils of the monster serpent. It was the lion of trees perishing in the embrace of a vegetable boa.

Since life is short, it becomes us to be diligent. As the way was steep and difficult, we proceeded slowly. When shame is lost, all virtue is lost. "Stop!" said the German, in a tone of anger. "I do not mean," said the antiquary, "to intrude upon your Lordship." "You are a tyrant," he answered, with a sigh. Happiness is found in the arm-chair of dozing age, as well as in the sprightliness of the lance, or the animation of the chase. The first turkeys ever seen in Europe were taken there by Cabot, on his return from the voyage in which he discovered Newfoundland. It is stated that two scientific gentlemen of France, having quarrelled about something, fought a duel in balloons.

REVIEW QUESTIONS ON CHAPTER X.

291. Of what are words signs? Define thought. What is a sentence? What is the subject of a sentence? the predicate? What is the copula? the attribute? the grammatical subject? the grammatical predicate? the logical subject? the logical predicate? How may the grammatical subject be modified? the grammatical predicate? What is a proposition? Give an example. What is a simple sentence? Give an example.

292. What is a leading proposition? Give an example. What is a clause? Give an example. What is a complex sentence? Give an example. 293. What is a member? What is a compound sentence? Give an example and name the members. Illustrate the difference between members, clauses, and leading propositions. 294. What is a phrase? What is an adjunct? Illustrate by examples the difference between phrases and adjuncts. 295. What is an element? How may elements be classified?

Name the principal kinds of clauses. 296. What is a substantive clause? How may substantive clauses be used? Give examples. 297. Of what are quotations a part? What is a direct quotation? Give an example. What is an indirect quotation? Give an example. How are quotations introduced? How are quoted questions introduced? What are substantive clauses used to denote? 298. What is an adjective clause? How are adjective clauses introduced? 299. What is an adverbial clause? Give examples. Name the classes of adverbial clauses? How are adverbial clauses of place introduced? Give an example. How are adverbial clauses of time introduced? Give an example. How are adverbial clauses of manner introduced? Give an example. How are adverbial clauses of cause introduced? Give an example. How is the relation

11

of cause generally expressed? How are adverbial clauses of condition introduced? Give an example. How are adverbial clauses of intensity introduced? Give an example.

300. Name the kinds of phrases. What is a substantive phrase? Give an example. How may substantive phrases be used? Give examples. What is an adjective phrase? Give an example. What is an adverbial phrase? Give an example. What are independent expressions? Give examples. What words are used independently?

301. What are contracted sentences? How may they be analyzed? How may they be classified? 302. What parts of speech are not modified by other words? 303. By what may a noun be modified? a pronoun? 304. A verb or participle? 305. An adjective? 306. An adverb? 307. A preposition? Give examples. Give the forms for parsing. Give the rules for analysis. Give the forms for analysis. Analyze according to the models the sentences:—I. Large trees of the forest grow rapidly in summer. II. You will depart with but a small retinue, said the baronet. III. I thought that Titus was your friend. IV. A soft answer turneth away wrath; but grievous words stir up anger.

THE RULES OF SYNTAX.

RULE I. APPOSITION.

A noun or pronoun annexed to another noun or pronoun, and denoting the same person or thing, is put, by apposition, in the same case: as, "Paul the *apostle*." "Ye *men* of Rome."

RULE II. SUBJECT-NOMINATIVE.

The subject of a finite verb is in the nominative case; as, "*He* loves." "*I* rule."

RULE III. SUBJECT OF THE INFINITIVE.

The infinitive mode sometimes has a subject in the objective case; as, "I believe *the sun* to be the centre of the solar system." "I know *him* to be a man of veracity."

RULE IV. SUBSTANTIVE IN THE PREDICATE.

A noun or pronoun in the predicate after an intransitive verb, and the passive of certain transitive verbs, is in the same case as the subject, when both words refer to the same person or thing; as, "He has become a *poet*." "*He* was made *king*."

RULE V. VERB AND SUBJECT.

A verb agrees with its subject-nominative in person and number; as, "I *am*." "He *walks*."

RULE VI. SINGULAR NOMINATIVES TAKEN TOGETHER.

Two or more subject-nominatives, singular, connected by *and* expressed or understood, generally require a plural verb; as, "Charles, Thomas, and George *are* brothers." "Charles, Thomas, George, are brothers."

RULE VII. SINGULAR NOMINATIVES TAKEN SEPARATELY.

Two or more subject-nominatives, singular, connected by *or* or *nor*, require a singular verb; as, "Ambition or pride *controls* him."

RULE VIII. COLLECTIVE NOUNS.

A collective noun used as a subject-nominative takes a verb in the singular or plural, according as the noun denotes unity or plurality; as, "The *class was* large." "My *people do* not consider."

RULE IX. POSSESSIVE CASE.

A noun or pronoun which limits the meaning of a noun denoting a different person or thing, is put in the possessive; as, *Noah's* ark; *Peter's wife's* mother; *your* house; *their* prayers.

RULE X. OBJECTIVE AFTER VERBS AND PREPOSITIONS.

The object of a transitive verb or a preposition is put in the objective case; as, "The sun, imparting *warmth* to the *ground*, renders *it* fertile."

RULE XI. OBJECTIVE OF TIME, &c.

Nouns that denote *time, quantity, measure, distance, value,* or *direction*, are often put in the objective case without a preposition; as, "He is ten *years* old." "The rule is a *foot* in length." "She is worth a hundred *dollars*." "The ship sailed *south*."

RULE XII. TWO OBJECTIVES.

The verbs *ask, teach, call, allow, make, constitute, cost, charge*, and some others, frequently govern two nouns in the objective; as, "He asked *me* a *question*." "God called the *firmament Heaven*." "Nature made *Milton* a *genius*." "They elected *him clerk*." "It cost *me* much *labor*." "He charged *me* a *dollar* for the book."

Rule XIII. Substantive and Participle.

A noun or pronoun modified by a participle, and not dependent for its case on any other word, is put in the nominative absolute; as, "The *oration* having been delivered, the assembly was dismissed." "*Tarquinius* reigning, Pythagoras came into Italy." "*Thou* being my guide, I do not fear."

Rule XIV. Objects Addressed.

Nouns and pronouns denoting objects addressed, or used in exclamations, or without grammatical dependence on other words, are put in the nominative absolute; as, "Welcome, *stranger!*" "Oh! the *morals* of the day!" "*St. George* and *victory!*"

Rule XV. Pronouns.

Pronouns agree with their antecedents, or with the words for which they stand, in person, number, and gender; as, "Robert broke *his* knife." "Men often destroy *themselves.*" "Thou *who* speakest art the man."

Rule XVI. Adjective and Substantive.

An adjective belongs to the noun or pronoun whose meaning it qualifies or limits; as, "a *sour* apple;" "it is *sour.*"

Rule XVII. Pronominal Adjectives.

Pronominal adjectives belong to the nouns which they limit, or are used alone as pronouns; as, *this* man, *these* men, *both* men, *these* think, *both* come.

Rule. XVIII. An or A, The.

The definitive adjective *an* or *a* is used before nouns in the singular only; *the* is used before nouns in both numbers; as, *a* man, *the* man, *the* men.

Rule XIX. The Infinitive.

A verb in the infinitive mode generally limits the meaning of a verb, noun, or adjective; as, "I hope *to succeed.*" "Have a desire *to improve.*" "She is anxious *to hear.*"

Rule XX. The Infinitive, without the Sign.

When the verbs *bid, dare* [meaning *venture*], *hear, feel, make, need, see,* in the active voice, or *let,* in either the active or the passive, are followed by an infinitive, the sign *to* is omitted before it; as, "You bid me come [not *to come*]." "I saw him fall [not *to fall*]." "He durst do anything." "They let me recite." "The curtain was let fall."

RULE XXI. PARTICIPLES USED AS ADJECTIVES.

Participles belong to nouns or pronouns which they limit or modify; as, "I hear the birds *singing.*"

RULE XXII. PARTICIPLES USED AS NOUNS.

Participles used as nouns have the construction of nouns, while they are modified in the same way and govern the same case as the verbs from which they are formed; as, "I am in favor of *giving* him the situation."

RULE XXIII. THE SUBJUNCTIVE.

The subjunctive mode is used to express future contingency; also, after the conjunctions *lest* and *that* annexed to a command, and after *that* denoting a wish; as, "Though he *slay* me, yet will I trust in him." "Sin no more, lest a worse thing *come* upon thee." "See that thou *reform.*" "Oh! that I *were* at home!"

RULE XXIV. USE OF THE TENSES.

In using verbs, different tenses should not be confounded, nor should any tense be employed except in such connections as are consistent with the time it denotes.

RULE XXV. ADVERBS.

Adverbs generally modify verbs, participles, adjectives, and other adverbs; as, "We *seldom* see *very* old men walking *rapidly*; they are *too easily* tired."

RULE XXVI. PREPOSITIONS

Prepositions show the relations of things; as, "*From* Boston, we proceeded *by* railroad *to* Portland."

RULE XXVII. CONJUNCTIONS.

Conjunctions connect single words, adjuncts, clauses, members, and sentences; as, "He reads, *or* writes." "I sought the Lord, *and* he heard me."

RULE XXVIII. INTERJECTIONS.

Interjections have neither governing power nor dependence on other words.

CHAPTER XI.

THE RULES OF SYNTAX

309. Words combined in sentences bear different relations to each other.

Some words agree with others in certain accidents, as, *I am, you are.* *Am* is first person, singular number, because its subject *I* is first person singular. *Are* is second person, plural number, because its subject *you* is second plural. These are cases of agreement.

Some words govern others, — that is, require them to be put in a certain part. *I love her; her* is the objective case, governed by the transitive verb *love.* *Do it for me; me* is the objective case, governed by the preposition *for.* These are cases of government.

310. Syntax is that department of grammar which treats of the agreement, government, and arrangement of words in sentences.

311. To determine the agreement, government, and arrangement of words in sentences, we have certain rules, known as the Rules of Syntax.

We shall consider the Rules of Syntax in turn, and give exercises under them in analysis and parsing, as well as for correction. Particular attention should be paid to these exercises by those who wish to speak and write correctly. In parsing apply the rules, and in correcting the false syntax give the reasons for making changes.

Rule I. Apposition.

312. A noun or pronoun annexed to another noun or pronoun, and denoting the same person or thing, is put, by apposition, in the same case; as, "Paul the *apostle;*" "ye *men* of Rome."

Apostle is annexed to *Paul*, and denotes the same person; it is therefore said to be in apposition with *Paul*, and agrees with it in case. — *Men* is annexed to *ye*, and denotes the same persons; it is therefore put, by apposition, in the same case as *ye*.

APPOSITION. 167

Remarks.

313. The noun or pronoun in apposition defines, describes, or explains the one to which it is annexed, and always stands in the same part of the sentence as the latter, either subject or predicate. If two nouns denote the same thing, but stand the one in the subject and the other in the predicate, they are not said to be in apposition. " Kepler was called the legislator of the heavens." *Legislator* refers to the same person as *Kepler*, but is not in apposition with it, because the one is in the subject of the sentence and the other in the predicate.

314. A noun in apposition is frequently connected with the one to which it is annexed by the conjunction *as;* as, " My father intended to devote me *as* the *tithe* of his sons."

315. A preposition is sometimes introduced before the modifying noun, in which case the latter ceases to be in apposition; as, " the city *of Boston;*" " the title *of king.*"

316. A noun sometimes stands in apposition with a verb in the infinitive, a phrase, a clause, or the leading proposition of a sentence; as, " To travel comfortably, a very necessary *thing* in my case, was impossible." " The eldest son was always brought up to that employment, a *custom* which he and my father followed."

317. In like manner, a verb in the infinitive, a phrase, or a clause, is sometimes put in apposition with a noun preceding it; as, " My motion, *that the whole subject should be laid upon the table*, prevailed."

318. When two nouns denoting the same object come together in the possessive case, the sign is omitted after the first; as, "*John* the Baptist's head."

319. A noun in apposition is sometimes used without the possessive sign, to limit a noun or pronoun in the possessive case; as, " His office as *judge* must be responsible." In this sentence, *judge* refers to *his*, and agrees with it in the possessive case, the sign of the possessive being omitted.

320. A noun in apposition with two or more nouns, is put in the plural; as, " Romulus and Remus, the *grandsons* of Numitor."

321. A pronominal adjective used as a pronoun may be put in apposition in the singular number with a plural noun or pronoun; as, " They mourned *each* for his mate." " They dislike *each* other." " They play with *one* another."

The last two sentences show the mode of expressing a reciprocal action. The former of the two is equivalent to " They each dislike the other." *Each* is in apposition with *they* in the nominative case; *other* is in the objective case governed by the verb *dislike*. The latter of the two sentences is equivlaent to " They play one with another." *One* is in the nominative case, in apposition with *they;* *another* is in the objective, governed by the preposition *with.*

THE RULES OF SYNTAX.

Analysis and Parsing.

MODEL. — " My dog Fido is sick." *Fido* is a proper noun, third, singular, masculine, nominative; put, by apposition, in the same case as *dog*, according to the Rule, "A noun or pronoun annexed to another noun or pronoun, and denoting the same person or thing, is put, by apposition, in the same case."

Herschel, the *astronomer*, discovered the planet *Uranus*. Washington, the *commander-in-chief* of the American army, was born near the banks of the Potomac. It can be found at Jones the bookseller's shop. Webster, a dramatic *poet* of the seventeenth century, was clerk of the parish of St. Andrew. The Tippecanoe, a river of Indiana, is rendered famous by a battle between the Americans and Indians. I dined with him at our friend Davies's. Exhort one another daily. You are too humane and considerate; things which few people can be charged with. I am pleased with your appointment as chaplain. Righteousness and peace have kissed each other.

To be Corrected.

GENERAL FORM FOR CORRECTING FALSE SYNTAX.

1. Read the sentence.
2. Correct the sentence.
3. State the correction.
4. Give the reason for the correction.
5. Parse the words changed.

MODEL. — " The prime minister of Augustus was Mæcenas, him who was spoken of by Virgil." The sentence should read, *The prime minister of Augustus was Mæcenas, he who was spoken of by Virgil.* *Him* should be changed to *he*. It is in the objective case, and should be in the nominative, to be in the same case with *Mæcenas*, with which it is in apposition, according to Rule I., "A noun or pronoun annexed," &c.

He is a personal pronoun, thus declined: Sing. — Nom. *he*; Poss. *his*; Obj. *him*: Plural — Nom. *they*; Poss. *theirs*; Obj. *them*: it is found in the third person, singular number, and is in the nominative case, because the noun *Mæcenas* is, with which it is in apposition, according to Rule I., "A noun or pronoun annexed," &c.

They killed the chief, he who was at the fort yesterday. The chief is here, him who was at the fort yesterday. Let us crown her again, she who has so often been our queen of May. Relieve us, we who once relieved you. Such was the career of Burns, he who delighted a whole nation with his songs. Burns is still remembered as him who delighted a whole nation with his songs.

Rule II. Subject-Nominative.

322. The subject of a finite verb is in the nominative case.

Remarks.

323. In declarative sentences, the subject-nominative usually precedes the verb; as, "*He* reads." "The *rain* falls." In interrogative and imperative sentences, it follows the verb, or in compound tenses the first auxiliary; as, " Believest *thou* this?" " Who art *thou* ?" " Has *Cæsar* triumphed?" In exclamatory sentences, the subject may either precede or follow the verb; as, " How slowly yon tiny *vessel* sails!" or, " How slowly sails yon tiny *vessel!*"

324. The subject-nominative follows the verb or its first auxiliary when a supposition is expressed without the conjunction *if;* as, " Had *I* been there, this would not have happened." It also follows the verb in declarative sentences when *there, here, then, neither, nor,* &c., precedes; as, " There is an old *house.*" " Ye shall not eat of it, neither shall *ye* touch it."

Rule III. Subject of the Infinitive.

325. The infinitive mode sometimes has a subject in the objective case; as, "I believe *the sun* to be the centre of the solar system." "I know *him* to be a man of veracity."

Remarks.

326. This form of expression is equivalent to a subordinate clause introduced by *that;* "I believe him to be dishonest [that is, *that he is dishonest*]."

327. The infinitive with its subject is sometimes introduced by *for;* as, "*For* him to die was gain." In such expressions, the infinitive and the words connected with it constitute a substantive phrase which is used as the subject of the verb. *For him to die* is the subject of *was*.

Rule IV. Substantive in the Predicate.

328. A noun or pronoun in the predicate, after an intransitive verb, and the passive of certain transitive verbs, is in the same case as the subject, when both words refer to the same person or thing; as "*He* has become a *poet.*" "*He* was made *king.*"

Remarks.

329. This rule applies chiefly to nouns in the predicate after the intransitive verbs *to be, to become, to grow, to remain, to seem, to appear,* and after such transitive verbs in the passive voice as signify *to name, to render, to make, to esteem, to choose, to appoint,* and the like.

330. A noun in the predicate, according to this rule, may be in either the nominative or the objective case; for it must be in the same case as the subject, and we have just learned (Rule II.) that a finite verb has a subject in the nominative, while (Rule III.) a verb in the infinitive mode sometimes has a subject in the objective. "He has become a knave;" *knave,* standing in the predicate after the intransitive verb *has become,* must be in the same case as its subject, *he,* — that is, nominative. "I know him to be a knave;" here, *knave,* standing in the predicate after the infinitive *to be,* is in the same case as its subject *him,* — that is, objective. — " It was me;" *it,* the subject of the verb *was,* being in the nominative case, *me,* standing in the predicate should be in the same case, and must therefore be changed to *I.* "They suspected it to be me;" here, *me* is right; standing in the predicate after the infinitive *to be,* it must be in the same case as its subject *it,* — that is, objective.

331. Participles being parts of the verb, this rule applies to them also. A noun standing after a participle of an intransitive verb or a passive participle of a transitive verb, is in the same case as the noun or pronoun that the participle modifies; as, "Being a *soldier,* I could not resist the call." *Soldier,* standing after the present participle of the intransitive verb *to be,* is in the nominative case, because *I,* which the participle *being* modifies, is nominative.

332. An exception, however, is found in sentences in which the participle is preceded by a noun or pronoun in the possessive; as "He is angry with me on account of *my* being a *friend* to his enemy." Here, since *my* precedes the participle *being* in the possessive case, we would expect to find *friend* in the possessive after it, instead of which it is in the nominative. *On account of my being a friend* is an abridged expression equivalent to *because I am a friend,* in which *friend* is in the nominative case. The following is a parallel construction: "I am suspicious *of his being a rogue,"* — that is, *that he is a rogue.*

In the abridged form, the entire expression, *my being a friend,* or *his being a rogue,* is the object of the preposition; but the words *friend* and *rogue* may be regarded as in the same case in which they would be in the unabridged form, — that is, the nominative.

The construction of a noun after the verbs *to be, to become,* &c., when together they form a substantive clause, may be explained in a similar way. In the sentence, " To be a learned *man* is no easy attainment," *to be a learned man* is the subject of *is;* and the noun *man* may be considered as in the nominative case after *to be*.

333. A verb in the infinitive, a substantive clause, or phrase, is sometimes used as the predicate-nominative; as, " To steal is *to break the law.*" " The question is *whether we shall go or remain.*"

334. The usual order is, first the subject, then the verb, and then the predicate-nominative. In some sentences, however, this order is reversed; as, " *Who* is *he?*" Occasionally we find both the subject and the predicate-nominative before the verb; as, "*Monster* as *thou* art, I will yet obey thee:" or, both after it; as, "Art *thou he?*" "Am *I* a *traitor?*"

Analysis and Parsing.

Clement was the *name* of many popes. A coronation is a solemn *inauguration* of a monarch. The diamond is the most valuable *gem*. The youth will become a poet. Stephen died a martyr to his faith. What is the hour? We suspected him to be an impostor. Historians represent Brutus as having been an ardent lover of liberty.

Washington is called the father of his country. Napoleon Bonaparte, a native of Corsica, was styled Emperor of France. In England, a kind of trident is used for catching eels, called an eel-spear. Cicero and Antonius were elected consuls. I am tired of being an idler. I cannot bear the thought of being an exile from my country.

To be Corrected.

I that speak unto thee am him. It was not him that said it. It cannot be him. Whom are you? Whom do men say that I am? Who do they represent me to be? I do not think it is him. Did you believe it to be he? I did not think of its being him. If I were him, I would not tolerate it. I could not believe it was her. I could not believe it to be she.

Rule V. Verb and Subject.

335. A verb agrees with its subject-nominative in person and number; as, " I *am.*" " He *walks.*"

THE RULES OF SYNTAX.

Remarks.

336. A substantive clause, phrase, or a verb in the infinitive, may be used as the subject of a verb; as, "*That falsehood is met with more frequently than truth*, cannot be denied." "*To plow* is hard work."

337. An intransitive verb between two nominatives of different numbers or persons commonly agrees with the one that precedes it; as, " His *meat was* locusts and wild honey." Sometimes, however, it is made to agree with the one that follows; as, " The wages of sin *is death*."

338. The verbs *need* and *dare*, when intransitive, are sometimes used in the plural form with a singular nominative; as, She *need* [instead of *needs*] not go." "He *dare* [instead of *dares*] not repeat those words."

339. *As regards, as concerns, as respects, as appears, as follows.* — In these common expressions, *as* is an adverb; *regards, concerns, respects, appears*, and *follows* are impersonal verbs, the pronoun *it* being understood before them. Sometimes *it* is expressed; as, " The prisoner was not there, as *it* appears from the following evidence."

340. The verbs *need* and *require* are sometimes used before their subjects with a passive signification in the active voice; as, There *required* haste in the business." " There *needs* no argument for proving," &c. In such expressions, *there* is an introductory expletive. *Haste* and *argument* are the subjects with which the verbs agree, and *required* and *need* are used with a passive signification. Expressed in the usual way, these sentences would read, " Haste was required in the business." " No argument is needed for proving," &c. — "*There wanted* not men to fight in such a cause," is a parallel construction, equivalent to " Men were not wanting," &c.

341. The verb that agrees with the nominative case is sometimes omitted; as, " To whom the monarch;" *replied* is omitted.

Analysis and Parsing.

Varro *was esteemed* a learned man, but Aristides *was called* just. Titus *has been called* the delight of the human race. Shall a barbarian have these cultivated fields? To see the sun is pleasant. Robert need not practice such economy. To excel in knowledge is honorable; but to be ignorant is base. That you may enjoy felicity is my fervent prayer. Promising, and not performing, is an evidence of insincerity. Methinks this single consideration will be sufficient to extinguish all envy.

The first impression made by the proceedings of the American Congress on our people in general, was greatly in our favor. Methought I was admitted into a long, spacious gallery. I am indifferent as regards my personal security. She dare not remain. As appears from the evidence, he is guilty of an atrocious crime. Let there be no strife betwixt me and thee. There wanted not proof of the conspiracy. "'Marry,' says* I, 'if it be so, I am very well rewarded for all the pains I have been at.'" — *Addison.*

To be Corrected.

The clouds has dispersed. The rivers has overflowed their banks. There was three Indians in the company. A variety of blessings have been conferred upon us. In piety and virtue consist the happiness of man. What names has the planets? There follows from thence these plain consequences. There is men who never reason. The smiles that encourage severity of judgment hides malice and insincerity. So, thinks I, I will remain. Some foggy days, and about ten or twelve days in January, was cold and icy. How does your plans succeed? What signifies good opinions when our practice is bad? There was more impostors than one. The virtue of these men and women are indeed exemplary. Too great a variety of amusements create disgust.

Rule VI. Singular Nominatives taken together.

342. Two or more subject-nominatives, singular, connected by *and*, expressed or understood, generally require a plural verb; as, "Charles, Thomas, and George *are* brothers." "Charles, Thomas, George, are brothers."

343. Subject-nominatives connected by *and* are said to be taken together; but when preceded by *each, every, no,* and *not*, even though connected by *and*, they are taken separately. Singular subjects taken separately require a verb in the singular; as, "No man, no woman, *says* this with truth." "Every officer and every soldier *claims* a superiority."

344. In like manner, singular subjects connected by *and also, as well as*, and other expressions that serve to distinguish them emphatically, take a verb in the singular; as, "Ambition, and also the safety of the state, *was* concerned." "The nephew, as well as the uncle, *has* trampled on the rights of his countrymen."

---

* Irregular expressions are occasionally met with, which usage sanctions rather than analogy; such as, "*says I*," "*thinks I*," &c. These, however, are ungrammatical, and should not be used.

345. A singular subject-nominative, connected with another noun by *with, in company with, together with,* &c., requires a singular verb, though the idea of plurality is conveyed in the logical subject; as, "The king, with the lords and commons, *constitutes* [NOT *constitute*] an excellent government." Here, *lords* and *commons*, being the objects of the preposition *with*, are in the objective case; *constitutes* agrees with *king* alone, and must be in the singular number.

346. When singular subject-nominatives connected by *and* refer to the same person or thing, the verb must be singular; as, "The wife and mother [meaning one person who is both wife and mother] *kneels* in prayer."

347. When several singular subject-nominatives connected by *and* are separated by the introduction of the verb after the first, the verb is put in the singular, agreeing with the first and being understood with the rest; as, "Your beauty *captivates* me, your wit, and your amiability."

348. If two subject-nominatives connected by *and not, and also,* or *as well as,* are of different numbers, the verb agrees with the first; as, "Diligent industry, and not mean savings, *produces* honorable competence." — If subject-nominatives connected by *and* are of different persons, the verb prefers the second person to the third, and the first to both the second and third; as, "Thou [2d person], James [3d person], and I [1st person], *are attached* [1st person] to our country." "Thou [2d] and he [3d] *shared* [2d] it between you."

349. Under this rule, two or more infinitives, clauses, or phrases used as subject-nominatives, require a plural verb; as, "To steal and lie *are* base." "Whether capital punishment should be abolished, and whether the election of judges by the people is expedient, *are* open questions."

Analysis and Parsing.

[PARSING MODEL. — *Tranquillity and love dwell here.*

Tranquillity is a common noun, third, singular, neuter; nominative case, because it is one of the subjects of the verb *dwell;* according to the Rule, "The subject of a finite verb is in the nominative case."

And is a conjunction, connecting the words *tranquillity* and *love.*

Love is a common noun, third, singular, neuter; nominative case, because it is one of the subjects of the verb *dwell;* according to the Rule, "The subject of a finite verb is in the nominative case."

Dwell is an intransitive verb; the principal parts are *dwell, dwelt* or *dwelled, dwelt, dwelled;* irregular, active voice; indicative, present, third, plural, and agrees with its subject-nominatives *tranquillity* and *love;* according to the Rule, "Two or more subject-nominatives, singular, connected by *and*," &c.

Here is an adverb of place, and modifies the verb *dwell*.

According to the above model, repeat the rules whenever they apply in the parsing.]

Reason and truth *constitute* intellectual gold. Riches, honors, and pleasures *steal* away the heart from religion. You and I *look* alike. The planetary system, boundless space, and the immense ocean, affect the mind with sensations of astonishment. He and I are foes. His ready wit, together with his varied acquirements, makes him an agreeable companion. The useful arts improved by science, and science itself improved by philosophy, confer power on civilized and instructed man, and enable him to triumph over his fellows and over nature.

To be Corrected.

[The reason for the correction should be given in every instance.]

Idleness and ignorance is the parent of many vices. Time and tide waits for no man. Patience and diligence, like faith, removes mountains. The forehead, the eyes, and the countenance often deceives. Castor and Pollux were seen to fight on horseback. To fish and hunt is pleasant. The following treatise, with those which accompany it, were written many years ago. His wisdom, not his riches, produce esteem. Not wealth, not rank, not arrogance, constitute a gentleman. My uncle, with his son, were in town yesterday. That able scholar and grammarian have been refuted. The discomfiture and slaughter was very great. Temperance as well as obedience, were enjoined.

> Forth in the pleasing spring
> Thy beauty walk, thy tenderness, and love.

Rule VII. Singular Nominatives taken separately.

350. Two or more subject-nominatives, singular, connected by *or* or *nor*, require a singular verb; as, "Ambition or pride *controls* him."

351. If one of the subject-nominatives thus connected is plural and the rest are singular, the plural nominative should be placed next to the verb, and the verb should agree with it in the plural; as, "Neither poverty nor *riches were* injurious to him."

352. If the subject-nominatives thus connected are of different persons, the pronoun of the first person is placed nearest to the verb, and the verb

agrees with it; as, "Neither thou, he, nor *I am* tall." If, of two subject-nominatives thus connected, one is second person and the other third, the latter is placed nearest to the verb, and the verb agrees with it; as, "Either thou or *he is* mistaken."

Such sentences, however, as those just given as examples, although correct, are inelegant. The nominatives should be separated, the verb used with the first, and either repeated or understood with the rest. "Neither are you tall, nor he, nor I." "Either thou art mistaken or he is."

Analysis and Parsing.

Ignorance or negligence *has caused* the mistake. Neither the captain nor the sailors *were acquainted* with the coast. Death or some worse misfortune soon *divides* them. History or geography is a proper study for youth. Intense heat or extreme cold is painful. Man's happiness or misery is in a great measure put into his own hands. One or both of the witnesses were present. Thou mayst go, or he, but not both.

To be Corrected.

James or Charles were in fault. Neither authority nor analogy support such an opinion. Either ability or inclination were wanting. Neither the father nor the son were saved. Neither the general nor the soldiers was charged with cowardice. Have the dictionary, the spelling-book, or the grammar been found? Has the dictionaries, the spelling-book, or the grammar been found? No tyrant or robber enjoy peaceful sleep. To lie or even to deceive are inconsistent with honesty. I or thou art wrong. He or thou shouldst go. Robert or thou is the offender. Were this philosopher and poet or his critic in the wrong?

Rule VIII. Collective Nouns.

353. A collective noun used as a subject-nominative takes a verb in the singular or plural, according as the noun denotes unity or plurality; as, "The *class was* large." "My *people do* not consider."

Remarks.

354. A collective noun, though in the singular number, denotes a body of individuals. When an action or state is affirmed of the whole as a body, the verb is singular; as, "The regiment *was* cut up [that is, the

whole body, not each of the individuals composing it]." When it is affirmed of each individual composing the body, the verb is plural; as, "The peasantry *wear* no shoes [that is, the individual peasants]. In doubtful cases, use the plural; as, "The people *have* spoken."

355. When the definitive *this* or *that* precedes the noun, the verb must be singular; as, "This people *has* spoken."

Analysis and Parsing.

A part *mount* their horses. A great multitude *hurl* stones and darts. The court *has* just *ended* its session. In France, the middle class make use of wooden shoes. Why do the heathen rage and the people imagine a vain thing? The nobility are the pillars that support the throne. A company of troops was detached. The whole party are in favor of the measure. Does this party favor the measure? The majority were in favor of remaining.

To be Corrected.

The British Parliament are composed of king, lords, and commons. A council were called. The crowd were very great. That party were in error. This company are handsomely uniformed. The court of Rome were not without solicitude. The French cavalry were more formidable than the infantry. Congress meet on the first Monday of December. Are the senate or the lower house to consider the question first?

REVIEW QUESTIONS ON CHAPTER XI. — RULES I. - VIII.

309. What is said of the relations of words combined in sentences? Give an example of agreement. Of government. 310. What is syntax? 311. What is the use of the rules of syntax?

312. Repeat Rule I. Show its application. 313. What does the noun or pronoun in apposition do? How does it stand, as regards the leading noun or pronoun? 314. How are the two nouns frequently connected? 315. In what case does the limiting noun cease to be in apposition? 316. With what does a noun sometimes stand in apposition? 317. What sometimes stands in apposition with a noun? 318. State the principle relating to the omission of the sign of the possessive case? 319. In what other case is the sign of the possessive omitted? 320. In what number is a noun that stands in apposition with two or more nouns? 321. State the principle relating to a pronominal adjective used as a pronoun. Explain such constructions as *they dislike each other.*

THE RULES OF SYNTAX.

322. Repeat Rule II. 323. How does the subject-nominative stand in declarative sentences? In interrogative and imperative sentences? In exclamatory sentences? 324. In what cases does the subject-nominative follow the verb? 325. Repeat Rule III. 326. To what is this form of expression equivalent? 327. By what is the infinitive with its subject sometimes introduced? 328. Repeat Rule IV. 329. To what does this rule chiefly apply? 330. According to this rule, in what case may a noun in the predicate be? Give examples. 331. In what case is a noun that stands after the participle of an intransitive verb? Give an example. 332. What exception is there to the principle just stated? How is the nominative case after the participle accounted for? What parallel construction is explained in the same way? 333. What is sometimes used as the predicate-nominative? 334. In most cases, what is the relative position of subject, verb, and predicate-nominative? How is this order sometimes changed? 335. Repeat Rule V. 336. What may be used as the subject of a verb? 337. State the principle that applies to an intransitive verb between two nominatives of different numbers. 338. How are the verbs *need* and *dare* sometimes used? 339. Explain such expressions as *as regards*. 340. How are the verbs *need* and *require* sometimes used? 341. What is sometimes omitted?

342. Repeat Rule VI. 343. When are subject-nominatives said to be taken together, and when to be taken separately? What must be the number of a verb agreeing with singular subjects taken separately? 344. State the principal applying to singular subjects connected by *and also*. 345. What is the principle relating to a singular subject-nominative connected with another noun by *with?* 346. What is the principle relating to singular subject-nominatives referring to the same object? 347. What is the principle relating to singular subject-nominatives separated by the verb? 348. When the subject-nominatives are of different numbers and persons, which does the verb prefer? 349. What, used as subject-nominatives, require a plural verb?

350. Repeat Rule VII. 351. What principle applies when one of the subject-nominatives is plural and the rest are singular? 352. When the subject-nominatives are of different persons, how must they be arranged, and with which must the verb agree? What more elegant form is suggested?

353. Repeat Rule VIII. 354. When is the noun said to denote unity, and when plurality? In doubtful cases, what number should the verb be? 355. What number is the verb when *this* or *that* precedes the subject-nominative?

Rule IX. Possessive Case.

356. A noun or pronoun which limits the meaning of a noun denoting a different person or thing is put in the possessive; as, *Noah's* **ark;** *Peter's wife's* **mother;** *your* **house;** *their* **prayers.**

Remarks.

357. The limited noun is often omitted when it can be easily supplied; as, "We dined at Garrick's [that is, *Garrick's house*]." "Paradise Lost" is a work of Milton's [that is, *of Milton's works*]."

358. When two or more nouns in the possessive, standing together, imply joint ownership, the sign of the possessive ('s) is generally omitted after all but the last; as, "Sanborn and Carter's bookstore." *Sanborn* and *Carter's*, limiting the meaning of *bookstore*, are both in the possessive; but, since joint ownership is implied, the sign of the possessive is annexed only to the latter noun.

When, on the other hand, separate ownership is implied, each noun takes the sign; as, *Cowper's*, *Thomson's*, and *Coleridge's* works.

359. When nouns denoting the same object stand together in the possessive, the sign is annexed to the last only; as, "Paul the *apostle's* journey;" "at our friend Sir Robert *Hinckley's*."

360. So, when an adjunct is very closely connected in sense with the noun which it modifies, forming with it, as it were, one compound term, the sign of the possessive is annexed to the noun in the adjunct, instead of the leading noun; as, "the king of *Great Britain's* prerogative;" "the captain of the *guard's* house." In these expressions, *king* and *captain* are in the possessive case, governed by *prerogative* and *house;* *Great Britain's* and *guard's* are in the objective case, governed by the preposition *of.* — A neat way of parsing such expressions is to take noun and adjunct together, and call the whole a substantive phrase; as, *king of Great Britain's* is a substantive phrase, third, singular, neuter, possessive, according to the Rule, "A noun or pronoun which limits the meaning of a noun," &c.

361. In the case of possessives in apposition, if the limited word is omitted, the sign is annexed to the first, especially if it is modified by more than one word; as, "I dined at *Walton's*, an amiable and worthy man." "I left the parcel at *Smith's*, the bookseller and stationer."

362. The preposition *of* with the objective case is often equivalent to the possessive. "The advice of my father" means the same thing as "my father's advice." Since these constructions are equivalent, instead of repeating either too often in a sentence, it is best to alternate them. It would be awkward to say either "Peter's wife's mother's sister" or "the sister of

the mother of the wife of Peter;" we should say " the sister of Peter's wife's mother." In like manner, harshness or obscurity is sometimes avoided by substituting the verb *belong* for the possessive case. " This farm belonged to my father and brother," is better than " This was my father and brother's farm."

363. Avoid bringing in a clause between the limiting and the limited noun; as, " They condemned the prodigal's, as he was called, extravagant conduct;" — it should be, " They condemned the extravagant conduct of the prodigal, as he was called."

364. A noun or pronoun which precedes and limits a participle, or a clause containing one, is put in the possessive; as, " I insist upon these *rules*' being enforced." " We heard of *your* going away." " Much depends on the *patient's* observing these rules." In such constructions, the participle retains its verbal properties, and may govern the objective case, or be modified by an adverb or adjunct, like the verb from which it is derived. This will be seen in the above examples.

Analysis and Parsing.

I asked for *Buskerville's* edition of *Barclay's* Apology. *My* ways are not thy ways. He accompanied me to St. Mary's Church. His lady was the daughter of Johnson's first schoolmaster. He pathetically described the parent's and the son's misfortune. I gave him an account of my having examined the chest of books which he had sent to me. There was also a book of De Foe's, and another of Dr. Mather's.

This took place at our friend Sir Joshua Reynolds's, the great painter. The manner of a young lady's employing herself usefully in reading will be the subject of another paper. Very little time was necessary for Johnson's concluding a treaty with the bookseller. Whose children deserve attention at my hands, if my own do not? We have heard of our army's having been defeated. Smith Brothers and Thompson's stores are the handsomest in our town. The Emperor of Russia's proclamation has just reached his army.

To be Corrected.

Webster or Johnson's Dictionary. Washington and Taylor's courage. Bancroft or Prescott's History. Ferdinand's and Isabella's reign. Hyde's, Lord's, and Duren's bookstore. Mr. Murphy mentioned Dr. Johnson having a design to publish an edition of Cowley. There is no danger of that complaint being made at present. The Bishop's of Landaff excellent works. I will not, for David's thy father's sake.

Such was the stupid fellow's, as he was commonly regarded, proposition. This was a discovery of Sir Isaac Newton. This property was my father's, my brother's, and my uncle's wife's. A mother's tenderness and a father's care are nature's gifts for man's advantage. The medicine was procured at Brown, the apothecary and chemist's.

Rule X. Objective after Verbs and Prepositions.

365. The object of a transitive verb or a preposition is put in the objective case; as, "*The sun, imparting warmth* to the *ground*, renders *it* fertile."

This rule applies to the active participles of a transitive verb, as may be seen in the example given above.

Remarks.

366. This rule applies to an objective case after an intransitive verb used transitively; as, " Look *danger* in the face, and it will flee from you." " We talked the *hours* away." " Groves whose trees wept odorous *gums.*" Intransitive verbs are frequently construed in this way with a noun of kindred signification to their own; as, " Let him *die* the *death.*" " He went his *way.*"

367. The objectives *whom, which,* and *that* should stand before the verb that governs them, and also before its subject: as, "*whom* ye seek;" "the story *which* he told."

368. Transitive verbs in the active voice govern the objective case without the intervention of a preposition. Such expressions as the following are wrong:—"This allows *of* no trifling." "I do not wish *for* any more." The prepositions *of* and *for* must be expunged.

369. Two prepositions, or a transitive verb and a preposition, may be construed with the same object when obscurity or harshness does not result; as, "Payment shall be made *on* or *before* the first of August." ' He *is studying,* and bestowing much attention *on,* this subject." But such constructions are often offensive to the ear, and in that case should be avoided; as, " She does not pay the slightest attention *to,* or rather she acts in open defiance *of,* my commands." " Take an interest *in,* and try to benefit, your friends." Such sentences are easily corrected: — " She does not pay the slightest attention to my commands, or rather she acts in open defiance of them." " Take an interest in your friends, and try to benefit them."

370. Prepositions governing the objective case are frequently omitted.

1. *To* is generally omitted after *near* and *like:* as, " Near [*to*] me sat a Mexican general." " Like [*to*] the rest of the world."

2. *Of* is sometimes omitted after *worthy* and *unworthy*; as, "a work worthy [*of*] his great genius;" "actions unworthy [*of*] his fair fame."

3. *To* and *for* are omitted when the noun or pronoun they govern is introduced between a transitive verb and its object; as, "Hand [*to*] the lady a chair." "Buy [*for*] me a knife." "Please to find [*for*] me the place."

4. Several objects connected by a conjunction generally have the preposition expressed before the first only; as, "The works of Milton and [*of*] Shakespeare are read with admiration and [*with*] delight."

Analysis and Parsing.

Disappointment depresses the *heart* of *man*. Foolish pursuits delight some *persons*. Coursing in its pebbly channel, the brook ran nectar. A variety of pleasing objects charms the eye. Those whom opulence has made proud, and whom luxury has corrupted, cannot relish the simple pleasures of nature. The President's speech is so important to the public, that I know you will be anxious to see it as early as possible. I will resign my office and remain with you. Her lips blushed deeper sweets. Some men would rather sleep the sleep of death, than live a life of idleness. He gave me an order to buy him a dozen grammars.

To be Corrected.

Who did they send? He that is idle reprove. He invited my brother and I to examine his library. Ye hath he quickened. Who shall I call you? He who committed the offence, you should correct, not I who am innocent. He who is in fault I will chastise. Who shall I direct this letter to? Who will you vote for? He and they we know, but who are you? Lend to me your book, and I will give to you my pencil. I premise with a few remarks which the subject has suggested. Do not halt in, or give up, the race. He set his face against, and violently denounced, all innocent amusements. Sicily lies over against, and not far from, Italy. Will you accept of my gift? Consider of it.

Rule XI. Objective of Time, &c.

371. Nouns that denote *time*, *quantity*, *measure*, *distance*, *value*, or *direction*, are often put in the objective case without a preposition; as, "He is ten *years* old."

"The rule is a *foot* in length." "She is worth a hundred *dollars.*" "The ship sailed *south.*"

Remarks.

372. The word *home* after *come, go,* and other verbs of motion, is put in the objective case without the preposition *to;* as, " My intention is to return *home.*" But if an adjective is introduced to qualify or limit *home,* the preposition is used; as, " My intention is to return *to my home.*"

373. Nouns that denote particular points of time are generally used with a preposition, but not always; as, " *at* that *hour ;* " " *in* the *morning ;* " " He arrived on *Wednesday* last; " " He arrived last *Wednesday.*"

Analysis and Parsing.

Congress has been in session three *months*. He was absent from his native country six *years*. They excavated a pit twenty *feet* in depth. One morning we walked out together. Wednesday, Nov. 1st, we left Paris. The storm burst upon us three leagues from land. They travelled north, south, east, and west. The people looked this way and that way, but discovered no means of escape. A flatterer's praise is not worth a farthing.

Rule XII. Two Objectives.

374. The verbs *ask, teach, call, allow, make, constitute, cost, charge,* and some others, frequently govern two nouns in the objective; as, " He asked *me* a *question.*" "God called the *firmament Heaven.*" " Nature made *Milton* a *genius.*" " They elected *him clerk.*" " It cost *me* much *labor.*" " He charged *me* a *dollar* for the book."

Remarks.

375. An infinitive, a substantive clause, or a phrase, is often used as one of the objectives; as, " He asked me *to give him money.*"

376. The direct object of a verb in the active voice becomes the subject when the verb is changed to the passive voice; as, " Columbus discovered America." " America was discovered by Columbus."

Verbs signifying *to ask, to teach,* &c., have two direct objects in the active voice, one of a person, the other of a thing; as, " He asked me a question."

After the passive voice of these verbs either of these objects remains in the objective case; as, " I was asked a question," or, " A question was asked me."

Verbs signifying *to offer, to promise, to give,* &c., have two objects in the active voice, one direct and the other indirect; as, " He offered me [indirect] a chair [direct]." When these verbs are used in the passive voice, the indirect object remains in the objective case; as, " A chair was offered me; " NOT, " I was offered a chair."

Verbs signifying *to make, to choose, to constitute,* &c., have two objects in the active voice, one direct, the other the object of effect; as, " They chose him [direct] king [object of effect]." After the passive of these verbs, the object of effect becomes the predicate-nominative; as, " He was chosen king."

Analysis and Parsing.

In long journeys, ask your *master leave* to give ale to your horses. God called the *light day*, and the *darkness* He called *night*. While they promise themselves liberty, they themselves are the servants of corruption. He fashioned it with a graving tool, after he had made it a molten calf. He allowed his son the third part of his inheritance. His son was allowed the third part of his inheritance. Simon he surnamed Peter. If the wicked offer you anything, beware how you accept it. A good situation has been offered him.

Rule XIII. Substantive and Participle.

377. A noun or pronoun modified by a participle, and not dependent for its case on any other word, is put in the nominative absolute; as, " The *oration* having been delivered, the assembly was dismissed." " *Tarquinius* reigning, Pythagoras came into Italy." " *Thou* being my guide, I do not fear."

Remarks.

378. Adverbial phrases like the above are abridged expressions, equivalent to clauses introduced by *after, while, when, if, since*, or some other conjunctive adverb or conjunction. Thus, in the above examples, we may substitute the following clauses for the abridged expressions: " After the oration had been delivered; " " While Tarquinius was reigning; " " Since thou art my guide."

379. The noun or pronoun in such expressions is sometimes omitted; as, " Generally speaking [that is, *we* speaking generally], vice is wedded to misery."

380. The participle is sometimes omitted; as, "The war over [that is, *being over*], Francis disbanded his army."

Analysis and Parsing.

[In parsing nouns or pronouns thus construed, call them *nominative absolute*. Thus, in the first sentence below, *We* is a simple personal pronoun, first, plural, masculine or feminine, nominative absolute; according to the Rule, "A noun or pronoun modified by a participle," &c.]

We being exceedingly tossed, they lightened the ship. Edwards walked along with us, *I* eagerly assisting to keep up the conversation. The *sun rising*, darkness disappears. The preliminaries being settled, we proceeded on our business. This done, we set out for Liverpool. Looking at it in the most favorable light, it was a disgraceful act. Danger once past, even the coward becomes brave. Waterloo having proved fatal to his hopes, Napoleon could but retreat.

Exercise in Construction.

[In the following sentences, substitute for the clauses in italics equivalent clauses containing a participle and noun or pronoun in the nominative absolute.

MODEL.— Whose gray top shall tremble *as he descends*.
Whose gray top shall tremble, *he descending*.]

While I and my partner were absent, everything went wrong. *As the drought had destroyed the crops*, apprehensions were entertained of a famine. *Since he was the light of our household*, we miss him exceedingly. No country can enjoy prosperity *when a tyrant reigns*. *Since he and I were at sword's points*, there was a general constraint on the company. *If you except us*, there are no lawyers in the town. *After war had been proclaimed*, an engagement soon took place. *When schools are plenty*, there is comparatively little ignorance. *When she fled*, Augustus soon gained the battle.

Rule XIV. Objects Addressed.

381. Nouns and pronouns denoting objects addressed, or used in exclamations, or without grammatical dependence on other words, are put in the nominative absolute; as, "Welcome, *stranger!*" "Oh! the *morals* of the day!" "*St. George* and *victory!*" "The *boy*,— Oh! where was he?"

382. The simple personal pronoun of the first person, used in exclamations, instead of always standing in the nominative absolute, according to this rule, is sometimes put in the objective, governed by some verb or preposition understood; as, "*Me* miserable! [that is, *behold* me miserable! *pity* me miserable!]" "Woe is *me!* [that is, woe is *to* me! woe is *for* me!]"

Analysis in Parsing.

[An exclamation which contains no verb may be called, in analyzing, an Exclamatory Expression. Its leading word should be pointed out, and the clauses, adjuncts, &c., by which it may be modified.]

O *light* of Trojans and *support* of Troy! O sacred *city!* O valiant heroes! Religion! what a treasure divine! Your fathers, where are they? and the prophets, do they live forever? The name of a procession! what a great mixture of independent ideas, of persons, habits, tapers, orders, motions, sounds, does it contain! O happy we! Miserable they! O me! Ah me! My friend, disregard not my advice!

REVIEW QUESTIONS.—RULES IX.-XIV.

356. Repeat Rule IX. 357. In what case is the limited noun often omitted? 358. When two or more nouns standing together imply joint ownership, which takes the sign of the possessive? Which takes the sign, when separate ownership is implied? 359. When nouns denoting the same object stand together in the possessive, which takes the sign? 360. In what case is the sign of the possessive annexed to a noun in an adjunct, instead of to the noun which the adjunct modifies? Give examples. What neat way of parsing such expressions is suggested?

361. When we have possessives in apposition, if the limited word is omitted, which takes the sign? 362. What other construction is often equivalent to the use of the possessive? How may we avoid the too frequent use of the possessive case? How is harshness or obscurity proceeding from the use of the possessive sometimes avoided? 363. What must not be separated by a clause? 364. State the rule that applies to a noun or pronoun preceding and limiting a participle.

365. Repeat Rule X. To what does this rule apply? 366. In what case is an intransitive verb followed by the objective? 367. How should the objectives *whom*, *which*, and *that* stand? 368. In what case must a preposition be expunged? 369. State the principle with respect to connecting two prepositions, or a transitive verb and a preposition, with the same object. 370. In what four cases may prepositions governing the objective case be omitted?

371. Repeat Rule XI. 372. State the usage with respect to the word *home*. 373. State the usage with respect to nouns denoting particular points of time. 374. Repeat Rule XII. 375. What may be used as one of the objectives after these verbs? 376. What is the construction of these verbs in the passive voice? Give examples. 377. Repeat Rule XIII. 378. To what are clauses containing a nominative absolute and a participle equivalent? 379. What is sometimes omitted in such clauses? Give an example. 380. Give an example of the omission of the participle. 381. Repeat Rule XIV. 382. What exception is there to this rule?

Rule XV. Pronouns.

383. Pronouns agree with their antecedents, or with the words for which they stand, in person, number, and gender; as, "Robert broke *his* knife." "Men often destroy *themselves*." "Thou *who* speakest art the man."

In the first example, *his* agrees with the noun *Robert*, for which it stands, in the third person, singular number, and masculine gender. In the second example, *themselves* agrees with the noun *men*, for which it stands, in the third person, plural number, and masculine gender. In the third example, *who* agrees with its antecedent *thou*, in the second person, singular number, and masculine gender.

384. Pronouns referring to two or more singular nouns taken together, must be in the plural number; as, "George and Thomas excel in *their* studies."

If the nouns referred to are of different persons, the pronoun, on being put in the plural, prefers the first person to the second, and the second to the third; as, "Thou, he, and I, excel in *our* studies." "Thou and he excel in *your* studies."

385. Pronouns referring to two or more singular nouns taken separately must be in the singular number; as, "Neither James nor John is diligent in *his* [not *their*] studies." "James, and also John, is diligent in *his* [not *their*] studies." "James, as well as John, is diligent in *his* [not *their*] studies." — But if one of the nouns referred to is plural, the pronoun also must be plural; as, "Neither the captain nor the sailors were acquainted with *their* danger."

386. A collective noun takes a pronoun in the singular or plural, according as it denotes unity or plurality; as, "The senate resolved *itself* into a committee of the whole." "The party generally thought that *their* leaders were wrong."

387. When the singular nouns taken separately are of the third person and different genders, as no pronoun of the third person is found in all the genders, different pronouns must be used, referring to the different nouns respectively; as, "No boy or girl must talk to *his* or *her* neighbor, when *he* or *she* hears the bell ring." Such constructions are very awkward, yet it would be ungrammatical to use a plural pronoun of common gender, as is sometimes done; "No boy or girl must talk to *their* neighbor, when *they* hear the bell ring." The best way is to avoid the use of such expressions by substituting for the two nouns of different genders some general term applicable to both, and making the pronoun agree with this general term in the masculine; as, "No *pupil,* [*scholar, child*] must talk to *his* neighbor when *he* hears the bell ring."

388. *It* is often used independently as the subject of a verb, referring to some noun, pronoun, infinitive, or clause, in the predicate, without regard to the person, number, or gender of the latter; as, "*It* is *I.*" "*It* is *thou.*" "*It* is *she.*" "*It* is Robert's *children.*" "*It* is the mark of a generous spirit *to forgive injuries.*" "*It* is strange *that you have forgotten me.*"

389. The compound personals, *myself, thyself,* &c., are sometimes used in apposition with a noun or pronoun for the sake of emphasis; as, "I *myself* saw it." "They killed Cicero *himself.*"

390. *What* is sometimes used adverbially in the sense of *partly;* as "*what* with the war;" "*what* with the sweat," &c.

391. *What* and *but what* are often improperly used for *that;* as, "They will not believe but *what* [*that*] I have been to blame." "I have no doubt *but what* [*that*] she did it."

392. Every relative must have an antecedent, either expressed or understood; as, "Who is partial to others, is so to himself." In this sentence, *who* refers to some indefinite antecedent understood; as, the *man* who, the *person* who, *he* who.

393. The relative frequently refers to a whole clause; as, "You have overcome envy with glory, *which* is very difficult."

394. The relative is sometimes omitted. 1. In the nominative case; as, "It is he [*that*] bids you forbear." 2. In the objective case; as, "The greatest curiosity [*that*] we saw was the burning spring."

395. When there are two antecedents of different persons, denoting the same object, the relative, though it may refer to either, agrees with the nearer one. "I, who made all things, am the Lord." Here, *who* agrees

with *I*, in the first, singular. " I am the Lord, who made all things." Here, *who* agrees with *Lord*, in the third, singular.

396. The relative *which*, though generally used with reference to irrational animals or things, may be applied to young children. It was formerly applied to persons also (as " Our Father, *which* art in heaven"), and is still so used when the antecedent has reference merely to the character or profession of the person, or is a name used merely as such; as, " He has at length become a good performer, *which* he has long aimed to be." " I hate to hear you say Nero, *which* is another name for cruelty."

As an interrogative pronoun, *which* is applied directly to persons; as, " *Which* of you was there? "

397. The relative *that*, may refer either to persons or things. It is generally used in preference to *who* or *which*, in the following cases: —

1. After an adjective in the superlative degree; as, " Humility is one of the *most amiable* virtues *that* we can possess."

2. After *same, very,* and *all*; as, " They are the *same* persons *that* we saw yesterday." " You are the *very* man *that* I wanted to see." "*All that* were aboard, were injured."

3. After the interrogative *who*, and an antecedent introduced by *it is ;* as, " *Who that* is prudent would conduct in such a manner? " "*It* is you *that* must bear the responsibility; not I."

4. When the antecedent consists of two or more words denoting both persons and things; as, " My memory fondly clings to the dear *friends* and *country that* I have left."

398. Relatives in different clauses, referring to the same antecedent, should be the same; as, " It is remarkable, that Holland, against *which* the war was undertaken, and *that* in the very beginning was reduced to the brink of ruin, lost nothing." *Which* should be used in the latter relative clause, because it is used in the former.

399. The relative is generally placed after its antecedent, and should stand as near it as possible. " He often overreaches himself that tries to overreach others." In this sentence we have a faulty arrangement; the relative and its clause should stand immediately after the antecedent *he*, — " He that tries to overreach others, often overreaches himself."

400. We can sometimes tell what a relative refers to only by its position. " I have seen a shawl made of silk which came from China." Is it the *shawl* or the *silk* that came from China? The position of the relative indicates that it is the *silk*. If we wish to state that the *shawl* came from China, we must make such a change as will bring the relative immediately after *shawl*, — " I have just seen a silk shawl that came from China."

401. A relative is sometimes introduced in such a way as to divide a

clause which constitutes its antecedent; as, "There was, therefore, *which* is all we assert, a course of life pursued by them different from that which they before led."

Analysis and Parsing.

[In parsing a relative, two rules must be given; one for its person, number, and gender, and another for its case.

MODEL. — I shall never forget a friend who entertained me so hospitably and whom I love so much.

Who is a simple relative pronoun, thus declined: Sing. and Plural, Nom. *who;* Poss. *whose;* Obj. *whom.* It is in the third person, singular number, and masculine or feminine gender, because its antecedent *friend* is, with which it agrees according to Rule XV., — " Pronouns agree with their antecedents, or with the words for which they stand, in person, number, and gender." It is in the nominative case, being the subject of the verb *entertained;* according to Rule II., — "The subject of a finite verb is in the nominative case."

Whom is a simple relative pronoun, thus declined: Sing. and Plural, Nom. *who;* Poss. *whose;* Obj. *whom.* It is in the third person, singular number, and masculine or feminine gender, because its antecedent *friend* is, with which it agrees according to Rule XV., — "Pronouns agree with their antecedents," &c. It is in the objective case, being the object of the transitive verb *love;* according to the Rule, — "The object of a transitive verb or a preposition is in the objective case."]

The little bill must be paid, but I confess *it* alarms me. The expense of my son here is greater than *I* ever imagined. Although *his* company is almost all the pleasure I have in life, yet I should not have brought him if I had known the expense. The cookery, and the manner of living here, which you know Americans were taught by their masters to dislike, are more agreeable to me than you can imagine. It is the care of a very great part of mankind to conceal their indigence from the rest; they support themselves by temporary expedients, and every day is lost in contriving for the morrow.

The public are respectfully informed that their friend and servant continues his business at the old stand. It is the little foxes that spoil the vines. Saints themselves could hardly have witnessed this with patience. Columbus had a promising child, in which centered all a father's love. They are now tavern-keepers, which is all they are fit for. Who steals my purse, steals trash. The pleasantest voyage we made was on the Mediterranean. The men and things that he treats of, he handles like a philosopher. I hear, which has surprised me much, that hostilities have actually commenced. Idleness and vice go hand in hand; that is the parent, this the child.

To be Corrected.

Rebecca took goodly raiment, and put them upon Jacob. One should not think too favorably of themselves. The multitude eagerly pursue pleasure, as its chief good. The council were divided in its sentiments. The moon appears, but the light is not his own. The men which seek wisdom will find him. One cannot be too careful of their reputation. My brother and I are employed in their proper business. George and Charles are diligent in his studies. Neither James nor John has gained for themselves much credit. Each of the sexes should be kept within their proper bounds.

No father or mother lives that does not love his or her children. The army was cut up, or at least they suffered much. Neither the baggage of this regiment nor their flags were captured. You, Robert, and I have been commended for your behavior. There can be no doubt but what gunpowder was known to the Chinese. All which I have said, you must consider confidential. The greatest curiosity which we saw was the very thing which I least expected o admire. Who who is a patriot can hesitate to take the field? The very men that had fought in the Peninsular War, and who had received the plaudits of all Europe, were defeated at New Orleans. Can any one, on their entrance into the world, be fully secure that they shall not be deceived? The child whom we have just seen is wholesomely fed.

Rule XVI. Adjective and Substantive.

402. An adjective belongs to the noun or pronoun whose meaning it qualifies or limits; as, " a *sour* apple ; " " It is *sour*."

Remarks.

403. Adjectives are sometimes used to modify other adjectives; as, " a *bright blue* pitcher; " " a *pale red* silk."

404. An adjective is sometimes used to modify a noun and another adjective taken together; as, "a *poor* old man;" "a *fine* bay horse." — In the use of such constructions, care must be taken that the adjective next to the noun express a quality which distinguishes it more than the other. It would be improper to say, "an old poor man," "a bay fine horse."

405. Adjectives are used to modify infinitives and substantive clauses; as, "To see the sun is *pleasant.*" "Whether we shall go is *uncertain.*"

406. Adjectives are sometimes used indefinitely, without direct reference to any noun or pronoun; as, "To be *wise* and *good*, is to be *great* and *noble.*" "Being *honest* is better than being *wealthy.*" A noun, however, can generally be supplied in such cases; as, "For a *person* to be wise and good," &c.

407. An adjective is used in the predicate of a sentence after an intransitive verb, when the subject is to be modified, and not the action or state expressed by the verb; as, "The wind is blowing *fresh.*" "The flowers smell *sweet.*" When the action or state expressed by the verb is to be modified, an adverb must be used; as, "The flowers are growing *rapidly.*"

Entirely different meanings are sometimes conveyed by the use of an adjective and its corresponding adverb in the predicate. *She looks cold* implies that she looks as if she felt cold, the subject *she* being modified. *She looks coldly on me* implies that she looks as if she did not care for me, the verb *looks* being modified.

An adjective following an intransitive verb is generally used correctly when the verb *to be* in a corresponding part can be substituted for the intransitive verb. "*He looks warm;*" we can say *he is warm*, therefore *warm* is correctly used. "*He walks rapid;*" *he is rapid* would make no sense, therefore *rapid* should be changed to the adverb *rapidly*. To this rule, however, there are many exceptions.

408. Adjectives are sometimes improperly used for adverbs; as, "*miserable* poor," for "*miserably* poor;" "*excellent* well," for "*excellently* well;" "He behaved himself *conformable* [instead of *conformably*] to that great example."

409. Such expressions as *the two first, the three last*, are authorized by good usage as well as *the first two, the last three*, although the latter are generally preferred.

410. An adjective denoting more than one must be joined to a plural, and not a singular noun; as, "three *shillings* [not *shilling*]."

When a noun and a numeral are united to form a compound adjective, the noun is generally used in the singular form; as, "A *two-gallon* jug." 'A *two-foot* rule."

Comparison of Adjectives.

411. When two objects, or more than two taken individually, are compared, the comparative degree should be used; when more than two not taken individually, the superlative; as, "John is the *taller* of the two." "John is *taller* than Richard." "John is *taller* than Richard or Timothy." "John is the *tallest* of the three."

Remarks.

The superlative is often used when only two objects are compared, but improperly; as, "the *weakest* [instead of *weaker*] of the two."

412. If the objects compared are of the same class, when the comparative degree is used, the object to which it is applied should be excluded from the rest by the use of the word *other;* as, "Sirius is brighter than any *other* fixed star." If *other* were omitted in this sentence, it would lead to a wrong impression, — that Sirius is not a fixed star.

When the objects compared are not of the same class, the object to which the adjective in the comparative degree is applied is sufficiently excluded without the use of the word *other;* as, "Venus is brighter than any fixed star." If *other* were inserted after *any*, it would lead to a wrong impression, — that Venus is a fixed star.

When the superlative degree is used, the object to which it belongs should not be excluded by the use of the word *other;* as, "Sirius is the brightest of all the [not *all the other*] fixed stars."

413. Double comparatives and superlatives should be avoided; as, "a *more serener* temper." It should be either a *more serene* or a *serener* temper.

414. In expressing a comparison, if both nouns relate to the same object, the definitive *an* or *a*, or *the*, should not be prefixed to the latter noun; if to different objects, it should not be omitted. If we say, "Wilson is a better blacksmith than carpenter," we refer to but one person, Wilson, and declare that he is better in the capacity of a blacksmith than in that of a carpenter. If we say, "Wilson is a better blacksmith than *a* carpenter," or "*the* carpenter," we compare two persons, Wilson and a carpenter, and declare that Wilson is the better blacksmith of the two.

415. *Such* is often improperly used for *so;* as, "He was *such* an extravagant person." It should be "*so* extravagant a person."

416. Adjectives denoting qualities that do not exist in different degrees should not be compared, or used after *so*, *as*, or any other word implying comparison. We should not say "a *more infinite* variety," "there is no law *so universal*," &c.; but, "a *greater* variety," "there is no law so *general*," &c. 13

Position of Adjectives.

417. Adjectives generally stand immediately before the nouns to which they belong; as, "A *generous* man."

Remarks.

The following cases are exceptions. The adjective generally stands after its noun, —

1. When it is limited by an adjunct or other words; as, "food *convenient* for me;" "a rule, a foot *long.*"
2. When it expresses a title; as, "Alexander the *Great.*"
3. When it is predicated of a subject; as, "This man is *generous.*" Sometimes, however, for the sake of emphasis, the predicated adjective is placed first; as, "*Great* is Diana of the Ephesians."
4. When the quality it denotes is the result of an action expressed by a verb; as, "God made all things *good.*"
5. An adjective belonging to a pronoun in the objective case stands after it; as, "We found her *well* and *happy.*"

An adjective modified by an adverb sometimes precedes and sometimes follows its noun; as, "a very *great* man;" "a man truly *great.*"

Several adjectives belonging to the same noun may either precede or follow it: as, "a *learned, wise,* and *brave* prince;" or, "a prince *learned, wise,* and *brave.*"

418. The definitive *all* is often separated from its noun by *the;* as, "*All the* people. *All* sometimes stands after several nouns, to impart energy to the sentence; as, "Ambition, interest, honor, *all* concurred."

419. All adjectives are separated from their nouns by *a,* when they are preceded by *so* or *as;* as, "*so* wise a man;" "*as* good a man."

Analysis and Parsing.

To advance was *difficult,* to retreat *dangerous. Great* is the Lord. He acted agreeably to my advice. Agreeable in her manners, amiable in her disposition, and obliging to all, she was a general favorite. How sweet the hay smells! The great brilliancy of the sun makes the stars invisible during the day. Solomon was wiser than any Roman king. Numa was wiser than any other Roman king. Numa was the wisest of all the Roman kings. Numa was wiser than Ancus Martius, but less warlike. He is the least volatile of all. Covetousness enters deeper into the soul of man than any other vice. Our beer has turned sour. Napoleon was a better general than statesman. The colonel rides better than the major. To die for one's native country is sweet and becoming. Firm in his attachments, but fearful in his revenge, the American Indian seldom forgot either friend or foe. Man is the noblest of animals. Man is nobler than any other animal.

To be Corrected.

A new barrel of flour. A clear spring of water. A green load of wood. A new pair of boots. I can never think so mean of him. They wandered about solitarily and distressed. She reads proper, writes neat, and composes accurate. They lived comformable to the rules of prudence. He was such an extravagant man, that he soon wasted his property. I never saw such large trees. Such a bad temper is seldom found. A tree fifty foot high. Twenty ton of hay. I have just bought a sorrel handsome horse, and a Durham large cow. Young promising men are often led astray by temptation.

'Tis more easier to build two chimneys than to maintain one. The tongue is like a race-horse, which runs the faster the lesser weight it carries. The nightingale sings; hers is the most sweetest voice in the grove. The Most Highest hath created us for His glory and our own happiness. Jupiter is larger than any planet. Jupiter is brighter than any other fixed star. The elephant has more instinct than any animal. Virtue confers the supremest dignity on man, and should be his chiefest desire. Having come without my overcoat, I began to feel coldly. Look sharp. I see good. We sat silently. His assertion was more true than that of his opponent; nay, the words of the latter were most untrue. There is no king so supreme as he. Eve was the fairest of all her daughters. Profane swearing is, of all other vices, the most inexcusable. A talent of this kind would, perhaps, prove the likeliest of any other to succeed. He spoke with such propriety that I understood him the best of all the others who spoke on the subject. Of my two daughters, Jane is the quickest to learn, but Ellen is the most affectionate in her disposition. Henry is the elder of my three sons. Mr. Brown is a better writer than a speaker. It was a hard to understand subject. They are exceedingly difficult questions to be answered.

Rule XVII. Pronominal Adjectives.

420. Pronominal adjectives belong to the nouns which they limit, or are used alone as pronouns; as, *this* man, *these* men, *both* men, *these* think, *both* come.

Remarks.

421. A pronominal adjective, if it denotes but one, must be used with a singular noun; if it denotes more than one, with a plural noun only; as, *this* sort, *these* sorts.

422. The pronominal adjectives *each, every, either,* and *neither,* require a noun, pronoun, or verb with which they are construed to be in the singular number; as, "Every tree is known by *its* fruit." This rule is often violated, as in the following examples:—"Let each fulfil *their* [instead of *his*] part." "Every passenger must hold *their* [instead of *his*] own ticket."

Every is sometimes joined to a plural noun preceded by a numeral adjective; as, "every *six months;*" "every *hundred years.*" As the noun and the numeral are together merely a complex term expressing a definite period, such examples do not constitute an exception to the rule.

Even when several nouns are connected as the subject of a verb, if they are severally limited by *each* or *every,* expressed or understood, the verb must be singular; as, "Every leaf, every twig, and every drop of water, *teems* with life."

423. *Either* is sometimes used for *each;* as, "Two thieves were crucified, on *either* side one."

424. *Either* and *neither* are used with reference to two things only; when more than two are referred to, *any* should take the place of *either,* and *none* of *neither.* We may say *either of the two, neither of the two;* but, *any of the three, none of the four. — Any* and *none,* let it be remembered, imply either one or more than one.

425. *Both* is sometimes used in apposition with a pronoun, for the sake of emphasis; as, "He forgave them *both.*" "I will teach you *both.*"

426. *One* is often used indefinitely, to signify persons in general; as, " *One* ought to pity the distresses of mankind."

427. The pronominals *former* and *latter, one* and *other, that* and *this,* may be used to represent two nouns or clauses in contrast, when there is no danger of obscurity; as, " Genius and talent must not be confounded: *the former* [or, *the one,* meaning *genius*] qualifies a person for the most exalted efforts; *the latter* [or, *the other,* meaning *talent*], for the active duties and employments of life."

428. *This here, that there,* and *them* for *those,* are common vulgarisms. *This here* book, should be *this* book; *that there* coat, should be *that* coat; *them* dishes, should be *those* dishes.

Analysis and Parsing.

PRONOMINAL ADJECTIVES.

One day Alonzo made a discovery that startled him. The boy hoped he had made *some* impression. *Every* feeling of gratitude is obliterated by one single interference with your wicked desires. He soon learned that it was one thing to see that his feelings were wrong, and another thing to feel right. These omissions were more frequent than he imagined. The eyes of them both were opened.

PRONOMINAL ADJECTIVES USED AS PRONOUNS.

And he went after the man of Israel into the tent, and thrust both of them through. The same is equally true of the past. In the evening he was occupied with some one of these enjoyments, and the next day he was planning another. This he could not but strongly shrink from. Let others serve whom they will; as for me and my house, we will serve the Lord. The dialogue between conscience and his heart was going on all the time; the latter finally prevailed. Many shall come in my name, saying, I am Christ, and shall deceive many. Jubal was the father of such as dwell in tents. More I cannot do, less I will not do. Either will answer my purpose.

To be Corrected.

These kind of indulgences. Those sort of favors. I have been waiting this two hours. Do you see those books lying on this table? These men that stand yonder are soldiers. Both the sun, moon, and planets turn on their axes. Do you see them people walking in the park? This 'ere boy and that 'ere girl are constantly in mischief. This here table needs dusting; but do not move them books. Every pebble and every blade of grass testify to the greatness of their Creator. Neither of the soldiers of the regiment has cause to complain. Neither of my three sisters can play on the pinao. Ask either of the twenty that survived, their feelings at that trying hour.

Rule XVIII. An or A, — The.

429. The definitive adjective *an* or *a* is used before nouns in the singular only; *the* is used before nouns in both numbers; as, *a* man, *the* man, *the* men.

Remarks.

430. *A* is sometimes used before the pronominal *few*, and some adjectives of number, such as *hundred, thousand, million,* &c., though a noun follows in the plural; as, *a few tears, a hundred men, a thousand dollars.*

431. *A* is followed by a singular noun, even when *many* precedes and more than one are implied; as, "Full many *a* gem;" "many *a* youth."

432. A nice distinction in the sense is made by the use or omission of *a* before the words *little* and *few.* "He has *a little* reverence;" this means that he has reverence in a slight degree. "He has *little* reverence;" this implies a doubt whether he has any.

433. *An* or *a* is sometimes used in the sense of *each* or *every* ; as, "twice *a* day."

434. The definitive *an* must not be confounded with the conjunction *an*, formerly used with the meaning of *if;* as, "*an* it please your honor."

435. When the meaning of the noun is general, and requires no limitation, the definitive is omitted; as, "Honor to whom honor is due." "Man is mortal." "He is called Count."

436. When two or more nouns are closely connected and have the same construction, *an, a,* or *the* may be used with the first and omitted with the rest, or may be repeated for the sake of greater emphasis with each; as, "I love *the* brightness, [the] noise, and [the] excitement of day." But if the nouns are contrasted, or have not a common construction, the definitive in question *must* be used with each; as, "I love *the* brightness, but not *the* noise, of day." It would be improper to omit *the* before *noise.*

437. When two or more adjectives are used to express different qualities of the same object, the definitives *an* or *a* and *the* may be used with the first, and omitted with the rest; as, "*a* large and convenient dwelling," referring to a single dwelling. But if they express qualities of different objects, the definitive must be used before each; as, "*A* large and *a* convenient dwelling," referring to two dwellings. "A white and black horse" means one horse partly white and partly black. "A white and *a* black horse" means two horses, one white and the other black.

When there is no danger of ambiguity, the latter definitive is sometimes omitted, and the noun put in the plural number; as, "the Old and New Testaments." Such constructions, however, though shorter and less formal, are to be avoided as not strictly correct.

438. *An* or *a* and *the* never by themselves stand after the nouns to which they belong. Sometimes, however, with another adjective, they are placed after it; as, "men *a* dozen, dames *a* few;" "Pliny *the* younger." But even when an adjective is introduced after the noun, the definitive may keep its place before the noun; as, "*an* estate larger than any other in the city."

To be Corrected.

Reason was given to a man to control his passions. A man is the noblest work of creation. He is a much better writer than a reader. The king has conferred on him a title of a duke. Wisest and best men sometimes commit errors. He has been censured for giving a little attention to his business. I like the quiet but not dews of evening. Look not at the appearance but merit of your visitors. A stream runs between the stone and brick house. We visited the American and Canadian fall. Among variegated flowers, none is prettier than a red and a white rose. He lamented that a few men love honor more than riches. A rosewood and a mahogany table has been presented to her.

REVIEW QUESTIONS.—RULES XV.-XVIII.

383. Repeat Rule XV. Give examples. 384. What is the rule for pronouns referring to two or more singular nouns taken together? If the nouns are of different persons, which does the pronoun prefer? 385. What is the rule for pronouns referring to two or more singular nouns taken separately? 386. In what number must a pronoun referring to a collective noun be put? 387. State the principle that applies to singular nouns of the third person and different genders, taken separately.

388. How is *it* often used? 389. How are the compound personals sometimes used? 390. How is *what* sometimes used? 391. What are often improperly used for *that?* 392. What must every relative have? 393. To what does the relative frequently refer? 394. Give examples of the omission of the relative. 395. When there are two antecedents of different persons, with which does the relative agree? 396. To what is the relative *which* applied? In what case is it applied to persons? As an interrogative, to what may *which* be applied?

397. To what may the relative *that* refer? In what cases is it generally preferred to *who* or *which?* 398. What is the rule for relatives in different clauses referring to the same antecedent? 399. How should the relative stand, as regards its antecedent? 400. What sometimes affords us the only means of determining the antecedent of a relative? 401. In what way is a relative sometimes introduced?

402. Repeat Rule XVI. 403. What are adjectives sometimes used to modify? 404. In such expressions as *a poor old man*, what does the former of the two adjectives modify? What is essential in the use of such constructions? 405. What else are adjectives used to modify? 406. Illustrate and explain the indefinite use of an adjective. 407. When is an adjective used in the predicate after an intransitive verb, and when an adverb? Show the difference of meaning resulting from the use of adjective and

THE RULES OF SYNTAX.

adverb. 408. For what are adjectives sometimes improperly used? 409. What forms of expression may be used instead of *the first two, the last three,* &c.? 410. With what must an adjective denoting more than one be used? 411. Give the rule that applies to the use of the comparative and the superlative. 412. Give the rule that applies to the use of the comparative degree, when the objects compared are of the same class. When the objects compared are not of the same class. State the principle that applies when the superlative degree is used. 413. What is said of double comparatives and superlatives? 414. When should *an* or *a* and *the* not be prefixed to the latter of two nouns compared, and when not omitted? 415. For what is *such* often improperly used? 416. What is the rule for adjectives denoting qualities that do not exist in different degrees?

417. How do adjectives generally stand? What exceptions are noted? How does an adjective modified by an adverb stand, as regards its noun? What is the position of several adjectives belonging to the same noun? 418. How does *all* often stand? 419. When are all adjectives separated from their nouns by *a?*

420. Repeat Rule XVII. 421. What must be the number of the nouns with which pronominal adjectives are joined? 422. State the rule relating to *each, every, either,* and *neither.* 423. For what is *either* sometimes used? 424. Explain the difference in use between *either, neither,* and *any, none.* 425. How is *both* sometimes used? 426. How is *one* often used? 427. For what may *former* and *latter, one* and *other, that* and *this,* be used? 428. What vulgarisms must be avoided?

429. Repeat Rule XVIII. 430. In what case may a noun in the plural follow *a?* 431. By what is *many a* followed? 432. Show the difference between *little, few,* and *a little, a few.* 433. In what sense is *an* or *a* sometimes used? 434. With what must the definitive *an* not be confounded? 435. When are *an* or *a* and *the* omitted? 436. State the principle that relates to the omission of *an* or *a* and *the* before the last of two or more nouns. 437. State the principle that regulates the omission of *an* or *a* and *the* when two or more adjectives are used. 438. How do *an* or *a* and *the* stand as regards their noun?

Rule XIX. The Infinitive.

439. A verb in the infinitive mode generally limits the meaning of a verb, noun, or adjective; as, "I hope *to succeed.*" "Have a desire *to improve.*" "She is anxious *to hear.*"

THE INFINITIVE.

Remarks.

440. A verb in the infinitive may also limit the meaning of, —

1. *As* or *than;* as, "He is so conceited as *to think* himself learned." "He desired nothing more than *to know* his imperfections."

2. *Adverbs;* as, "I know not how *to address* you." "He is too lazy to *study.*"

3. *Prepositions;* as, "My friend is about *to take* his departure." In old writings, we find the preposition *for* limited by an infinitive; as, "What went ye out *for to see?*" But this construction has gone out of use, and should be avoided.

441. The infinitive is also used independently; as, "*To say the least,* he has erred in judgment." "*To proceed* with our argument."

442. The expression *to be sure* is often used adverbially, in the sense of *surely* or *certainly.*

443. When the infinitive denotes purpose or design, it is frequently preceded by the words *in order*, but not always; as, "He went to Germany *in order to finish* his education," or *to finish* his education."

444. When two or more infinitives in the same construction stand near each other, the sign *to* may be omitted with all but the first; as, "He wishes to visit foreign countries, and thus [to] enlarge his views and [to] improve his mind." In such cases, the sign is repeated when emphasis is desired; as, "He has returned to his native country, to visit his friends, and — *to* die."

445. Never use *to* alone for a verb in the infinitive mode; as, "I have never intrigued for office, and I never intend *to.*" It should be, "I never intend *to do so.*"

Analysis and Parsing.

He was willing *to risk* all, for the excitement of a new revolution. Not far from the city of Avila, they caused a scaffold *to be erected*, of sufficient elevation *to be* easily *seen* from the surrounding country. Be not so greedy of popular applause, as to forget that the same breath which blows up a fire may blow it out again. I understand him better than to suppose he will relinquish his design. The abject mind of Henry was content to purchase repose, even by the most humiliating sacrifice. It is our duty to try, and our determination to succeed. I am following up the subject, to satisfy my own mind, enlighten others, and expose the baseness of those who have sought to deceive and betray us.

Rule XX. Infinitive without the Sign.

446. When the verbs *bid, dare* [meaning *venture*], *hear, feel, make, need, see,* in the active voice, or *let,* in either the active or the passive, are followed by an infinitive, the sign *to* is omitted before it; as, " You bid me come [not *to come*]." " I saw him fall [not *to fall*]." " He durst do anything." " They let me recite." " The curtain was let fall."

Remarks.

447. This rule applies also to the participle of the above-mentioned verbs; as, " Making me look [not *to look*] him in the face, he smiled."

448. Though generally omitted, the sign of the infinitive is sometimes retained after *need* and *dare;* as, " He needs *to* be restrained." " She has dared *to* speak ill of the king."

449. *To* is not omitted after *dare* meaning *challenge;* as, " He dared me *to* repeat the expression."

450. The verbs *watch, behold, know, observe have,* and some others, are occasionally followed by the infinitive without the sign *to;* as, " We watched him enter." " I have known him go two days without food."

Analysis and Parsing.

The name of Henry makes them *leave* me desolate. Dare any man *be* so bold to sound retreat or parley, when I command them *kill?* Hark! I hear the angels sing. And the multitude wondered when they saw the lame walk and the blind see. He had dared to think for himself. The haughty infidel banished from the schools all who had dared draw water from the living fountain. I found my friend express much satisfaction with the bargains he had made.

To be Corrected, according to Rules XIX., XX.

Your duty requires you to go, and I advise you to. I have never truckled to demagogues, and I never intend to. Wellington stormed the city because his officers urged him to. Lend me your pencil for to sharpen my knife. I tried for to see him, but without success. Be anxious for improving. You ought not walk too hastily. I need not to solicit him to do a kind action. I have seen some young persons to conduct themselves very indiscreetly. Robert dared his cousin fight him. Fabius durst not to come to a general engagement.

Rule XXI. Participles used as Adjectives.

451. Participles belong to nouns or pronouns which they limit or modify.

Remarks.

452. This rule applies to participles used in such a way as to partake of the properties of adjective and verb; as, " *Persuading* my brother to accompany me, I emigrated to Kansas." Like an adjective, *persuading* modifies *I*, and therefore belongs to it according to the above rule. It retains, at the same time, the governing power of the verb from which it comes, being followed by *brother* in the objective case.

453. A participle may belong to a clause or the leading proposition of a sentence; as, " *Owing* to the bad state of the roads, he was detained a day beyond the time." In this sentence, *owing* belongs to the leading proposition, *he was detained a day beyond the time.* — Observe that *owing*, though active in form, has a passive force, as if used for *owed*.

454. Participles are sometimes used indefinitely, without reference to any noun or pronoun expressed; as, "It is impossible to act otherwise, *considering* the weakness of our nature." " Generally *speaking*, his conduct was honorable."

Rule XXII. Participles used as Nouns.

455. Participles used as nouns have the construction of nouns, while they are modified in the same way, and govern the same case, as the verbs from which they are formed.

Remarks.

456. This rule applies to participles preceded by a preposition, the definitive *the*, a noun or pronoun in the possessive, or used as the subject or object of a verb; as in the following sentences: —

I am in favor of *going* at once.
The *adorning* of the person occupies too much of our time.
Much depends on the pupil's *obeying* promptly.
Cultivating the ground is hard work.
I like *travelling* rapidly.

By comparing these sentences with the example given under Rule XXI., it will be seen that the participle here has an entirely different office.

457. Even when thus used as nouns, the present and the compound participle active retain the governing power of the verb from which they come. "He was displeased with the king's *having bestowed* the office upon a worthless man." In this sentence, the compound participle, used as a noun, requires *king's*, the noun before it, to be in the possessive; at the same time, as a verb, it governs *office* in the objective.

458. As before remarked, a noun or pronoun preceding and limiting a participle is put in the possessive case; as, "*Cæsar's* having crossed the Rubicon spread consternation throughout Rome."

459. When preceded by the definitive *the*, the present participle active must, in most cases, be followed by *of*: as, "the gaining *of* wisdom;" "the supplying *of* our wants." The omission of the preposition after the participle makes expressions like the following incorrect: — *the preaching repentance, the writing an essay.*

The converse of this rule also holds good. When the participle is not preceded by *the*, *of* should not be introduced: as, "gaining wisdom;" "supplying our wants." The introduction of the preposition after the participle makes expressions like the following incorrect: *By preaching of repentance, In writing of an essay.* Use both *the* and *of* with the participle, or omit both.

Analysis and Parsing.

[The following examples will show how participles are to be parsed and the last two rules applied.

MODEL. — In bidding you God-speed after having just entered on the business of life, allow me to advise your avoiding all those temptations which young men find it so hard to resist. Reflecting on the past will often enable you to escape difficulties in the future.

Bidding is a participle of the verb *bid;* the participles are, pres. *bidding*, perf. *bid* or *bidden*, compound *having bid;* present active, used as a noun in the objective case, governed by the preposition *in*, according to the Rule, "Participles used as nouns have the construction of nouns," &c.

Having entered is a participle of the verb *enter;* the participles are, pres. *entering*, perf. *entered*, compound *having entered;* compound used as an adjective, and modifies the pronoun *you*, to which it belongs, according to the Rule, "Participles belong to nouns or pronouns which they limit or modify."

Avoiding is a participle of the verb *avoid;* the participles are, pres. *avoiding*, perf. *avoided*, compound *having avoided;* it is the present active, and is used as a noun in the objective case, after the transitive verb *to advise*, according to the Rule, "Participles used as nouns have the construction of nouns," &c.

Reflecting is a participle of the verb *reflect;* the participles are, pres.

reflecting, perf. *reflected*, compound *having reflected;* it is the present active, and is used as a noun in the nominative case, being the subject of the verb *will enable*, according to the Rule, " Participles used as nouns," &c.]

And they, *continuing* daily with one accord in the temple, and *breaking* bread from house to house, did eat their meat with gladness and singleness of heart, *praising* God, and having favor with all the people. He has left town for Ireland without taking leave of either of us. I have nothing to do with the President's having deprived your brother of office. We considered man as belonging to societies ; societies as formed of different ranks ; and different ranks as distinguished by habits. Having been very well entertained by your description of clubs, I shall take the liberty of furnishing you with a brief account of such a one as you have not seen.

To be Corrected.

By observing of truth. By the observing truth. By the sending proper information. Without the taking pains. Without taking of pains. The changing times and seasons, the removing and setting up kings, belong to Providence alone. Poverty turns one's thoughts too much upon the supplying one's wants. In tracing of his history, we discover little that is worthy of imitation. Do you advise the road being commenced at once ? The emperor being defeated by an army inferior to his own, occasioned no little surprise. I doubt these mountains ever having been crossed before.

Rule XXIII. The Subjunctive

460. The subjunctive mode is used to express future contingency ; also, after the conjunctions *lest* and *that* annexed to a command, and after *that* denoting a wish; as, " Though he *slay* me, yet will I trust in him." " Sin no more, lest a worse thing *come* upon thee." " See that thou *reform.*" " Oh! that I *were* at home!"

Remarks.

461. Contingency is denoted by *if, though, whether,* and other conjunctions. Futurity is implied when the leading verb is future, or when *shall* can be placed before the verb in the conditional clause without injury to

the sense. When both are implied, and only then, use the subjunctive mode in the conditional clause; as, " Though he [*shall*] *slay* me, yet will I trust in him." " If it [*shall*] *rain*, I will not go." " If he *do* but *touch* the hills, they shall smoke."

462. The subjunctive was formerly used in all cases to express contingency, whether the time denoted was past, present, or future. It is now used only when future time is implied; and even then, in familiar discourse, the tendency is to substitute the indicative.

463. A present supposition implying a denial of the thing supposed, is expressed by the imperfect subjunctive; as, " If I *were* Robert, I would go." "*Were* I in Robert's place, I would remain."

NOTE. — *Be* is sometimes equivalent to *may be*, and *were* to *would be* or *should be*; as, *What care I how fair she be. I were a knave to act thus.* In such cases *be* and *were* are in the potential mode.

To be Corrected.

[Using the indicative or the potential mode subjunctively does not involve any change of form in the tenses of these modes. Use the subjunctive only when required by the above rule. After correcting the following sentences, parse them.]

If he acquires riches, they will corrupt his mind. Though he urges me yet more earnestly, I shall not comply. I shall walk in the fields to-day, unless it rains. As the governess were present, the children behaved properly. Despise not any condition, lest it happens to be your own. Let him that is sanguine take heed lest he fails. Take care that thou breakest not any of the established rules. If he does but intimate his desire, it will be sufficient to produce obedience. At the time of his return, if he is but expert in the business, he will find employment. If he speak only to display his abilities, he is unworthy of attention.

If he be but in health, I am content. If thou have promised, be faithful to thy engagement. Though he have proved his right to submission, he is too generous to exact it. If thou had succeeded, perhaps thou wouldst not be the happier for it. Though thou did injure him, he harbors no resentment. Was he ever so great and opulent, this conduct would debase him. Was I to enumerate all her virtues, it would look like flattery. Though I was perfect, yet I would not presume. Unless thou can fairly support the cause, give it up honorably. Though thou might have foreseen the danger, thou could not have avoided it. Would that he was here!

Rule XXIV. Use of the Tenses.

464. In using verbs, different tenses should not be confounded, nor should any tense be employed except in such connections as are consistent with the time it denotes.

Remarks.

This rule is necessarily general. From the definitions of the different tenses and the illustrations that have been given of their use, it must be determined which it is proper to use in any particular case. The following remarks will put the pupil on his guard against the commonest errors: —

465. The perfect participle must not be used for the imperfect indicative. *I done* for *I did, she come* for *she came, he begun* for *he began, we drunk* for *we drank*, are all wrong in consequence of their violating this rule.

466. The imperfect indicative must not be used for the perfect participle. Hence the errors in the following sentences: —

The river *has froze* over; it should be *has frozen.*
The storm *has began;* it should be *has begun.*
The horse *was drove* hard; it should be *was driven.*
The thief *has stole* my watch; it should be *has stolen.*

467. The perfect must not be used with adverbs or adverbial clauses expressing past time; as, "I *have completed* the task two days ago," — it should be *I completed.*

468. The imperfect potential must not, as a general rule, be used in connection with the future indicative or the present potential. "Ye will not come to me, that ye might have life." This is wrong, because the imperfect potential *might have* is used in connection with the future indicative *will come.* If past time is referred to, it should be, "Ye *would* not come to me, that ye *might* have life;" if future, "Ye *will* not come to me, that ye *may* have life."

"I should be glad if he will write," is wrong for a similar reason; *will* must be changed to *would.* The present potential, however, may be used in connection with *should* meaning *ought,* or *could* meaning *was able to;* as, "He *should take* exercise, that he *may recover* his health." "It *may be* that he *could* not *come.*"

469. The present infinitive is used after verbs signifying *to hope, to intend, to desire, to command, to promise,* and the like; and also to express an action or state which is not prior to that denoted by the leading verb; as, "I hoped *to see* you." "I shall want *to hear* from you." "I had resolved *to remain.*" "He is said *to be* fifty years old."

If the action or state expressed by the verb in the infinitive is prior to that denoted by the leading verb, the perfect must be used; as, "Galileo is thought *to have invented* the thermometer."

470. Different auxiliaries must not be used with one and the same verbal form, unless it is appropriate to each. " I can accomplish as much in one day as he has in two." *Accomplish* is correctly used with the first auxiliary *can*, but not with the second *has*,—we cannot say *has accomplish*. The sentence should therefore read, " I can accomplish as much in one day as he has accomplished in two."

471. The intransitive verbs *sit* and *lie* must not be confounded with the transitive verbs *set* and *lay*. The difference in their conjugation is as follows:—

INTRANSITIVE.			TRANSITIVE.		
Sit,	sat,	sat.	Set,	set,	set.
Lie,	lay,	lain	Lay,	laid,	laid.

To sit means *to rest on a seat; to set* means *to place*. We *sit* down, but *set* things in order. We *sat* down yesterday; we *set* things in order yesterday. We *have* just *sat* down; we *have* just *set* the trap. — There is, also, an intransitive verb *to set;* as, " The sun *sets*."

To lie means *to recline; to lay* means *to place*. We *lie down;* we *lay* a thing down. I *lay* down yesterday; I *laid* a thing down yesterday. He *has* just *lain* down; he *has* just *laid* down his book.

To be Corrected.

It will give our parents much pain to have heard of your misconduct. They desired to have seen you respected and esteemed, but alas! their hopes have been unexpectedly cut off. They intended to have devoted you to the service of your country and mankind; but, when the sad intelligence reaches them, how would they sink under the burden of their disappointment! I expected to have seen them before the news should have reached them, but urgent duties will have prevented. I begun to think that I done wrong to conceal this from my father. He never drunk anything but water. His children have all forsook him. The bell has rang. You might have drove faster, I think. His style has formerly been admired. Robert has come to the same conclusion last week. They have resided in Italy till two months ago.

They laid down to rest. A beggar was setting by the wayside. A stone was laying in the street. The tree has laid there several days. Let us set down. It is injurious to health to set up late. He set up, and begun to speak. Sin layeth at the door. If he wishes, he might come. I will be much obliged to you if you would close that door. I might lead a better life, if you will stay with me. Man never has and never will be perfectly contented. He was slandering me behind my back, but he never will again. You are talking improperly, and have for the last half-hour. What nation has tolerated such cruelty or ever will? He sets a horse well.

REVIEW QUESTIONS.—RULES XIX.-XXIV.

439. Repeat Rule XIX. 440. What else may a verb in the infinitive limit? 441. How is the infinitive sometimes used? 442. How is the expression *to be sure* used? 443. When the infinitive denotes purpose or design, by what is it often preceded? 444. State the principle that relates to the omission of the sign *to*. 445. For what must the sign *to* not be used?

446. Repeat Rule XX. 447. To what does this rule apply? 448. After which of the verbs mentioned in the rule is *to* sometimes retained? 449. In what case is the sign of the infinitive retained after *dare?* 450. After what verbs is it occasionally omitted?

451. Repeat Rule XXI. 452. To what participles does this rule apply? 453. To what may a participle belong? 454. How are participles sometimes used?

455. Repeat Rule XXII. 456. To what participles does this rule apply? 457. What is said of the governing power of the participles? 458. In what case must a noun or pronoun preceding and limiting a participle be put? 459. When must the present participle active be followed by *of*, and when not?

460. Repeat Rule XXIII. 461. By what is contingency denoted? How can we tell when futurity is implied? 462. What is the difference between former and present usage, as regards the subjunctive mode? 463. What is the imperfect subjunctive used to imply?

464. Repeat Rule XXIV. How must we determine what tense to use in any particular case? 465, 466. What two parts must not be used for each other? Give examples. 467. With what must the perfect not be used? 468. With what, as a general rule, must the imperfect potential not be used? What exceptions to this rule are noted? 469. What principle determines the use of the present infinitive and the perfect infinitive? 470. What is said of the use of different auxiliaries with one verbal form? 471. What verbs are apt to be confounded? Conjugate them, and show the difference in their use?

Rule XXV. Adverbs.

472. Adverbs generally modify verbs, participles, adjectives, and other adverbs; as, "We *seldom* see *very* old men walking *rapidly;* they are *too easily* tired."

Remarks.

473. Adverbs sometimes modify prepositions, adjuncts, and phrases: as, "*just* below the surface;" "*independently* of these considerations;" "I lived *almost* in vain."

474. Adverbs may be used absolutely; that is, with reference to no particular word, but rather to a whole sentence. This is the case with *yes* and *no*, used as answers to questions, *amen, then* (in the sense of *to sum up the matter*), *therefore,* &c. *Why, well, there,* &c. are often used as expletives, — that is, to introduce a sentence without any special force; as, "*Why,* I had not heard this."

475. Adverbs are sometimes used as nouns: as, "until *now;*" "Since *when* has this state of things come about?"

476. Adverbs are sometimes used instead of adjectives to modify nouns: as, "*almost* a dollar:" "not *quite* a year;" "not *only* a house, but also a farm;" "the *above* discourse;" "the *then* ministry." In some cases, as in the first three examples given above, this construction is warranted by the best usage. When not well established, however, it should be strictly avoided. *The ministry then in office* is preferable to *the then ministry*.

477. The word modified by an adverb is sometimes omitted; as, "I'll [*go*] hence to London."

478. *From* is often used by good writers before *whence, hence,* and *thence;* but, being implied in their meaning, it is unnecessary. We can say either, "*Whence* art thou?" or, "*From whence* art thou?"

479. Two negatives in the same clause are equivalent to an affirmative; as, "*Nor* did they *not* perceive," — that is, *they did perceive.* Unless it is intended to convey an affirmation, two negatives should not be used. Such sentences as "I *don't* want *no* bread," are common vulgarisms. They may be corrected by leaving out one of the negatives; as, "I want no bread," or "I don't want any bread."

480. *Where* may be used for *in which* only when place is referred to. It is right to say, "That is the *spot where* I was born;" but not, "That is the *book where* I found the example."

Position of Adverbs.

481. The position of adverbs depends on the sense intended to be conveyed. As a general rule, they should stand near the words they modify.

Compare these two sentences: — " We *always* find them ready." " We find them always ready." The position of the adverb is right in both; but the meaning conveyed is different. From the first it is not certain that they are *always* ready, as is asserted in the second, but that we *always* find them so.

482. Adverbs generally stand before adjectives, after verbs in the simple tenses, and after the first auxiliary in the compound tenses; as, " He is *very* anxious." " He spoke *kindly*." " He is *busily* employed."

483. *Enough*, modifying an adjective, is placed after it; as, " He is not tall *enough*."

484. *Never, always, often,* and *seldom,* generally precede the verb in the simple tenses; as, " He *never* tells the truth."

485. When an adverb is used with the infinitive mode, it must not be introduced between the sign *to* and the verbal form; as, " He has learned to *handsomely* paint." " It is your duty to *never* despair." These sentences should be, " He has learned to paint handsomely." " It is your duty never to despair."

486. *Only* and *not only, merely* and *chiefly,* are often improperly placed, and thus give the sentence in which they stand a different force from what the writer intended it to have. For example, " He only washed my face;" this implies that he did nothing more to my face than to *wash* it, — he did not *dry* it. If I mean that no other part than my face was washed, I should place *only* near the word it is intended to modify, — " He washed my *face only*."

In like manner, there is an error in the following sentence; " He has not only bought a house, but also a farm." As it now stands, *not only* modifies the verb *has bought*, and we naturally expect a verb to follow, — has not only *bought* it, but *paid for it*, or something of the kind. But the author clearly intended it to modify *house*, since that is the word which is emphatically contrasted with *farm*. The sentence should therefore read, " He bought not only a house, but also a farm."

Analysis and Parsing.

There,* there,* now you have talked enough for one lecture "Well,* sir," said I, "how did you like little Miss? I hope she was fine enough." "Alas! madam," said he one day, "how few books are there, of which one ever can possibly arrive at the last page." The women and children only were saved from the conflagration. He then, having received the sop, went immediately out. Up and onward! there are no obstacles that courage and perseverance will not certainly surmount. From thence we proceeded directly to Berlin, as rapidly as steam could carry us. The wall tottered, and had wellnigh fallen right on their heads. Well, he brought him home, and reared him at the then Lord Valdez's cost. — *Coleridge.*

Stoop down, my thoughts that used to rise,
Converse awhile with death.

To be Corrected.

When he is in such moods, he will not see nobody. Nor is there no father that will tolerate such conduct. Can you turn to the page where you found it? The passage where I saw the word has escaped me. He has been deceived certainly. Roger Bacon was the inventor of spectacles undoubtedly. Milton has been acknowledged generally as one of the greatest poets the world ever has produced. Firm in his attachments always, Lafayette never forgot a friend. He reads the paper before breakfast always. I like never to hear a person slander his neighbors. I was tempted to forcibly take possession of the papers. Murat was seen to gallantly charge into the thickest of the fight. I have a mind to pleasantly upbraid you. Robespierre not only awakened the dislike, but the abhorrence, of the community. England not only produces rye and oats, but barley also. Turkey is chiefly indebted to the mutual jealousy of the other European powers, for its existence as an empire. Do not merely take me to thy arms, but to thy heart.

Rule XXVI. Prepositions.

487. Prepositions show the relations of things; as, "*From* Boston, we proceeded *by* railroad *to* Portland."

---

* These adverbs are used absolutely.

This rule should be given when a preposition is parsed. Thus, in the example given above: *From* is a preposition, and shows the relation between its object *Boston* and the verb *proceeded;* according to the Rule "Prepositions show the relations of things."

488. Appropriate prepositions must follow certain words.

In the sentence "I am interested with the book," *with* is improperly used after *interested* in place of *in*. As such errors are very frequent, a list of some common words and the prepositions that should be used after them is given below.

Abhorrence *of*.
Abound *with, in*.
Accompanied *with* an inanimate object; *by* anything that has life.
Accuse *of*.
Acquaint *with*.
Adapted *to*.
Agree *with* a person; *to* a proposition from another; *upon* a thing among ourselves.
Arrive *at, in*.
Attended *with* an inanimate object; *by* anything that has life.
Averse *to, from*.
Beguile *of*.
Capacity *for*.
Careful *of, in, about*.
Careless *of, in, about*.
Charge *on* a person; *with* a thing.
Compare *with* (in respect of quality); *to* (for the sake of illustration).
Connect *with*.
Conversant *with* men; *with* or *in* things: *about* and *among* are sometimes used.
Copy *after* a person; *from* a thing.
Correspond *with*.
Die *of* a disease; *by* an instrument or violence.

Differ *with* a person; *from* a thing.
Different *from*.
Disappointed *of* what we fail to obtain; *in* what does not answer our expectations, when obtained.
Entrance *into*.
Expert *in, at*.
Familiar *to* us; *with* a thing.
Followed *by*.
Impatient *of* control; *at* delay; *for* something expected; *under* wrongs.
Influence *on, over, with*.
Interfere *with*.
Militate *against*.
Participate *with* a person; *in, of*, things.
Profit *by*.
Provide a person *with* a thing; a thing *for* a person; *against* misfortunes.
Reconcile (in friendship) *to;* (to make consistent) *with*.
Reduce (subdue) *under;* (in other cases) *to*.
Rely *on, upon*.
Suitable *to; for*, before a present participle.
Unite *to, with*.

489. *Into*, and not *in*, must be used after verbs denoting entrance; as, "He burst *into* [not *in*] the room."

490. *Between* is applicable to two objects only; *among* should be used when more than two are referred to: as, "I will divide my money *between* George and Stephen; my land, *among* Jane, Ellen, and Sarah."

To be Corrected, and then Parsed.

Napoleon left the field, accompanied with Ney. Few volumes are now published on this subject, that are not accompanied by illustrations. We arrived to Liverpool on the 1st instant. Crossing the Alps is attended by many difficulties. They died from cholera. The scenery of the Rhine is different to what most persons suppose. We ought to profit from the errors of others. It is our duty to reconcile with each other those who are at enmity. Do not interfere among other people's concerns. Some geographies are adapted for very young pupils, while others are suitable for advanced classes. On his arrival, he divided his property among his two sons. I have three faithful friends, and have determined to distribute my money between them. There should be no quarrelling between us four. Dr. Kane penetrated far in the Arctic regions. Hannibal forced his way in Italy. Pass in the room, gentlemen. Go in the carriage and shut the door.

Rule XXVII. Conjunctions.

491. Conjunctions connect single words, adjuncts, clauses, members, and sentences; as, "He reads *or* writes." "I sought the Lord, *and* he heard me."

Remarks.

492. When conjunctions connect single words, they are words of the same class and in the same construction. Thus, nouns and pronouns in the nominative case are connected with nouns and pronouns in the nominative; nouns and pronouns in the objective case are connected with nouns and pronouns in the objective; verbs in the third singular, with verbs in the third singular; &c. — "Between you and I there should be no hard feeling;" this is wrong, because *I*, being connected with *you* by the conjunction *and*, is in the same construction; and, since *you* is in the objective, governed by the preposition *between*, *I* should be changed to *me*, to be in the objective also. — "Henry and Mary's father." *Henry* and *Mary's*, being connected by *and*, are both in the possessive case, though the sign of the possessive is omitted with the former.

CONJUNCTIONS. 215

493. Two or more verbs connected by a conjunction have the same subject-nominative; as, "I can read, write, and parse." The three verbs connected by the conjunction agree with the same nominative, *I*, in the first, singular. In such cases, the auxiliary is generally expressed with the first verb only, — as in the above example, in which *can* is omitted before *write* and *parse*.

When the verbs have different nominatives, the conjunction may still be used; but it connects clauses or sentences instead of individual verbs; as, "I can read, *but* my brother can write."

494. There is a tendency to put verbs in connected clauses in the same *tense*, even though they have separate nominatives. This often leads to error; as, "The alchemists taught that bodies were composed of salt, sulphur, and mercury." *Were composed* is here used in the imperfect tense, because *taught* in the leading clause is in the imperfect; but, since general truths are expressed by the present, it should be changed to *are composed*.

495. Conjunctions are often understood; as, "I knew [*that*] he would come." "We fought, [*and*] we conquered."

496. After the conjuction *than* (which is used after the comparative degree) there is generally an omission of some word or words necessary to the construction; as, "He that cometh after me is mightier than I," — that is, than I *am*. "He loveth his mother more than me," — that is, than *he loveth* me. "Cæsar's soldiers were better disciplined than Pompey's," — that is, than Pompey's *soldiers*.

It is on some word thus omitted that the case of the noun or pronoun after *than* generally depends. In the first of the examples just given, *I* is in the nominative, because it is the subject of *am* understood. In the second, *me* is in the objective, because it is the object of the verb *loveth* understood. In the third, *Pompey's* is in the possessive, governed by *soldiers* understood. When you have occasion to use a noun or pronoun after *than*, find on what omitted word its case depends, for errors are frequently made in this connection.

497. After expressions which denote *doubt, fear,* or *denial*, the conjunction *that* should be used; as, "I do not doubt *that* he is honest." It is a very common fault to use *lest*, or *but that*, instead of *that*, in such connections; as, "I do not doubt *but that* he will succeed." "I fear *lest* he will not recover."

498. A subsequent clause should not be connected by a conjunction with two antecedent clauses, unless it is consistent in construction with each. "I am taller, but not so heavy, as my brother." This sentence is incorrect, because the subsequent clause, *as my brother*, is inconsistent in construction with the first clause, *I am taller*. It should read thus: "I am taller than my brother, but not so heavy as he."

Corresponding Conjunctions.

499. Certain connectives in an antecedent clause or member are followed by certain conjunctions in a subsequent one. A list of these correlatives follows: —

1. CONJUNCTIONS CORRESPONDING WITH CONJUNCTIONS.

Both — and; as, " *Both* gold *and* silver abound there."
Either — or; as, " I will *either* send it *or* bring it."
Neither — nor; as, " He will *neither* listen *nor* obey."
Whether — or; as, " *Whether* he will go *or* not, is uncertain."
Though, although — yet, still, nevertheless; as, " *Though* he slay me, *yet* will I trust in him."

2. CONJUNCTIONS CORRESPONDING WITH ADVERBS.

As — as (expressing equality); as, " She is *as* amiable *as* her sister."
As — so (expressing comparison); as, " *As* the stars, *so* shall thy seed be."
So — as (after a negative); as, " He is not *so* wise *as* he thinks himself to be." " Pompey was not *so* great a man *as* Cæsar."
So — that (expressing a consequence); as, " He was *so* fatigued *that* he could scarcely move."
Not only — but also; as, " He was *not only* rich, *but also* generous."
Rather — than; as, " I would *rather* work *than* beg."

3. CONJUNCTIONS CORRESPONDING WITH THE ADJECTIVE *SUCH*.

Such — as; as, " We have seldom had *such* a season *as* the present."
Such — that; as, " *Such* is his energy *that* he must succeed."

Analysis and Parsing

Different men are constituted by the Creator with different aptitudes for different pursuits, *and* with different dispositions towards those pursuits. A great public *as well as* private advantage arises from every one's devoting himself to that occupation which he prefers, *and* for which he is specially fitted. It is also evident that, by each nation's devoting itself to that branch of production for which it has the greatest facilities, either original or acquired, its own happiness will be better promoted than in any other manner. She is as old as I, but not so tall as her sister. I'd rather be a dog and bay the moon, than such a Roman. The old philosophers knew that man is an animal. I cannot decide whether to go or remain. Misfortune visits no one oftener than me. No one experiences misfortune oftener than I.

To be Corrected.

There is no man so miserable who does not enjoy something. Neither he or I am able to do it. I know not if it was James or his brother that performed the work. He asked me if I would call and see his brother. The judge asked the foreman if the prisoner was guilty or not guilty. I have travelled both in Europe, in Asia, and in America. Quebec is not as far north as Paris. London is a larger, but not so splendid a city, as Paris. The camel has as much strength, and more endurance, than the horse. I would rather spend the summer in travelling as in working. Between you and I, there is something wrong there. Whom can we admire more than he? No one can get a lesson better than her. We rode much faster than them. About the commencement of the present century, it was discovered that water was composed of two gases.

Rule XXVIII. Interjections.

500. Interjections have neither governing power nor dependence on other words.

REVIEW QUESTIONS. — RULES XXV.-XXVIII.

472. Repeat Rule XXV. 473. What do adverbs sometimes modify? 474. How may adverbs be used? 475. Show how an adverb is used as a noun. 476. For what are adverbs sometimes used? What is said of such constructions? 477. What may be omitted? 478. What is said of the use of *from* before *whence, hence,* and *thence?* 479. In what case is it proper to use two negatives in the same clause, and in what case not? 480. Under what circumstances may *where* be used for *in which?*

481. On what does the position of adverbs depend? Show that a change in their position affects the meaning of a sentence. 482. How do adverbs generally stand? 483. What is the position of *enough?* 484. Give the rule for *never, always, often,* and *seldom.* 485. What is the rule for an adverb used with the infinitive mode? 486. State and illustrate the principle relating to the use of *only* and *not only, merely* and *chiefly.*

487. Repeat Rule XXVI. When should this rule be given? 488. By what must certain words be followed? Give an example. By what is *accompanied* followed? *Agree? Charge? Different? Disappointed?*

Provide? Reconcile? 489. By what must verbs denoting entrance be followed? 490. How do *between* and *among* differ in their application? 491. Repeat Rule XXVII. 492. What is said of the single words connected by conjunctions? 493. When two or more verbs are connected by a conjunction, what do they have in common? With which is the auxiliary expressed? When the verbs have different nominatives, what does the conjunction connect? 494. What error as regards the tense of a dependent verb is mentioned? 495. Give an example of the omission of a conjunction. 496. What generally accompanies the conjunction *than?* On what does the case of the word after *than* depend?
497. What conjunction should be used after expressions denoting doubt, fear, or denial? 498. State the principle relating to a subsequent clause connected by a conjunction with two antecedent clauses. 499. Give the rule relating to corresponding conjunctions. By what is *either* followed? *Though? Neither? Both? Whether? As? So? Rather? Not only? Such?*
500. Repeat Rule XXVIII.

GENERAL EXERCISES ON THE RULES OF SYNTAX.

EXERCISE I.

Analyze and parse the following sentences, which show how the same words may be used, in different connections, as different parts of speech:—

Calm was the day, and the scene delightful. We may expect a *calm* after a storm. To prevent passion is easier than to *calm* it.

Better is a *little* with content, than a great deal with anxiety. The gay and dissolute think *little* of the miseries which are stealing softly after them. A *little* attention will rectify some errors.

Though he is out of danger, he is *still* afraid. He labored to *still* the tumult. *Still* waters are commonly the deepest. A *still* is an instrument used in the process of distillation.

Damp air is unwholesome. Guilt casts a *damp* over our sprightliest hours. Soft bodies *damp* the sound more than hard ones.

Though she is rich and fair, *yet* she is not amiable. They are *yet* young, and must suspend their judgment *yet* a while.

Many persons are better than we suppose them to be. The *few* and the *many* have their prepossessions. *Few* days pass without clouds.

EXERCISE ON THE RULES OF SYNTAX.

The *hail* was very destructive. *Hail*, Virtue! thou source of every good! We *hail* you as friends.

Have you seen the book *that* I purchased yesterday? Give me *that* book. I study, *that* I may improve.

We had been to the *fair*, and seen a *fair* lady.

Much money is corrupting. Think *much* and speak little. He has seen *much* of the world, and been *much* caressed.

His years are *more* than hers; but he has not *more* knowledge. The *more* we are blessed, the *more* grateful we should be. The desire of getting *more* is rarely satisfied.

He has *equal* knowledge, but *inferior* judgment. She is his *inferior* in sense, but his *equal* in prudence.

Every being loves its *like*. We must make *like* spaces between the lines. Behave yourselves *like* men. We are too apt to *like* pernicious company. He may go or stay as he *likes*.

They strive *to* learn. He goes *to* and fro. *To* his wisdom we owe our privileges. The proportion is ten *to* one.

He is esteemed *both* on his own account and on that of his parents. *Both* of them deserve praise. *Both* houses are for sale.

Yesterday was a fine day. I rode out *yesterday*. I shall write *to-morrow*. *To-morrow* may be brighter than *to-day*. We shall arrive *to-day*.

You must *either* go or stay; and you may do *either*, as you please. *Behold!* how pleasant it is to see the sun! I *behold* men as trees, walking.

EXERCISE II.

Analyze and parse the following sentences from standard writers, embracing a variety of peculiar constructions: —

As.   *As if.*   *Such as.*   *So.*

In singing *as* in piping you excel. — *Dryden.*
Mad *as* I was, I could not bear his fate with silent grief. — *Id.*
I live *as* I did, I think *as* I did, I love you *as* I did. — *Swift.*
Darest thou be *as* good *as* thy word now? — *Shakespeare.*
As thou art a prince, I fear thee. — *Id.*
    The noise pursues me wheresoe'er I go,
    As fate sought only me. — *Dryden.*
At either end it whistled *as* it flew. — *Id.*
He answered their questions *as if* it were a matter that needed it. — *Locke.*

Each man's mind has some peculiarity, *as well as* his face. — *Id.*

These should be gently treated, *as though* we expected to be in their condition. — *Sharp.*

As for the rest of those who have written against me, they deserve not the least notice. — *Dryden.*

Is it not every man's interest, that there should be *such* a government of the world *as* designs our happiness ? — *Tillotson.*

A bottle swinging at each side, *as* hath been said or sung. — *Cowper.*

They pretend, in general, to great refinements *as to* what regards Christianity. — *Addison.*

I viewed in my mind, *so* far as I was able, the beginning and progress of a rising world.

We think our fathers fools, *so* wise we 're grown;
Our wiser sons no doubt will think us *so*.

Deliver us from the nauseous repetition of As and So, which some *so so* writers, I may call them *so*, are continually sounding in our ears. — *Felton.*

What.   Whatever.   Whatsoever.

Let them say *what* they will, she will do *what* she lists. — *Drayton.*

Mark *what* it is his mind aims at in this question, and not *what* words he expresses. — *Locke.*

What! canst not thou bear with me half an hour ? — *Sharp.*

What if I advance an invention of my own, to supply the defect of our new writers ? — *Dryden.*

Then balmy sleep had charmed my eye to rest,
What time the morn mysterious visions brings. — *Pope.*

The enemy, having his country wasted, *what by* himself and *what by* the soldiers, findeth succor in no places. — *Spenser.*

Whatever is read, differs from what is repeated. — *Swift.*

Whatsoever is first in the invention, is last in the execution. — *Hammond.*

What ho! thou genius of the clime, *what ho!* — *Dryden.*

When.   While.   Then.

I was adopted heir by his consent,
Since *when* his oath is broke. — *Shakespeare.*

Pausing *a while*, thus to herself she mused. — *Milton.*
One *while* we thought him innocent. — *Ben Jonson.*
The *then* Bishop of London, Dr. Laud, attended on his Majesty throughout that whole journey. — *Clarendon.*
Thee *then* a boy within my arms I laid. — *Dryden.*
Till *then* who knew the force of those dire dreams ? — *Milton.*

That.

He wins me by *that* means I told you. — *Shakespeare.*
What is *that* to us ? See thou to *that.* — *Bible.*
I'll know your business, *that* I will. — *Shakespeare.*
    Treat it kindly *that* it may
    Wish at least with us to stay. — *Cowley.*
O *that* those lips had language ! — *Cowper.*
There is no man *that* sinneth not. — *Bible.*

Each other.   *One another.*

Loveliest of women ! heaven is in thy soul, beauty and virtue shine forever about thee, bright'ning *each other.* Thou art all divine. — *Addison.*
The storm beats the trees against *one another.* — *Johnson.*
This is the message that ye heard from the beginning, that we should love *one another.* — *Bible.*

Save.   *But.*

All the conspirators *save* * only he,
Did that they did in envy of great Cæsar. — *Shakespeare.*
Night shades the groves, and all in silence lie,
All *save* the mournful Philomel and I. — *Young.*
    For who *but* He who arched the skies
    Could raise the daisy's purple bud ?
He that is washed needeth not, *save* to wash his feet. — *Bible.*
And all desisted, all *save* him alone. — *Wordsworth.*
    The boy stood on the burning deck,
    Whence all *but* him had fled. — *Hemans.*

---

* *Save* and *but*, when equivalent to *except*, are prepositions, and are followed by the objective case. Some writers, however, have used them as conjunctions, as in this sentence and the next two, in which they are followed by the nominative. This usage should be avoided.

EXERCISE III.

Correct the miscellaneous errors in the following sentences, according to the rules and remarks that have been given:—

I admire the generous sympathy of Lafayette, he who befriended America. The tomb we visited was Washington's, the man who is the boast and pride of America. They slew Varus, he that was mentioned before. Him it is whom they persecuted. Whom do you think it is? Who do you think it to be? Man, though he has a great variety of thoughts, yet they are all within his own breast. Trouble, though it may be long delayed, yet it will surely come.

There is a great many different ways of accumulating wealth. Nothing but vain and foolish pursuits delight some persons. What avails the best sentiments, if persons do not live suitably to them? Thou, who art the Author of life, can restore it. There is many occasions in life in which silence and simplicity is true wisdom. Great pains * were taken to reconcile the parties with each other. He need not to proceed in such haste. He dare not to touch a hair of Catiline. It is easy to dare a man fight, but not so easy to meet him in the lists.

To live soberly and piously are required of all. What signifies the counsel and care of teachers? One, added to nineteen, make twenty. Idleness and ignorance is the parent of many vices. In unity consists the welfare and security of society. One or both of the scholars was present at the transaction. The deceitfulness of riches, or the cares of life, has choked the seeds of virtue in many a promising mind. The people rejoices in that which should give them sorrow.

Such will ever be the effect of youth associating with vicious companions. Who have I reason to esteem so highly as you? Ye who are dead hath he quickened. And he that was dead set up and begun to speak. We have done no more than it was our duty to have done. I always intended to have rewarded my son. He appeared to have been a man of letters. It was a pleasure to have received this approbation. They whom he had most injured, he had the greatest reason to love.

---

* Good authority justifies the use of a verb in either the singular or plural with the noun *pains*. It seems to preponderate, however, in favor of the singular.

I am not recommending these kind of sufferings. By this means,* he had them more at vantage. There is no mean of escaping the persecution. And with this amend he was content. Peace of mind is an honorable amend for the sacrifices of self-interest. Some men think exceeding clearly, and reason exceeding forcibly. He acted in this business bolder than was expected. Every man and every woman were numbered. What black despair, what horror fills his mind!

His work is perfect; but his brothers is more than perfect. Which of them two persons was in fault? We have a great many of them flowers in the garden. Each of them in their turn receive favors. Every person, whatever be their station, are bound by the duties of morality and religion. Humility and love constitutes the essence of religion. Though the designs be laudable, it will involve much anxiety and labor. A large number of vessels is being built, the present season. The army is being concentrated to invade the capital.

I intended to have called on my way home. I had hoped to have seen the affair amicably settled. It was said by somebody, I know not who, that Charles was the person who they imputed the crime to. Neither despise the poor or envy the rich. I should be obliged to him if he will gratify me. The relations are so uncertain, as that they require much examination. I am not afraid but what he will return. Take care lest he finds you off your guard. I would rather die of the sword than by cholera. Such a day as this, I feel too warmly.

The old man was setting upon the ground on the side of the road. I differ entirely with you in this particular. He was resolved of going to the Persian court. He was eager of recommending it to his fellow-citizens. He accused the ministers for betraying the Dutch. It is a use that perhaps I should have thought on. He was made much on at Argus. Neither of them shall make me swerve out of my path.

The weakest of my eyes is now a little better; but the strongest one is beginning to be effected. I expected my father, brother, and sister to have arrived; but neither of them have yet come. Either

---

* *Means* (in the sense of *resources, instrument for gaining an end*) is used in both the singular and the plural, but always has the plural form. The same may be said of *amends*.

of the three books you mention will answer. Nothing is more preferable than retirement from the bustle of the world. I respect no one more than he. If any of the scholars has drawed a better picture than him, I am mistaken. Did you not know that insects had feeling ?

CHAPTER XII.

PUNCTUATION.

501. Punctuation is the art of dividing written language by points, that its meaning may be readily understood.

502. The points used in Punctuation are these:—

PERIOD,	.	SEMICOLON,	;
INTERROGATION POINT,	?	COMMA,	,
EXCLAMATION POINT,	!	DASH,	—
COLON,	:	PARENTHESES,	( )
	BRACKETS,	[ ]	

Besides these, the following characters are used:—

APOSTROPHE,	'	HYPHEN,	-
QUOTATION POINTS,	" "		

503. A Period must be placed,—

I. After every declarative and imperative sentence; as, "Beauty is fleeting." "Take heed."

II. After abbreviations; as, *Dr.* for *Doctor ; P. S.* for *postscript.*

504. An Interrogation Point must be placed after every interrogative sentence and member; as, "Is not nature beautiful?" "Nature is beautiful; shall we not, then, enjoy it?"

505. An Exclamation Point must be placed,—

I. After every exclamatory sentence and member;

as, "How beautiful is nature!" "There is the Hudson; how it sets off the landscape!"

II. After every interjection except O, unless it is very closely connected with some other word or words; as, "Alas! alas! I am undone." "O my friend!" "Hail, virtue!"

EXERCISE.

Insert periods, interrogation points, and exclamation points wherever they are required in the following sentences:—

Air is 828 times lighter than water — Were Mr Jones and his son Chas at the party — Dr Jas S Smith has gone to Nyack, Rockland Co, N Y — Microscopes were first used in Germany — What ho who comes — Where were looking-glasses first made — What a fine sight is a sunrise on the ocean — Indeed that's passing strange — Who spoke — I do not know who spoke — He is well, is he — Louis XIV, of France, first adopted military uniforms — O Mr Hall, can you believe this — What an impostor was Mohammed — How true is the saying, "Time flies" — The Alps abound in fine scenery; how I would like to visit them.

506. A Colon must be placed, —

I. Between the great divisions of sentences, when subdivisions occur, separated by the semicolon; as, "I admire you, my friend; I love you: but you must not expect me to make this sacrifice."

II. Before a quotation or an enumeration of particulars, when introduced by the words *thus, these, following,* or *as follows;* as "The following branches are taught: Geography, History, Grammar, &c."

507. A Semicolon must be placed, —

I. Between the members of a compound sentence, unless they are very closely connected; as, "Doubt and distraction are on earth; the brightness of truth is in heaven."

II. Between the great divisions of sentences, even

though closely connected, when subdivisions occur separated by the comma; as, "America, otherwise called the New World, was discovered in 1492; but it was not settled till some years afterwards."

III. Before the conjunction *as*, introducing an example, as in the last two paragraphs.

IV. Between enumerated particulars, preceded by a colon, when each consists of several words; as, "The value of a maxim depends upon these four things: the correctness of the principles it embodies; the subject to which it relates; the extent of its application; and the ease with which it may be practically carried out.

EXERCISE.

Insert colons and semicolons wherever they are required.

One thread does not make a rope one swallow does not make summer. — The Esquimaux feast on rancid fish; the Russian peasants consider themselves well fed, if they have rye bread and cabbage soup but more civilized nations are not so easily satisfied. — Our stock of defensive weapons was as follows one old sword, dull, jagged, and rusty one musket without a lock and two pitchforks, which my grandfather had received from his ancestors. — He reasoned thus All men are mortal I am a man therefore I am mortal. — The poem begins with these words "Arms and the man I sing," &c. — He is my friend, who tells me my faults he is my enemy, who speaks of my virtues. — Trouble neglected becomes still more troublesome a stitch in time saves nine. — There are eight parts of speech the noun, the pronoun, &c.

508. The Comma indicates less break in the connection than any other point. It must be used according to the following rules: —

I. Phrases, adjuncts, and clauses that are not restrictive, — that is, that may be left out without injury to the sense, — when they are introduced so as to break the connection between the component parts of a sentence, must be set off on each side with the comma; as, "He wishes, *in fine*, to see the world." "Mary, *by the way*, would like to hear from you." "Rome, *which then ruled the world*, was opposed to the measure."

Adverbs and conjunctions thrown in as described above, and used to modify a whole proposition and not any particular word, are also set off on each side with the comma; as, "France, *meanwhile*, was arming for the struggle." "Linen, *however*, was first made in England."

Phrases, adjuncts, clauses, and single words, like those described above, standing at the commencement of a sentence, take a comma after them; as, "*Moreover*, mathematics disciplines the mind." "*Dazzled by pleasure*, the young forget their duty." "*In general*, the best men are the happiest."

Restrictive clauses must not be set off with the comma; as, "I love not the man *that slanders his neighbor*." "We found her *discontented and unhappy*."

II. A comma must be placed before *and, or, if, but, that* (when equivalent to *in order that*), and some other conjunctions, when they connect, not words, but short members and clauses, closely allied in sense, yet requiring separation by some point; as, "Spring came, and the flowers bloomed more brightly than ever." "Avoid temptations, that you may not be led astray by their allurements."

III. A comma often takes the place of a verb or a conjunction omitted for the sake of avoiding repetition; as, "Sullivan commanded on the right flank; Greene, on the left," — a comma taking the place of the verb *commanded*, omitted after *Greene*. "He came, saw, and conquered;" a comma takes the place of the conjunction *and*, omitted after *came*.

IV. A comma is placed after the logical subject of a verb, when it consists of a great many words or ends with a verb; as, "The anarchy that had grown up in

England among all classes during these long and bloody wars, now bore its fruit." "Whatever breathes, lives."

V. Words used in pairs take a comma after each pair; as, "Brave but not rash, prudent but not timid, he soon gained the respect of his soldiers."

VI. A comma sets off a noun in apposition with some preceding noun, when it is accompanied with several modifying words; as, "Harvey, the discoverer of the circulation of the blood, was an eminent English physician."

VII. A comma generally separates words and clauses expressing contrast or opposition; as,

Liberal, not *lavish*, is kind Nature's hand.
Though *deep*, yet *clear;* though *gentle*, yet not *dull*.

EXERCISE.

Insert commas where they are required by the preceding rules.

When the graces of novelty are worn off admiration is succeeded by indifference. The ox knoweth his owner and the ass his master's crib. He who preserves me to whom I owe my being whose I am and whom I serve is eternal. We hear nothing of causing the blind to see the lame to walk the deaf to hear the lepers to be cleansed. The miseries of poverty of sickness of captivity would without hope be unsupportable. To err is human; to forgive divine. His wisdom not his talents attracted attention. Earth and sea rain and snow night and day summer and winter seed-time and harvest show forth the wisdom and goodness of the Creator. He was gigantic in knowledge in virtue in health.

Johnson had repeated a psalm which he had translated during his affliction into Latin verses. Cowper the gifted poet died in the year 1800. Miltiades the son of Cimon was an Athenian. Self-conceit presumption and obstinacy blast the prospects of many a youth. Translated to Heaven Enoch knew not death. Far down in the depths of the ocean the mermaid plied her song. I will tell the story that you may know how I have been injured. A man so insensible to kindness as not to manifest the slightest gratitude for the many favors you have bestowed on him is unworthy of any further notice. Those who were wounded have died.

509. The Dash is used, —

I. To denote that a sentence is unfinished, from hesitation in the speaker or writer, or some sudden interruption; as, " Pardon me for wounding your feelings, but — "

II. To denote a break in the construction; as, " The boy — oh! where was he? "

III. To denote an unexpected transition from grave to comic style; as, " He had a manly bearing and — an exceedingly red nose."

IV. After other points, to make them denote a somewhat higher degree of separation; as, "To be overlooked and misunderstood, to be envied and persecuted, — such is too often the fate of genius."

510. Parentheses are used to enclose words that explain or add to the leading proposition of a sentence, when introduced in such a way as to interfere with the harmonious flow; as, "The alligator (so the American crocodile is called) abounds in the bayous of Louisiana."

511. Brackets are generally used in quoted passages to enclose some word improperly omitted by the author, to correct a mistake, or to introduce some observation or explanatory word that does not belong to the quotation; as, " Few good men [the author might have said none at all] can escape calumny."

EXERCISE.

Insert dashes, parentheses, and brackets, wherever they are required.

Some men are afflicted with a grievous consumption of victuals. She is very intelligent, very refined, very affable, and withal very fat. "Here comes" "Your obedient servant," broke in my friend.

You are a a a I know not what to call you. This ignis fatuus for so we might rightly call it led many to their destruction. Byron and the same may be said of many a better man was the cause of his own unhappiness. This admitted and admitted it will have to be by honest minds I proceed to the next point of the argument. My brother is eager after for going. The finest oranges which that I ever ate came from St. Michael's. Just as the twig is bent alas! it is too often bent the wrong way the tree's inclined.

512. The Apostrophe is used, —

I. To denote the omission of one or more letters in a word; as, *o'er* for *over,* *'mid* for *amid,* *thro'* for *through.*

II. As the sign of the possessive case; as, *man's, men's.*

III. To form the plurals of letters, figures, and signs; as, +'s, *t's,* 7's.

513. The Hyphen is used, —

I. To connect simple words uniting to form a compound; as, *nut-brown, ever-to-be-remembered, ill-natured.*

When the compound comes into very common use, the hyphen is often omitted; as in *fireman, myself, railroad.*

II. To connect the syllables into which a word is separated, particularly at the end of a line; as, "Integrity is its own reward." *In-teg-ri-ty.*

When there is not room to get the whole of a word in a line, it must be divided according to syllables, and, the hyphen having been placed after a complete syllable, the rest is carried over to the commencement of a new line.

514. Quotation Points are used to enclose a passage quoted from a writer or speaker in his own words; as, Cowper says, "Oh for a lodge in some vast wilderness!"

Single Quotation Points (' ') are used to enclose a quotation within a quotation, or one in which the words of the writer or speaker are slightly altered; as, "Cowper says, 'Oh for a lodge in some vast wilderness!'"

EXERCISE.

Insert apostrophes, hyphens, and quotation points wherever they are required.

Well sit neath willows by the waters edge. Id not give a hapenny for such an ill tempered cur. Een tho the heavens should fall, Ill have no fear. As we approached the citys gates on that never to be forgotten day, my companions courage forsook him. Charless hat is better than Moses. The oftquoted passage, God tempers the wind to the shorn lamb, is taken from Sternes Sentimental Journey. I will say to you, continued my friend, what an old philosopher once said, Know thyself. Tired natures sweet restorer, as Young poetically styles sleep, is oerpowering me. A gem, says the Chinese proverb, is not polished without rubbing ; nor is a man perfected without trials.

Other marks are frequently used in printing and writing. The principal are, —

Marks of Reference.

THE PARAGRAPH,	¶	THE DAGGER,	†
THE SECTION,	§	THE DOUBLE DAGGER,	‡
THE ASTERISK,	*	THE PARALLELS,	‖

Marks of Ellipsis to show that something has been omitted ; as, K——g, K**g, K..g, for King.

LONG DASH,	(———)	DITTO MARKS,	(")
STARS,	(****)	CARET,	(ʌ)
DOTS,	(......)		

The Caret is used only in manuscripts, to direct attention to something written above the line; as, I have ^no^ home.

Marks of Pronunciation.

The cedilla (ç), placed under *c* to indicate the sound of *s*; as, *façade, garçon*.

The tilde (ñ), placed over *n* to indicate the sound of *ny*; as, *cañon, señor*.

The diæresis (¨) placed over the latter of two contiguous vowels to show that they must be pronounced separately; as, *aëronaut*.

The quantity marks, macron or long sound (-), as *hōly*; the breve or short sound (˘), as, *glŏrious*.

The marks of accent, grave (`), acute (´), and circumflex (ˆ); as, conˆflict, bruisèd. Will yóu wálk or ríde ?

Other Marks.

The brace (⏜) to connect terms having a common relation.
The index (☞) to direct attention.

REVIEW QUESTIONS ON CHAPTER XII.

501. What is punctuation? 502. Name the points used in punctuation. What other characters are employed? 503. Where must a period be placed? 504. An interrogation point? 505. An exclamation point? 506. Where must a colon be placed? 507. Where must a semicolon be placed? 508. What does the comma indicate? Give the rule for the use of the comma relating to phrases, adjuncts, and clauses that are not restrictive. What is the rule relating to certain adverbs and conjunctions? How are these phrases, adjuncts, &c., punctuated, when they stand at the commencement of a sentence? What is said of restrictive clauses?

Give the rule for the use of the comma before conjunctions. Give the rule for the use of the comma in place of an omitted word. Give the rule relating to the logical subject. Give the rule relating to words used in pairs. Give the rule relating to a noun in apposition. What is the comma sometimes used to separate? 509. For what is the dash used? 510. For what are parentheses used? 511. For what are brackets used?

512. For what is the apostrophe used? 513. For what is a hyphen used? When is the hyphen omitted in compound words? What must be done when there is not room to get the whole of a word in a line? 514. For what are quotation points used? Single quotation points? Name the marks of reference. Name the marks of ellipsis. When is the caret used? Name the marks of pronunciation, and state the office of each. When is the brace used? The index?

PART IV.

LETTERS.

CHAPTER XIII.

CLASSES, SOUNDS, AND COMBINATIONS OF LETTERS.

515. A Letter is a character employed in writing or printing, to represent some sound of the human voice used in speaking.

Before the invention of letters, pictures and symbols, called Hieroglyphics, were used to convey ideas. A battle, for example, was represented by a picture of two men fighting. Eternity was denoted by a circle; an appropriate symbol, for a circle, like eternity, has neither beginning nor end.

The number of letters is different in different languages. The letters of any given language arranged in order are called its Alphabet.

516. That part of Grammar which treats of letters is called Orthography.

SECTION I.

CLASSES OF LETTERS.

517. The English alphabet consists of twenty-six letters, which are divided into two classes, known as Vowels and Consonants.

518. A Vowel is a letter that represents a free, uninterrupted sound.

519. A Consonant is a letter that does not represent a free, uninterrupted sound.

520. Five of the letters are always vowels, — *a, e, i, o,* and *u*. Two, *w* and *y*, are sometimes vowels and sometimes consonants. The remaining nineteen are always consonants.

Since a vowel represents a complete sound, it can be uttered alone. Try whether this is so with *a, e, i*. Since a consonant does not represent a complete sound, it cannot be fully uttered without the aid of a vowel. Try whether this is so with *b :* you will find that it cannot be sounded till a vowel is joined to it, — *b-a, b-e, b-i, b-o, b-u*. Try, in the same way, to sound *p, t, d*.

SECTION II.
SYLLABLES. — ACCENT.

521. A Syllable is one or more letters forming a complete sound, and uttered with one impulse of the voice; as, *O, on, one, once*.

A syllable may constitute a whole word, as in the above examples: or part of a word; as, *on-ly, one-sided*.

522. A word of one syllable is called a Monosyllable; as, *on*.

A word of two syllables is called a Dissylable; as, *li-on*.

A word of three syllables is called a Trisyllable; as, *li-on-ess*.

A word of more than three syllables is called a Polysyllable; as, *li-on-ess-es, in-de-struc-ti-bil-i-ty*.

523. It was said above, that *w* and *y* are sometimes consonants and sometimes vowels. They are consonants when they come before a vowel in the same syllable; and otherwise, vowels. They are consonants in the words *wine, yet, re-ward, un-yoke*, &c. They are vowels in the words *now, pray, re-new, bold-ly, y-clept, show-y*, &c.

524. When a word consists of two or more syllables, one of them is naturally uttered with more force than the rest. This stress of the voice is called Accent.

In the words *profit, remedy, temporary*, &c., the first syllable receives the stress of the voice, and is therefore said to be accented. In the words *dispute, propeller, laborious*, &c., the second syllable receives the stress of the voice, and is said to be accented. In the words *palisade, California*, &c., the third syllable receives the stress of the voice, and is said to be accented.

The acute accent (′), placed after a syllable, denotes that it receives the stress of the voice; as, *thun′-der, rec-i-ta′-tion*.

SECTION III.
SOUNDS OF THE LETTERS.

525. Each vowel has several different sounds; as, *a* in the words *fate, fat, all, arm, what*.

The sound of *a* in each of the above examples may be obtained by pronouncing the whole word first, and then leaving off the sounds of all the letters except *a*.

526. Most of the consonants have one sound only, but some have more than one; as, *s* in *sit* and *his*.

527. *C* and *G* have two sounds each.

C is said to be *soft* when it sounds like *s*, as in the word *recite;* *hard*, when it sounds like *k*, as in the word *cat*.

G is said to be *soft* when it has the sound of *j*, as in *gin, gesture*. In other cases, it is *hard*, as in *go, gun*.

As a general rule, *c* and *g* are soft before the vowels *e, i*, and *y*, hard before *a, o*, and *u*.

528. A letter is said to be *silent* when it is not sounded; as, *h* in *hour, e* in *fate, b* in *dumb*.

SECTION IV.
SUBDIVISIONS OF CONSONANTS.

529. The consonants are subdivided into Mutes and Semivowels.

A Mute is a consonant that cannot be uttered at all without the aid of a vowel. To this class belong *b, c* hard, *d, g* hard, *k, p, q,* and *t.*

A Semivowel is a consonant that can be imperfectly uttered without the aid of a vowel. To this class belong *c* soft, *f, g* soft, *h, j, l, m, n, r, s, v, x,* and *z.*

530. *L, m, n, r,* are also called Liquids, because their sound flows with peculiar ease.

In the following tabular arrangement of consonant sounds, the classes show the position of the organs in emitting the sound, the orders show the relative amount of breath used, and the way in which it escapes.

Orders.	CLASS I. Labials.	CLASS II. Linguo-Dentals.	CLASS III. Dentals.	CLASS IV. Palatals.
1. Smooth,	p	t		k
1. Middle,	b	d		g
3. Rough,	v, w	th(is), th(in) / zh, ch	l, r	j, y
4. Aspirates,	f, wh	s, sh		h
5. Nasals,	m	n		ng
Double Consonants,		z		x

SECTION V.

DIPHTHONGS AND TRIPHTHONGS.

531. A Diphthong consists of two vowels united in one syllable; as, *oa* in *oar, ee* in *meet, ow* in *now, ay* in *day.*

532. A Diphthong is said to be Proper when both of its vowels are sounded; as, *ou* in *noun, oi* in *toil.*

A Diphthong is said to be Improper when but one of its vowels is sounded; as, *ea* in *beat, ay* in *may.*

533. A Triphthong consists of three vowels united in one syllable; as, *eau* in *beauty, ious* in *pugnacious.*

CAPITAL LETTERS. 237

EXERCISE.

A list of words follows. 1. Tell, with respect to each, whether it is a monosyllable, dissyllable, trisyllable, or polysyllable. 2. Tell on which syllable the accent falls. 3. Pick out the silent letters. 4. Pick out the diphthongs, and tell whether they are proper or improper. 5. Pick out the triphthongs. 6. Tell whether *w* and *y*, as they successively occur, are consonants or vowels. 7. When *c* and *g* occur, tell whether they are hard or soft.

Millionaire, treacherously, get, viewing, wonderful, dewy, youthful, Sicily, gregarious, goat, gymnasium, phlegmatic, recitation, wristband, yellow, Knickerbocker, Yankee, cite, beautifully, yawned, woodpecker, impenetrability, peaceable, buoy, yclad, spacious, oyster, automaton, egregious, historically, newly, herb, hurricane, browbeat, wooest, early, analogically, Ptolemy, gaol, gallop.

SECTION VI.

CAPITAL LETTERS.

584. As regards their form, letters are divided into two classes, Small Letters and Capitals. Almost all printed and written matter consists of small letters; but, for the purpose of distinction, capitals are used at the commencement of words in certain cases.

Rules for the Use of Capitals.

Begin with a capital, —

1. Every sentence.

2. Proper nouns, and common nouns personified; as, *George, York, the Strand, the Alps, the Thames, hail, bounteous Autumn!*

The names of the days of the week should begin with capitals; those of the seasons with small letters. The names of the points of the compass when denoting direction should commence with small letters; when applied to certain districts of a country or their inhabitants, with capitals; as, *Monday, summer, The wind blows north, The South is ardent and impetuous.*

3. Titles of office and honor, and also the names of religious sects and public bodies; as, *Governor Jones,*

Judge, Esquire, Baptists, Friends, Congress, the Supreme Judicial Court.

4. Adjectives derived from proper nouns; as, *European, Roman, Newtonian.*

5. Appellations of the Deity and personal pronouns standing for His name; as, *God, Jehovah, the Almighty, the Supreme Being, Providence, the Messiah, the Holy Spirit.*

6. Direct quotations forming complete sentences; as, " Our great Lawgiver says, 'Take up thy cross daily, and follow me.'"

Quotations introduced indirectly by a conjunction need not commence with a capital; as, "Solomon observes that 'pride goeth before destruction.'"

7. The nouns and other important words in the titles of books; as, *Johnson's Dictionary of the English Language; Rollin's Ancient History.*

8. Every line of poetry.

9. The pronoun *I*, and the interjection *O*, must be written in capitals.

10. Words that are the principal subjects of discourse, or that denote well-known events, historical eras, public documents, or extraordinary phenomena; as, *the Revolution, the Middle Ages, Magna Charta, the Aurora Borealis.*

EXERCISE.

In the following sentences, use capitals when they are required by the above rule. If a capital is improperly used, substitute a small letter for it.

Employ thy time Well. to-morrow's sun may Never rise. portugal and spain constitute what is called the peninsula. Pride breakfasted with plenty, dined with poverty, and supped with infamy. The hungarian chief next crossed the danube and sought to Escape into turkey. The ozark mountains cross the Boundary that separates missouri from arkansas. great is the lord. General Brown and major morgan have been invited to dine with the private secretary of president buchanan.

On monday, september 5th, the steamer waterwitch will be launched; o how i would like to see It! The omnipotent father has made all these worlds. In howitt's "homes and haunts of the most eminent british poets," i have read an Interesting Account of joanna baillie. Smile on me, beauteous spring. Poor richard says "three removes are as bad as a fire." Poor Richard says that "three removes are as bad as a fire."

> he that by the plough would thrive,
> himself must either hold or drive.

The court of common pleas is now sitting in the city hall. The honorable justice nodine observes that There is great uncertainty in the Law. The central american question seemed at one time about to embroil the united states in a war with several of the leading powers of europe. dunderdale's "Tour through the argentine republic" has been pronounced a capital Book by the brazilian minister.

CHAPTER XIV.
SPELLING.

535. Spelling is the art of expressing words by their proper letters.

SECTION I.
RULES FOR SPELLING.

536. So arbitrary is the spelling of English words, and so inconsistent oftentimes with their sound, that but little assistance can be derived from rules. The following, however, should be remembered: —

RULE I. — Monosyllables ending with f, l, or s, preceded by a single vowel, double their final letter; as, *stiff*, *hill*, *miss*.

EXCEPT *of, if, as, gas, has, was, yes, is, his, this, us, pus, thus.*

RULE II. — Words ending with any other consonant

than *f, l,* or *s*, do not double their final letter; as, *rub, hat, in.*

EXCEPT *ebb, add, odd, egg, inn, bunn, err, purr, butt, buzz, fuzz.*

RULE III. — Compounds retain the spelling of the simple words that compose them; as, *fireman, school-master.*

EXCEPTIONS. — In compounds whose parts are so perfectly incorporated that they have but one syllable accented, *full* and *all* drop one *l;* as, *careful, always.*

SECTION II.
FORMATION OF DERIVATIVES.

537. Derivatives are formed from simple or compound words by the addition of a letter or letters; as, *horse, horse-s; horseman, horseman-ship.*

538. Words from which derivatives are formed are called Radicals.

539. The letter or letters added to form a derivative may be placed before or after the radical; in the former case, they are called a Prefix; in the latter, a Suffix.

Thus, *act* is a radical; *transact* is a derivative formed by adding the prefix *trans;* *actor* is a derivative formed by adding the suffix *or.*

By learning the meaning of the principal prefixes and suffixes, we at once become acquainted with the signification of a great number of derivatives. Thus, if we know that *or* means *one who,* we shall also know that *actor* means *one who acts; visitor, one who visits; instructor, one who instructs,* &c., &c.

540. The prefixes are derived mainly from the Saxon, Latin, and Greek. They are classed below according to their origin.

List of the Principal Prefixes.
Saxon.

A, *on, in, to, at;* as, *afoot, on* foot.
Be, *near, by, at, on, to make;* as, *becalm, to make* calm.
Fore, *before;* as, *foretell,* to tell *before.*
Mis, *wrong;* as, *misconduct, wrong* conduct.

LIST OF THE PRINCIPAL PREFIXES. **241**

Out, *beyond, more;* as, *out*run, run *beyond.*
Over, *above, beyond, too; over*hang, hang *above.*
Un (before adjectives), *not; un*certain, *not* certain.
  (before nouns), *to take off;* as, *un*mask, *to take off* a mask.
Under, *beneath, inferior;* as, *under-*teacher, *inferior* teacher.
Up, *aloft, on high;* as, *up*lift, lift *aloft.*
With, *against, from;* as, *with*stand, to stand *against.*

Latin.

A, ab, abs, *from;* as, *a*vert, turn *from.*
Ad, a, ac, af, ag, al, an, ap, ar, as, at, *to;* as, *af*fix, fix *to.*
Ante, *before;* as, *ante*cedent, going *before.*
Circum, *around;* as, *circum*navigate, navigate *around.*
Con, co, cog, col, com, cor, *with, together;* as, *com*press, press *together.*
Contra, counter, *against;* as, *counter*act, act *against.*
De, *down, from;* as, *de*duce, draw *from.*
Dis, di, dif, *apart, not, to deprive of;* as, *dis*like, *not to* like.
E, ex, ef, ec, *out, out of, from;* as, *e*ject, cast *out.*
Extra, *beyond, more than;* as, *extra*ordinary, *more than* ordinary.
In, im, ig, il, ir (before adjectives), *not;* as, *in*active, *not* active.
  (before verbs), *in, into, to make;* as, *im*brown, *to make* brown.
Inter, *between, among;* as, *inter*vene, come *between.*
Ob, oc, of, op, *before, against, in the way;* as, *oc*cluse, closed *against;* *ob*trude, thrust *in the way.*
Per, *through;* as, *per*vade, go *through.*
Pre, *before;* as, *pre*judge, judge *before.*
Pro, *for, forth, forward;* as, *pro*noun, *for* a noun.
Re, *again, back;* as, *re*enter, enter *again.*
Sub, suc, suf, sug, sup, sus, *under, from;* as, *sub*scribe, write *under.*
Super, *above, over;* as, *super*scribe, write *over.*
Trans, *across, over, beyond;* as, *trans*fer, carry *over.*

Greek.

A, an, *without, want of;* as, *an*onymous, *without* name.
Anti, *against;* as, *anti*pathy, feeling *against.*
Apo, aph, *from;* as, *aph*elion, (the point) *from* the sun.
Dia, *through;* as, *dia*meter, measure *through.*
Hemi, *half;* as, *hemi*sphere, *half* a sphere.
Hyper, *over;* as, *hyper*critical, *over* critical.
Peri, *around;* as, *peri*meter, measure *around.*
Syn, sy, syl, sym, *together, with;* as, *sym*pathy, feeling *with.*

16

EXERCISE.

Spell the following derivatives; analyze them and give their meaning, according to the following model:—

UNNATURAL.—*Unnatural* is a derivative, formed of the radical *natural* and the prefix *un*, meaning *not*; *unnatural*, *not* natural.

Abed, ashore, beside, foreknow, misguide, misarrange, outshoot, overleap, ungracious, uncrown, unrobe, under-agent, undergo, upraise, withhold, adjoin, assign, accredit, antechamber, antedate, circum-meridian, conjoin, cotenant, contradistinguished, counter-current, disarm, express, extra-regular, ignoble, irresponsible, immature, indelicate, impress, imbitter, prewarn, premeditate, recall, suppress, superabundant, transatlantic, antifederal, antimason, antichristian, anteroom, hemicycle, hypercriticise, bespot, forewarn, mismanagement, withdraw.

List of the Principal Suffixes.

S, es, *more than one;* as, boy*s*, *more than one* boy.
Er, *more;* as, bright*er*, *more* bright.
Est, *most;* as, bright*est*, *most* bright.
S, es, *does;* as, walk*s*, *does* walk.
Est, *dost;* as, walk*est*, *dost* walk.
Ed, *did;* as, walk*ed*, *did* walk.
Ing, *continuing to;* as, walk*ing*, *continuing to* walk.
Ate, en, ize, *to make;* as, hard*en*, *to make* hard.
Ar, er, or, an, ian, *one who;* as, beggar, *one who* begs.
Ess, ine, ix, *a female;* lion*ess*, *a female* lion.
Ness, ty, ity, *the quality or state of being;* soft*ness*, *the state of being* soft.
Ion, ment, *the act of;* as, agita*tion*, *the act of* agitating.
Al, ic, an, ian, ar, ary, *pertaining to;* as, hero*ic*, *pertaining to* a hero.
Ous, ful, y, *full of;* as, peril*ous*, *full of* peril.
Able, ible, *that may be;* as, eat*able*, *that may be* eaten.
Ly, *in a — manner;* as, warm*ly*, *in a* warm *manner*.
Less, *without, that cannot be;* as, penni*less*, *without* a penny.
Ish, some, *somewhat;* as, sweet*ish*, *somewhat* sweet.
Y, ry, ery, *the art or practice of;* as, glutton*y*, *the practice of* a glutton.
Ward, *towards;* as, north*ward*, *towards* the north.
Ive, ory, *tending to;* as, instruct*ive*, *tending to* instruct.
Let, et, ule, cule, *a little;* as, brook*let*, *a little* brook.

RULES FOR THE FORMATION OF DERIVATIVES. 243

EXERCISE.

Spell the following derivatives; analyze them and give their meaning, according to the following model:—

WISHING.— *Wishing* is a derivative, formed of the radical *wish* and the suffix *ing*, meaning *continuing to;* wishing, *continuing to* wish.

Boxes, plays, warmer, warmest, wanders, pushes, wanderest, wandering, wandered, pushed, sweeten, invalidate, christianize, passer, sailor, baroness, heroine, executrix, sweetness, oddity, action, baronial, hysterical, dangerous, courageous, spiteful, fleshy, wonderful, drinkable, instructible, politely, gallantly, passionless, tameless, tartish, cookery, eastward, sportive, floweret, streamlet, globule, animalcule, formal, fishery, utterable, owner, smaller, ownest, smallest, humorous, lonesome, darksome, acknowledgment.

Rules for the Formation of Derivatives.

541. When a prefix is added to a radical, no change is made in the latter. When a suffix is added, sometimes a change is made, and sometimes not.

Thus, when we add *er* to *hat*, we double the *t*,—*hat, hatter ;* but when we add *er* to *heat*, we make no change, —*heat, heater.*

542. In forming derivatives with suffixes, the following are the principal rules to be observed:—

RULE I.— The final *e* of a radical is rejected before a suffix beginning with a vowel ; as, *ride, rid-er ; move, mov-ing.*

Exception I.— Final *e*, when preceded by *c* or *g*, is not rejected before a suffix beginning with *a* or *o;* as, *peace, peaceable ; courage, courageous.*

Exception II.— Final *e*, when preceded by *e* or *o*, is not rejected before *ing ;* as, *see, seeing ; hoe, hoeing.*

Remark.— Final *e* is sometimes rejected when the suffix begins with a consonant; as, *true, truly ; judge, judgment.*

RULE II.— The final consonant of a monosyllable, if preceded by a single vowel, is doubled before a suffix beginning with a vowel ; as, *sin, sinner ; beg, begg-ing.*

Remark. — Observe that the final consonant, if preceded by two vowels, is not doubled; as, *beat, beaten ; toil, toiling.*

RULE III. — The final consonant of any word accented on the last syllable, if preceded by a single vowel, is doubled before a suffix beginning with a vowel ; as, *refer', referr-ed ; repel', repell-ing.*

Remark. — There are about fifty words ending in *l*, which, though accented on the first syllable, are made by many to double their final consonant before a suffix commencing with a vowel; as, *travel, travel-er; quarrel, quarell-ing.* Others prefer the single *l*, which is more in accordance with analogy; as, *traveler, quarreling.*

RULE IV. — The final *y* of a radical, when preceded by a consonant, is changed into *i*, before a suffix that does not commence with *i* ; as, *happy, happier ; glory, glorious.*

Remark. — Observe that, if the final *y* is preceded by a vowel, or the suffix commences with *i*, there is no change; as, *enjoy, enjoyed; cry, crying.*

RULE V. —Words ending with *ll* drop one *l* before the suffixes *less* and *ly ;* as, *skill, skil-less ; hill, hil-ly.*

EXERCISE.

I. *Write out the derivatives formed from the following radicals by adding* ING : — Thrive, face, rage, sow, spin, hit, stop, stoop, propel, abhor, debar, hinder, sunder, deter, shut, shoot, espy, cry, play, agitate, fee, see, shoe, buy, lie,* die,† dye.‡

II. *Write out the derivatives formed from the following radicals by adding* ABLE : — Surmount, peace, trace, value, move, efface, secure, suit, ply, destroy, admire, measure, deny.

III. *Write out the derivatives formed from the following radicals by adding* OUS : — Danger, continue, courage, outrage, parsimony, ceremony, contumely, contumacy.

IV. *Write out the derivatives formed from the following radicals by adding* ED : — Care, remove, thin, pass, hop, hope, hoop, heap, tender, commit, thunder, detest, fee, woo, tarry, decry, prey, toy, sigh, fancy, obey, huzza, whip, allure, stay, subdue, render, inter, emit, occur.

---

* Irregular, — *lying.*   † Irregular, — *dying.*   ‡ Irregular, — *dyeing.*

REVIEW QUESTIONS ON CHAPTERS XIII., XIV.

515. What is a letter? What were used to convey ideas before the invention of letters? What is meant by the alphabet of a language? 516. What is orthography? 517. Into what two classes are letters divided? 518. What is a vowel? 519. What is a consonant? 520. Which letters are always vowels? Which are always consonants? Which are vowels in some words and consonants in others? Can *a* be uttered alone? Can *b*?

521. What is a syllable? What may a syllable constitute? 522. What is a monosyllable? A dissyllable? A trisyllable? A polysyllable? 523. When are *w* and *y* consonants, and when vowels? 524. What is accent? Mention six words in which the accent is on the first syllable. Six in which it is on the second. Six in which it is on the third. How is the syllable that receives the stress of the voice denoted?

525. How many sounds has each vowel? Give examples with *a*. 526. How many sounds have the consonants? 527. How many sounds have *c* and *g*? When is *c* said to be soft, and when hard? When is *g* said to be soft, and when hard? As a general rule, before what vowels are *c* and *g* soft? Before what vowels are they hard? 528. When is a letter said to be silent?

529. How are the consonants subdivided? What is a mute? Mention the mutes. What is a semivowel? Mention the semivowels. 530. Mention the liquids. Why are they so called? 531. Of what does a diphthong consist? 532. When is a diphthong said to be proper? When improper? 533. Of what does a triphthong consist? 534. As regards their form, how are letters divided? Give the ten rules for the use of capitals.

535. What is spelling? 536. Repeat Rule I., and the exceptions. Repeat Rule II., and the exceptions. Repeat Rule III., and the exceptions. 537. How are derivatives formed? 538. What are radicals? 539. What is a prefix? What a suffix? Give examples. What is the advantages of learning the meaning of the prefixes and suffixes? 540. From what languages are the prefixes mainly derived?

541. When a prefix is added to a radical, what change is made in the latter? Is any change made when a suffix is added? 542. Repeat Rule I., relating to final *e*. What two exceptions are there to this rule? Is *e* ever rejected when the suffix begins with a consonant? Repeat Rule II., relating to the final consonant of a monosyllable. Repeat Rule III., relating to the final consonant of words accented on the last syllable. What remark is made about some words ending with *l*? Repeat Rule IV., relating to final *y*. Repeat Rule V., relating to words ending with *ll*.

PART V.

COMPOSITION.*

CHAPTER XV.

GENERAL DIRECTIONS TO TEACHERS. — The exercise of Composition should be commenced as soon as the pupil has fairly entered upon the study of Grammar. Rules for punctuation and capitals will be found in another part of this book, and may be learned at the pleasure of the teacher. The pupil should apply the rules as fast as they are learned. At the outset, little more should be required beyond good English sentences than correct spelling and general neatness. The exercises are progressive, and are designed to furnish object-lessons as a means of developing thought. Like all object-lessons, they should be commented upon and amplified by the teacher, until the pupil has learned to think for himself. The pupil should not be allowed to pass from one exercise to another until he has learned the preliminary matter well. In the judgment of the Editor, there is matter enough in this part to furnish the pupil an exercise in composition each week for a whole year. As the pupil progresses, he should be taught to be more and more critical, until he can readily apply all the rules of Syntax, and the directions in Exercises XIII. and XIV.

EXERCISE. — SIGHT.

DIRECTION. — Place an object before you. Examine it carefully with your eyes alone. Then write what you have learned.

---

* For a portion of the following pages, the author is indebted to a small work on Composition, published in Edinburgh, and edited by W. & R. Chambers.

TASTE. — SMELL.

Model. A Piece of Sealing-wax.

This piece of sealing-wax is about four inches long, half an inch broad, and a quarter of an inch in thickness. It is of a very bright red, and stamped with the name of the manufacturer. Its surface shines like glass, so that I suppose it is smooth, though I cannot be sure of this without touching it. One end is rough, as if broken, and the other is smoked from having been in the flame of a candle.

Describe in a similar manner the following objects: —

A book.	An inkstand	A chair.
A pen-knife.	A sheet of paper.	A looking-glass.

EXERCISE II. — TASTE.

DIRECTION. — Taste the object, and write the result.

Model. A Cup of Tea.

The substance in the cup is called tea, though, properly speaking, it is only an infusion of the leaves of that plant. Its taste is peculiar, but pleasant. It is naturally somewhat bitter, but the sugar prevents it from being unpleasantly so. The flavor is aromatic and agreeable.

Objects to be described: —

Onion.	Vinegar.	Coffee.	Strawberries.
Potato.	Honey.	Liquorice.	Apples.
Lemon.	Orange.	Cinnamon.	Cheese.

EXERCISE III. — SMELL.

DIRECTION. — Exercise the sense of smell on the given object, and write the result.

Model. A Full-blown Rose.

This beautiful flower is called the rose. Its buds are gradually opening, and from each proceeds a most delightful odor. But the chief perfume is from the petals of the full-blown flower. The essence which is extracted from the rose-leaves forms a fragrant scent termed otto of roses.

Objects to be described: —

Violet.	Pine-apple.	Strawberry.	Burnt feather.
Peach.	Lilac.	Geranium,	New-mown hay.
Orange.	Cologne,	Hartshorn.	Tobacco-smoke.

EXERCISE IV. — FEELING.

DIRECTION. — With eyes shut, touch the object, and write the result.

Model. An Octavo Volume.

I perceive by feeling, that this book is about ten inches long, six broad, and three in thickness. The book is smooth and hard, with raised ornaments on the back. I think it has been near the fire, for it feels somewhat warm.

Objects to be described: —

A door.	A bell.	Paper.	Woollen cloth.
Sponge.	A hair-glove.	Silk.	A doll.
Bread.	Marble.	A shilling.	Soap.

EXERCISE V. — HEARING.

DIRECTION. — Strike the object, or listen to its natural sounds, and describe what you hear.

Model. The Wind.

Last night I listened to the wind. Sometimes it whined like a dog, then it gave a sort of a shrill whistle. That was followed by a hollow moaning, and then there was a loud rush like a waterfall. This ceased, and afterwards there was a mixture of whistling and hissing. At last, it died away in gentle murmurs.

Objects to be described: —

A choir.	The sea.	Singing of birds.
A violin.	Bells.	Rustling of leaves.
A trumpet.	Thunder.	Sounds in a barn-yard.
A drum.	Hail.	Sounds in a street.

EXERCISE VI. — ALL THE SENSES.

DIRECTION. — Place the object before you, examine it carefully with all your senses in turn. Then write down the information which each organ has given you. Finish what you have learned from one sense, before you proceed to the next.

Model. A Pencil.

1. My eyes tell me that the pencil is about five inches long and a quarter of an inch in thickness. Its shape is round like a pillar, quite flat

STATEMENTS AND EXPERIMENTS.

at one end, and tapering to a point at the other. Its color is a beautiful light brown with dark streaks. It is at present lying on a sheet of white paper, with an old pen on one side, and a short piece of red sealing-wax on the other.

2. By feeling, I perceive its shape to be exactly that my eyes led me to suppose. But I ascertain something which my eyes could not tell; namely, that the pencil is as hard as this sealing-wax. It is smooth on one side, and rough on the other.

3. When I put it to my nostrils, I perceive that it has a very slight pleasant odor, like that of cedar-wood. 4. The taste is sweetish. 5. It utters no sound.

Objects to be described: —

A coin.	A flower.	A lemon.	*A pen.
An orange.	An apple.	A book.	A ball.
A watch.	A shell.	A thistle.	A clock.

EXERCISE VII. — STATEMENTS AND EXPERIMENTS.

DIRECTION. — Place an object before you. Try it with your senses, as before. Then make experiments on it, and write down the result.

Model. A Piece of India-rubber.

This piece of India-rubber, or caoutchouc, is three inches long, two broad, and one thick. It is in shape a sort of solid oblong. Its color is nearly black, with whitish or grayish parts in the middle, while some portions of it seem somewhat brown. Its smell is strong and somewhat disagreeable. It has no peculiar taste, though some boys are fond of chewing it. I shall now make some *experiments* with it. While I hold one end, you must pull out the other. When you let go, it returns to its former shape. Then I find it is *elastic.* Next, I put a small piece into the flame of a candle, and I perceive it takes fire very readily, burning with brilliant light, white at the bottom, and red at the top, emitting a considerable quantity of black smoke. I therefore ascertain that it is *inflammable.* By putting it into water, I perceive it floats; so its specific gravity must be *less* than that of water. I further observe that it does not diminish its bulk, from which I infer that it is *insoluble* in water. I have been informed, however, that tar will dissolve it. I have found it very useful in rubbing out pencil-marks.

According to direction and model, describe, —

1. A Small Piece of Glass.

QUALITIES, as proved by the senses. Size. Shape. Color. Weight Heat. Hardness. Smell. Taste. EXPERIMENTS.— By breaking marking, &c.

2. Coal.

QUALITIES. — Size. Shape. Color. Weight. EXPERIMENTS. — With water, with fire, with a hammer.

3. A Sheet of Paper.

QUALITIES. — Size. Shape, &c. EXPERIMENTS. — With water, with fire, with paint, with pencil, with ink.

4. Sealing-wax.

QUALITIES. — Shape. Size. Color. Weight, &c. EXPERIMENTS. — With flame, with water, &c.

EXERCISE VII.— SOURCES OF THINGS.

DIRECTION. — Place an object before you. Think from what source it came. If you do not know, ask your teacher or consult a book. Then put down all that you have heard. Add an account of its appearance, qualities, &c. Your description may conclude with some experiments.

Model. A Piece of Lead.

The substance before me is a metal called lead. I procured this piece at the plumber's, and he bought it of the owner of the lead-works. Lead is obtained by melting the ore, which is dug out of mines by men employed for that purpose. Lead is bluish white, very bright when cut or newly melted; but it becomes dull and dim after it has been in the air for some time. It has no taste, but if you rub it you will perceive a slight smell. It is very soft, and may be hammered into thin plates. It is easily melted, as you may prove by putting a piece into the fire.

Objects to be described : —

1. A Piece of Bread.

Suggestions. — *Baker*, oven, flour; *miller*, mill, stream, horses, water; *farmer*, ground, plough, harrow, horses, men, sun, rain, harvest, thrashing winnowing; soft, white, sweet, wholesome, nutritious.

2. A Coat.

Suggestions.— Tailor, cloth, merchant, manufacturer, wool, dyeing

PARTS OF THINGS. 251

spinning, weaving; wool-grower, sheep-washing, shearing. Shape, color, quality, &c.

3. Sugar.

Suggestions. — Grocer, merchant, ship, sailors, oven; West Indies, plantation, negroes, sugar-cane; refining. Shape, color, size, smell, taste, &c.

4. Paper.

Suggestions. — Stationers, paper-maker's mill, water or steam, rags, boiling, sizing, &c.; rag-merchant, linen, flax, plant, mode of preparation, &c. Shape, size, color, quality.

EXERCISE IX. — USES OF THINGS.

DIRECTION. — Place the object before you, and think for what purpose it is usually employed. If you do not know, ask your teacher or consult a book.

Model. A Piece of Lead.

This metal is of very great use. Water-pipes, cisterns, and roofs of houses, are made of it. Chemists form two substances out of it, called red and white lead, both of which are poisonous. If we mix it with tin, the result is that useful compound called pewter, of which some table-spoons are made. When blended with antimony, it affords a composition from which printers' types are cast.

Mention the uses of the following objects: —

Iron and steel.	Mahogany.	Sheep.	Wood.
Cotton cloth.	Leather.	Water.	Gold.
Steam-engine.	Silver.	Glass.	Cows.

EXERCISE X. — PARTS OF THINGS.

DIRECTION. — Place the object before you. Inquire how it came there, say where you bought it, whence the merchant procured it, &c. Tell whether it is natural or artificial, describe its parts, &c.

Model. A Penknife.

There is a penknife on the table before me. I bought it at the cutler's. He either made it himself or procured it of the manufacturer. It consists of two parts, each formed of a different substance. The handle is of horn, probably that of a stag. It is of a brown color, rough and hard.

It has several small rivets in it, for the purpose of holding its sides together. On one side there is a small plate, on which the owner's name may be engraven. The second substance is steel, of which the blade is composed. Steel is an artificial metal, the result of iron prepared with charcoal. It is very hard and smooth. When properly tempered, it makes very sharp blades.

Treat according to the direction and model —

1. A Room.

Suggestions. — Floor-boards, carpet-maker, pattern, color, texture, size, shape, walls, plaster, paper, color, figure, quality.

2. A Book.

Suggestions. — Leaves, pages, margins, title-pages, edges, plates, woodcuts, binding, author, printer, bookbinder, bookseller.

3. A Fire-place.   4. An Inkstand.

EXERCISE XI. — SIMPLE DESCRIPTION.

DIRECTION. — Select some subject about which you have or can get some definite information. Whatever the object, test it by your senses as far as the subject will admit. Ascertain its parts, qualities, sources, uses, value, &c. If the object selected is a plant, inquire further in regard to its structure, classification, seed, propagation, and mode of growth. If the object is an animal, inquire still further in regard to its food, habits, movements, instinct, place of abode, means of defence, varieties, &c. Collect all your thoughts and classify them before commencing to write.

Model. My Father's Horse.

My father's horse is a large and powerful animal. His body and legs are covered with glossy black hair. He has one white foot, and has a white star in his forehead. His head is quite small. His nostrils are large and full. His eyes are of a dark hazel color. His ears are short and thin, and are generally erect. His neck is beautifully arched, and is surmounted by a long, thick mane. His tail is bushy, and so long that it almost sweeps the ground.

My father bought him several years ago of a trader, who had obtained him of a farmer in Vermont. He is a proud and very courageous animal; but is, at the same time, gentle, kind, and faithful. He can walk, trot, canter, and run. When father puts the baby on his back, he is very careful not to move fast; but when I am mounted on him, he canters as fast as I desire to have him. We feed him on oats and hay. He does not like corn, but will eat bits of bread and apples from my hand. He sometimes sleeps while standing, but more frequently lies down to rest. Whenever I turn him into the pasture, he runs about as though he was crazy with joy. When provoked, he attempts to bite and kick. He knows a great many things as well as I do, and, on a dark night, can find his way home without any guidance.

I have been informed that horses were originally brought from Asia, and that no horses are native to this country, although there are many droves of wild horses on the prairies. The Arabian horse is the best for speed, but the English cart-horse is the largest and stoutest. On account of his speed and strength, the horse is very useful as a beast of burden.

According to the direction and model, describe, —

1. My writing-desk.

Suggestions. — Parts, legs, sides, lid, compartments; qualities, shape, size, color, &c.; material, uses, value.

2. A cherry-tree.

Suggestions. — Parts, trunk, roots, branches, leaves, &c.; blossoms, fruit, seed, propagation, growth, uses, &c.

3. A cow.

Suggestions. — Parts, head, body, legs, &c.; color, size, food, habits, qualities, place of abode, means of defence, use, age.

4. Our class-room.   6. An oak-tree.   8. An elephant.
5. A bird's nest.   7. A rose-bush.   9. An eagle.
   10. The house I live in.   11. England.

EXERCISE XII. — NARRATION.

DIRECTION. — Select for a theme some transaction or event with which you are familiar. Think over all the particulars connected with the event, and note them down. Select from these, — 1. Only those particulars that relate directly to the theme; 2. Only those which are necessary to convey all the information intended. Do not, however, omit any necessary particular. Arrange the particulars in the order of time. In narrating, it is often necessary to describe the actors or scenes connected with the event, but the description should not be carried too far. Those themes should be first selected which relate to what the writer has seen, felt, heard, or dreamed; then those may be taken which relate to the experience of others, to the history of nations, to changes in nature, or to purely imaginary events.

Model. What I did to-day.

I rose this morning at sunrise, and took a long walk into the country before breakfast. My spirits were buoyant, and everything I saw filled me with delight. The birds sang their sweetest songs, and the fields were covered with beautiful flowers. I returned home just in time for my breakfast, which I ate with a hearty relish. After breakfast, I learned my lesson in History, and then went to school. At nine I recited the lesson which I had prepared, and devoted the time that remained before recess to my lesson in Arithmetic. At recess, we played ball, but I am sorry to say that our side was beaten. Then came my recitation in Arithmetic, which lasted until twelve.

At noon, by permission of my parents, I dined with my cousins, and returned at two with them. The afternoon was pleasantly spent in studying and reciting grammar. I believe that I now understand something about verbs.

After school, I harnessed the horse to the rockaway, and drove with my sisters to the river to see a new sloop launched. When all was ready, the master waved a flag, and the workmen knocked away the fastenings, and she slid like a duck into the water. Sister Ellen then hurried us home to tea, although neither Mary nor I felt hungry in the least. After tea, we went into the garden arbor, where I am now engaged in writing this.

According to the direction and model, narrate,—

1. How I went a-fishing.

Particulars. — Purchasing my hook and line, searching for bait, walk to the river, selection of a place, the first nibble, success, other incidents, return home.

2. The story of King Alfred.

Particulars. — His misfortunes, his employment as cowherd, direction to watch the baking of the cakes, his inattention, anger of the woman, his reply.

3. History of a sheet of paper.

Particulars. — Rags, paper-mill, bookstore, purchaser, use, present condition.

4. Travels of Dr. Kane.
5. Life of William Tell.
6. Growth of Corals.
7. Travels of a Humming-bird.
8. My Autobiography.
9. Story of Daniel Boon.
10. Destruction of Tea in Boston Harbor.

EXERCISE XIII.—ANALYSIS.

Analysis is the division of the theme with reference to its class, or to the parts which compose it. Before analyzing, it is necessary to decide whether the theme should be considered as a class, or as a single object composed of separate parts. It is also necessary to determine the object which you have in view in making the divisions.

Thus the theme Plant may be divided, as a class, into Flowering Plants and Flowerless Plants; considered as a whole, it may be divided into root, stalk, branches, leaves. These principal divisions may be again subdivided.

The following directions will afford aid:—
Think long and patiently on the subject which you have chosen. Write down the leading thoughts as fast as they occur to you. Decide upon the object you have in view. Arrange your thoughts so as to present only a single theme. Have only one principle of division at a time. Select those particulars which are applicable to the end in view. Arrange the particulars in their natural order; that is, in the order of resemblance to each other, or in the order of nearness in position. Arrange the subordinate parts under the principal divisions. Be careful not to omit any essential part of the division, or to introduce as principal that which is merely subordinate.

Thorough analysis is of great service in all departments of composition, but especially so in description. When the analysis of the theme has been finished, such particulars may be added as tend to introduce the subject, to sustain interest, or to produce conviction. The analysis and such added particulars form the skeleton of the composition.

ANALYSIS OF SUBJECTS.

THEME. — *The Horse.* As a class the horse may be considered with reference to, —

1. Race: Arabian, Spanish, mustang, wild, &c.
2. Size: large, medium, small or ponies.
3. Color: black, white, gray, spotted, &c.
4. Uses: saddle, carriage, draught horses, &c.
5. Movements: trotting, pacing, running, &c.

These principal divisions may be enlarged by introducing the subordinate parts when appropriate; as, Arabian: 1. qualities, 2. habits, 3. peculiarities, 4. food, 5. place of abode, 6. means of defence, 7. history, &c. As a final step these subordinate parts may be again divided; as, Qualities: 1. faithful, proud, courageous; 2. speed, 3. strength, &c.

As a composite whole, the horse may be considered with reference to its parts: I. 1. head, 2. neck, 3. body, 4. legs, 5. tail; or, II. 1. bones, 2. muscles, 3. nerves, 4. skin.

These principal divisions may be subdivided as in the preceding examples. Of course it is not expected that all these particulars should be embraced in a single essay. Only those should be taken " which are consistent with the end in view."

Write a composition on
    The Arabian horse.   The movements of horses.
    The Shetland pony.   The utility of horses.
    A dray-horse.

SUBJECT. — Duties of children.
1. Definition of duty.   4. Duty to their parents.
2. Duty to themselves.   5. Duty to God.
3. Duty to their fellows.

These may be enlarged by enumerating the several duties, and specifying the reasons.

Write a composition with the aid of this analysis.

EXERCISE XIV. — THE COMPOSITION.

When the analysis has been carefully finished, each division of it may be enlarged and its relations distinctly shown. Do not write merely to fill up the page; but take heed that each sentence have some thought in it pertaining to the subject under consideration. Avoid nonsense.

I. MECHANICAL EXECUTION. — Write on the first and third pages of each sheet. Leave a margin on the left-hand side three fourths of an inch wide. Write the subject on the first line. State whether your object is to describe, narrate, or prove the theme. Begin the first paragraph on the third line, one and a half or two inches from the left-hand edge. Make a distinct paragraph for every topic in the analysis, or at convenient breaks in the thought. Write legibly. Do not make blots or write words that require to be erased. When the composition is written, fold the paper neatly. Put your name and the date on one side of the fold near the top.

II. GRAMMATICAL ACCURACY. — Guard against errors in spelling, in the use of capitals, in punctuation, and in syntax. Revise your manuscript carefully.

III. RHETORICAL FINISH. — 1. After the first draught has been made and carefully revised, re-examine, as critically as possible, the mechanical execution, the orthography, capitals, punctuation, and syntax of the whole. 2. Try to make each sentence stronger, clearer, and more harmonious. 3. Strike out unnecessary, unmeaning, and ill-sounding words. 4. Condense as much as possible. 5. Make the whole work as perfect as you can.

IV. Now make a careful, correct, and clean transcript of your essay.

Abbreviations used in Correcting.

O. = Orthography.
C. = Capitals.
R. = Reconstruct.
T. = Tautology.
N. = Nonsense.
S. = Syntax.

P. = Punctuation.
Rid. = Redundancy.
Pl. = Pleonasm.
Obs. = Obscure.
W. = Word to be changed
V. = Omission.

EXERCISE XV.—SUGGESTIVE TOPICS.

No one should attempt to write upon a subject which he does not understand; hence a young writer should avoid abstract themes. He will also find it to his advantage to select specific rather than general themes. Above all, he should always bear in mind that the object of composition is to express thought, not to multiply words. The preceding exercises are designed to develop thought, by suggesting inquiries as to parts, qualities, sources, and uses of things. These inquiries should be made whenever it is practicable, and, in addition, the theme should be viewed in every possible relation, so as to make the thought as exhaustive as possible. The following topics are added as a means of suggesting thought. Definitions. The *relation* of one subject to another; the *circumstances* of the persons concerned, the place, the time, the principles involved, the consequences and inferences, the purpose or design, comparison with other similar themes, the truth or falsehood involved, the objections proposed, historical illustrations effects, conclusions drawn.

Make analyses and then write compositions on the following themes: —
The city in which I live.   My right hand.
The home of Washington.   A swallow's nest.
How to play ball.   The story of a looking-glass.

The State in which I live.
The story of Romulus and Remus.
The story of Damon and Pythias.
The history of the steam-engine.
The effects of climate on character.
The story of the Prodigal Son.
How a fretful temper may be cured.

Description of a looking-glass.
Female heroism.
The trade-winds.
The Argonauts.
The Pilgrims.
On the last book that I read.

EXERCISE XVI.—VARIETY OF EXPRESSION.

The same idea may be expressed in different ways; and it will be both useful and entertaining for the learner to practise such exercises as the following:—

Model. The soul is immortal.
The soul will never die.
The soul will never cease to exist.
The soul will live forever.
The soul is destined to an endless existence.

Sentences for Practice.

A wise son maketh a glad father.
When we have finished our work, we will play.
Intemperance is ruinous to the mind as well as to the body.
A wolf, let into the sheepfold, will devour the sheep.
True religion teaches us to be gentle and affable.
My friend died last night, without a struggle or a groan.

In the same way, write in your own language stories that you have read. Change into prose, extracts in poetical narration and description like the following:—

Excelsior.—*Longfellow.*
Casabianca.—*Hemans.*
Well of St. Keyne.—*Southey.*

Burial of Sir John Moore.—*Wolfe.*
Wreck of the Hesperus.—*Longfellow.*
The Pied Piper of Hamelin.—*Browning.*

EXERCISE XVII.—LETTER-WRITING.

Few kinds of composition demand more care than letter-writing, or usually receive so little. A letter should be written in an easy, natural manner, adapted to the age and attainments of the recipient, as well as the circumstances which call it forth. All letters should be courteous, truthful, and free from extravagant professions of esteem. Business letters should be brief and to the point, and should be answered as soon as practicable after they have been received. In the mechanical execution and grammatical accuracy, the utmost pains should be taken. When finished, the superscription should be very plainly and neatly written. Care should be taken not to apply to a person two titles meaning the same thing; as, *Mr.* Robert Jones, *Esq. Dr.* E. Smith, *M. D.* In formal notes of invitation, both the invitation and answer should be written in the third person. The following is a proper example for imitation, in respect to the dating, beginning, and closing of a letter.

OLNEY, June 16, 1769.

My dear Friend:—

    I am obliged to you for your invitation, but being long accustomed to retirement, which I was always fond of, I am now more than ever unwilling to visit those noisy scenes which I never loved, and which I now abhor. I remember you with all the friendship I ever professed, which is as much as I ever entertained for any man.

    I love you and yours; I thank you for your continued remembrance of me, and shall not cease to be their and your

Affectionate friend,
WILLIAM COWPER.

JOSEPH HILL, Esq.

    Write a letter announcing your intended visit to the country. Write a letter recommending a person as a good servant. Write a note requesting a loan of twenty dollars. Write a *real letter* to some one of your friends.

PART VI.

PROSODY.

CHAPTER XVI.

547. Prosody treats of accent, quantity, and the laws of versification.

548. Accent is a particular stress of voice laid on a certain syllable in a word; as on the syllable *ban* in *abandon*.

<small>Accent should not be confounded with Emphasis. *Emphasis* is a stress of voice on a word in a sentence, to mark its importance. *Accent* is a stress of voice on a syllable in a word.</small>

549. The Quantity of a syllable is the time which is required to pronounce it. A short syllable requires half the time of a long one.

Kinds of Verse.

550. A Verse consists of a certain number of accented and unaccented syllables, arranged according to certain rules.

551. Rhyme is the correspondence of the last sound of one line with the last sound of another.

552. Blank Verse is poetry without rhyme.

553. A Stanza consists of several lines, and is sometimes improperly called a *verse*.

554. A Couplet, or distich [pronounced *dis-tik*], consists of two poetical lines which make complete sense.

KINDS OF VERSE.

555. A Foot is a division of a verse consisting of two or three syllables.

556. Metre is a measured arrangement of words in verses.

557. Scanning is dividing a verse into the feet of which it is composed.

SECTION I.

FEET.

558. The principal feet in English verse are the I-am-bus, the Trochee (*tro'-ke*), the Spondee, each consisting of two syallables; the Dac-tyl, the An-a-pest, and the Am-phi-brach, each consisting of three syllables.

559. An Iambus has the first syllable unaccented, and the last accented; as, *betráy, consíst.*

A Trochee has the first syllable accented, and the last unaccented; as, *háteful, pe'ttish.*

A Spondee has both syllables accented; as, *fáte we'll, vast' weight'.*

560. A Dactyl has the first syllable accented and the last two unaccented; as, *hap'pily, fear'fully.*

An Anapest has the first two syllables unaccented, and the last accented; as, *contravéne, acquiésce.*

An Amphibrach has the first and third syllables unaccented, and the second accented; as, *endeávor, redúndant.*

561. Different kinds of verse are named from the foot that predominates in them, and are called Iambic, Trochaic, Dactylic, Anapestic, &c. The following lines from Coleridge's Metrical Lesson to his Son will illustrate the different kinds of verse.

"Tróchee | trips from | lóng to | short;
From long to long in solemn sort,
Slów Spón | deé stálks | stróng foót, | yet ill able
Ever to | cóme up with | Dáctyl tri | sýllable;
Iám | bics márch | from shórt | to lóng,
With a leáp | and a boúnd | the swift An | apest thróng;
One syllable long, with one short at each side,
Amphíbra | chys hástes with | a státely | stride."

562. Verse containing different kinds of feet is termed composite.

SECTION II.
IAMBIC VERSE.

563. In reading Iambic verse, the accent is laid on the second syllable of each foot, — that is, on the even syllables; as,

To mé | the róse.

Iambic verses may be divided into several varieties, according to the number of feet of which they are composed.

I. The shortest form of Iambic verse in English consists of *one* Iambus, with an additional short syllable; as,

Disdain | ing,
Complain | ing,
Consènt | ing,
Repènt | ing.

We have no poem in this measure, but it is intermingled with other varieties in stanzas.

II. The second form of Iambic verse is also too short to be continued through any great number of lines. It consists of *two* Iambuses.

What pláce | is hère!
What scénes | appeár!

It sometimes takes an additional short syllable.

Upón | a moúnt | ain,
Besíde | a foúnt | ain.

III. The third form consists of *three* Iambuses.

> In plá | ces fár | or neár,
> Or fá | mous ór | obscúre.

It sometimes takes an additional short syllable.

> Our heárts | no lón | ger lán | guish.

IV. The fourth form consists of *four* Iambuses. Four lines of this form constitute a stanza of *Long Metre.*

> Broad ís | the roád | that leáds | to deáth,
> And thoú | sands wálk | togéth | er there;
> But wís | dom shóws | a nár | row páth,
> With hére | and thére | a tráv | ellér.

V. The fifth form consists of *five* Iambuses.

> How lóved, | how vál | ued ónce | avaíls | thee nót,
> To whóm | relát | ed ór | by whóm | begót.

This is called Heroic Measure. In its simplest form, it consists of five Iambuses; but, owing to the admission of other feet, it appears in several different forms.

VI. The sixth form of Iambic verse is commonly called Alexandrine Measure. It consists of *six* Iambuses.

> For thoú | are bút | of dúst; | be húm | ble ánd | be wíse.

VII. The seventh and last form consists of *seven* Iambuses.

> The Lórd | descénd | ed fróm | abóve, | and bówed | the heáv | ens hígh.

This was formerly written in one line, but is now divided into two, the first containing four feet, and the second three; as,

> The Lórd | descénd | ed fróm | abóve,
> And bówed | the heáv | ens hígh.

Four lines thus written constitute a stanza of *Common Metre.*

564. A stanza of *Short Metre* consists of four lines, the third of which contains four Iambuses, and the others contain three each.

I love thy kingdom, Lord,
The house of thine abode;
The church our blest Redeemer saved
With his own precious blood.

A stanza of *Hallelujah Metre* consists of eight lines. The first four contain three Iambuses each; the last four, two Iambuses each.

Welcome, delightful morn;
Sweet day of sacred rest,
I hail thy kind return;
Lord, make these moments blest:
From low desires | I soar to reach
And fleeting toys, | Immortal joys.

SECTION III.
TROCHAIC VERSE.

565. In reading Trochaic verse, the accent is laid on the first syllable of each foot, — that is, on the odd syllables; as,

On' the | moúntain.

The chief varieties of Trochaic verse are as follows: —

I. The shortest form consists of *one* Trochee and a long syllable.

Túmult | cease,
Sínk to | peace.

This measure is deficient in dignity, and can seldom be used in connection with serious subjects.

II. The second form consists of *two* Trochees, and is likewise so brief that it is rarely used in serious poetry.

On the | moúntain,
Bý a | foúntain.

It sometimes takes an additional long syllable.

In the | dáys of | old,
Fábles | plaínly | told.

12

III. The third form consists of *three* Trochees.

  Whén our | heárts are | moúrning.

It sometimes takes an additional long syllable.

  Réstless | mórtals | tóil for | naught,
  Blíss in | vaín from | eárth is | sought.

IV. The fourth form consists of *four* Trochees.

  Roúnd us | roárs the | témpest | loúder.

It sometimes takes an additional long syllable.

  Idle | áfter | dínner | ín his | chair,
  Sát a | fármer, | rúddy, | fát, and | fair.

This measure is very uncommon.

V. The fifth form is likewise uncommon. It is composed of *five* Trochees.

  Áll that | wálk on | foót or | ríde in | cháriots,
  Áll that | dwéll in | pála | cés or | gárrets.

VI. The sixth form of Trochaic verse consists of *six* Trochees.

  Ón a | moúntain, | strétched be | neáth a | hoáry | wíllow,
  Láy a | shépherd | swaín, and | viéwed the | rólling | bíllow.

This seems to be the longest trochaic line in use.

SECTION IV.
ANAPESTIC VERSE.

566. In reading Anapestic verse, the accent is laid on the third syllable of each foot; as,

  I would hide | with the beást | of the cháse.

The chief varieties of Anapestic verse are as follows:—

I. The shortest form consists of *two* Anapests.

  But his coúr | age 'gan faíl,
  For no árts | could avaíl.

This form admits of an additional short syllable.

  Then his coúr | age 'gan faíl | him,
  For no árts | could avaíl | him.

II. The second form consists of *three* Anapests.

O ye woóds, | spread your bránch | es apáce!
To your deép | est recéss | es I flý;
I would híde | with the beásts | of the cháse,
I would ván | ish from év | ery eyé.

This is a very pleasing measure, and much used both in solemn and lively style.

III. The third form consists of *four* Anapests.

May I góv | ern my pás | sions with áb | solute swáy,
And grow wís | er and bét | ter as lífe | wears awáy.

This measure will admit an additional short syllable.

On the wárm | cheek of yoúth, | smiles and ró | ses are blénd | ing.

SECTION V.

AMPHIBRACHIC VERSE.

567. In reading Amphibrachic verse the accent is laid on the second syllable of each foot; as,

Miss Flóra | McFlímsey | of Mádi | son Square.

The chief varieties of Amphibrachic verse are as follows: —

I. The shortest form consists of *one* Amphibrach.

Hearts beáting   Tears stárting
At meéting;   At párting.

II. The second form consists of *two* Amphibrachs.

We 've beáten | all foémen,
We 've túrned back | on nó men.

III. The third form consists of *three* Amphibrachs.

A cónquest | how hard and | how glórious.

IV. The fourth form consists of *four* Amphibrachs.

[Thanks,] my lórd, for | your vénison; | for fíner | nor fátter
Ne'er ránged in | the fórest | nor smóked on | the plátter.

SECTION VI.

DACTYLIC VERSE.

568. In reading Dactylic verse the accent is laid on the first syllable of each foot; as,

Whére shall the | lóver rest,
Whóm the fates | séver.

I. The first form consists of *two* Dactyls.

Bórne on her | nórthern pine,
Lóng o'er the | fóaming brine.

II. The second variety consists of *three* Dactyls.

Weáring a | wáy in his | yoúthfulness,
Lóveliness, | beaúty, and | trúthfulness.

III. The third variety consists of *four* Dactyls.

Bóys will an | tícipate, | lávish, and | díssipáte
All that your | búsy pate | hoárded with | care.

IV. The fourth variety is the Dactylic Hexameter, which consists of five Dactyls and one Spondee.

Over the | moúntain a | lóft ran a | rúsh and a | róll and a | roáring,
Dównward the|breéze came in|dígnant and|leápt with a|hówl to the|wáter.

CHAPTER XVII.

FIGURES.

569. Poetry owes much of its effect to the peculiar style in which it is dressed. It indulges more freely than prose in figurative expressions, in contractions and transpositions, in exclamations, antiquated words, and other peculiarities.

570. These peculiarities are generally considered under the head of Prosody. They may be divided into Figures of Etymology, Figures of Syntax, and Figures of Rhetoric.

571. A Figure of Etymology is an intentional deviation from the usual form of a word.

572. A Figure of Syntax is an intentional deviation from the usual construction of a word.

573. A Figure of Rhetoric is an intentional deviation from the usual application of a word.

SECTION I.
FIGURES OF ETYMOLOGY.

574. The principal Figures of Etymology are *Elision, Synæresis, Diæresis, Paragoge, Prosthesis,* and *Tmesis.*

575. ELISION is the omission of part of a word.

Elison includes, — 1. *Aphæresis,* or the omission of a letter or letters at the beginning of a word; as, *'gainst* for *against, 'squire* for *esquire.* 2. *Syncope,* or the omission of a letter or letters in the middle of a word; as, *list'ning* for *listening, lov'd* for *loved.* 3. *Apocope,* or the omission of a letter or letters at the end of a word; as, *th'* for *the, tho'* for *though.*

576. SYNÆRESIS is the contraction of two syllables into one; as, *seest* for *see-est, drowned* for *drown-ed.*

577. DIÆRESIS is the separation of two vowels that might form a dipthong; as, *aërial,* not *ærial; coöperate,* not *cooperate.*

Diæresis is denoted by two dots placed over the latter of the two vowels, as in the examples just given.

578. PARAGOGE is the addition of a letter or letters at the end of a word; as, *without-en* for *without, bound-en* for *bound.*

579. PROSTHESIS is the prefixing of an expletive letter or letters; as, *beloved* for *loved, a-down* for *down, y-clad* for *clad.*

580. TMESIS is the separation of a compound into its parts by some intervening word; as, *To us ward* for *toward us.*

SECTION II.

FIGURES OF SYNTAX.

581. The principal Figures of Syntax are *Ellipsis, Pleonasm, Enallage,* and *Hyperbaton.*

582. ELLIPSIS is the omission of some word or words necessary to the construction of a sentence, but not to its meaning.

Almost all sentences are more or less elliptical, as may be seen in the following examples: —

1. Ellipsis of the *noun*; as, The laws of God and man, — that is, The laws of God and the *laws* of man.
2. Ellipsis of the *pronoun*; as, I love and fear him, — that is, I love *him* and fear him.
3. Ellipsis of the *adjective*; as, A delightful garden and orchard, — that is, A delightful garden and *a delightful* orchard.
4. Ellipsis of the *verb*; as, The man was old and crafty, — that is, The man was old and the man *was* crafty.
5. Ellipsis of the *adverb*; as, He spoke and acted wisely, — that is, He spoke *wisely* and he acted wisely.
6. Ellipsis of the *preposition*; as, He went into the abbeys, halls, and public buildings; — *into* is omitted before *halls* and *public buildings.*
7. Ellipsis of the *conjunction*; as, They confess the power, wisdom, goodness, and love of the Creator; — *and* is omitted before *wisdom* and *goodness.*
8. Ellipsis of the *interjection*; as, O pity and shame! — that is, O pity! and *O* shame!

583. PLEONASM is the use of more words than are necessary either to the construction or the meaning; as,

Peace, O virtue! Peace is all thy own.

584. ENALLAGE is the use of one part of speech for another; as,

The fearful hare limps *awkward.*
They fall *successive* and *successive* rise.

585. HYPERBATON is the transposition of words; as,

The muses fair, these peaceful *shades among.*
He wanders *earth around.*

SECTION III.
FIGURES OF RHETORIC.

586. The principal Figures of Rhetoric are *Simile, Metaphor, Personification, Allegory, Metonymy, Vision, Apostrophe, Hyperbole, Synecdoche, Irony, Antithesis,* and *Climax.*

587. A SIMILE is an express and formal comparison of one object to another, and is generally introduced by *like* or *as ;* as,

> The actions of princes are like those great rivers, the course of which every one beholds, but their springs have been seen by few.
>
> As from the wing no scar the sky retains,
> The parted wave no furrow from the keel,
> So dies in human hearts the thought of death.

588. A METAPHOR is an implied comparison, in which the term denoting the similitude is omitted; as,

> I will be unto her a *wall* of fire round about.
> Thou art my *rock* and my fortress.
> Thy word is a *lamp* to my feet and a *light* to my path.

589. PERSONIFICATION, OR PROSOPOPŒIA, is that figure by which we attribute life, sex, or action to inanimate objects; as,

> Jordan *was driven* back! The *mountains skipped* like rams, and the little hills like lambs.
>
> Rome, for empire far renowned,
> *Tramples* on a thousand states;
> Soon her pride shall *kiss* the ground —
> Hark! the Gaul is at her gates.

590. An ALLEGORY is a continued metaphor; for examples, see Ezekiel xvii. 22-24, and Psalm lxxx. 8-17.

591. METONYMY is the substitution of one word for another; as the cause for the effect; the container for the contained; the sign for the thing signified; the abstract for the concrete; as,

> *Gray hairs* (i. e. *old age*) should be respected.
> The toper loves his *bottle* (i. e. *the contents*).

> He gained the *palm.*
> We wish *Labor* to be respected.

592. Vision is a figure by which something imaginary is represented as real, and present to the senses; as,

> I seem to myself to behold this city, the ornament of the earth, and the capital of all nations, suddenly involved in one conflagration. I see before me the slaughtered heaps of citizens lying unburied in the midst of their ruined country. The furious countenance of Cethegus rises to my view, while, with a savage joy, he is triumphing in your miseries.

593. Apostrophe is turning off from the regular course of the subject, to address some person or thing; as,

> Soul of the Just! Companion of the Good.
> O sun! thy everlasting light.

594. Hyperbole consists in magnifying or diminishing a thing beyond the truth; as,

> I saw their chief, tall as a rock of ice; his spear, the blasted fir; his shield, the rising moon; he sat on the shore, like a cloud of mist on the hill.

595. Synecdoche is putting the name of the whole of anything for a part, or a part for the whole; as the *waves* for the *sea,* the *roof* for the *house,* the *head* for the *person,* &c.

596. Irony is the intentional use of words in a sense contrary to that which the writer or speaker intends to convey.

> The prophet Elijah, when he challenged the priests of Baal, "mocked them and said, Cry aloud, for he is a god; either he is talking, or he is pursuing, or is on a journey, or peradventure he sleepeth, and must be awaked."

597. Antithesis is the placing of opposites in contrast; as,

> If you wish to enrich a person, study not *to increase his stores,* but *to diminish his desires.*
>
> Though *poor, luxurious;* though *submissive, vain.*
> Though *deep,* yet *clear;* though *gentle,* yet not *dull.*

598. CLIMAX is a figure in which the sentiment rises in regular gradation; as, "Add to your faith virtue; and to virtue, knowledge; and to knowledge, temperance;" &c. See 2 Pet. i. 5 – 7.

REVIEW QUESTIONS ON PART VI.

547. Of what does prosody treat? 548. What is accent? With what must accent not be confounded? What is the difference between accent and emphasis? 549. What is quantity? 550. Of what does a verse consist? 551. What is rhyme? 552. What is blank verse? 553. What is a stanza? 554. A couplet? 555. A foot? 556. What is metre? 557. What is scanning?
558. Name the principal feet in English verse. 559. What is an Iambus? A trochee? A spondee? 560. What is a dactyl? An anapest? An amphibrach? 561. How are different kinds of verse named? What is iambic verse? Trochaic verse? Anapestic verse? 562. What is composite verse? 563. In reading iambic verse, where is the accent laid? How may iambic verses be divided? Describe each variety, and give an example of each. 564. What is a stanza of short metre? A stanza of hallelujah metre? 565. In reading trochaic verse, where is the accent laid? Describe each variety of trochaic verse, and give an example of each. 566. In reading anapestic verse, where is the accent laid? Describe each variety of anapestic verse, and give an example of each. 567. In reading amphibrachic verse, where is the accent laid? Give an example of each variety of amphibrachic verse. 568. In reading dactylic verse, where is the accent laid? What is the dactylic hexameter? Give examples of each variety of dactylic verse.
569. To what does poetry owe much of its effect? 570. How are figures divided? 571. What is a figure of etymology? 572. What is a figure of syntax? 573. What is a figure of rhetoric? 574. Name the principal figures of etymology? 575. What is elision? What does elision include? What is aphæresis? What is syncope? What is apocope? 576. What is synæresis? 577. What is diæresis? How is diæresis denoted? 578. What is paragoge? 579. What is prosthesis? 580. What is tmesis?
581. Name the principal figures of syntax. 582. What is ellipsis? Give an example of the ellipsis of a noun. Of a pronoun. Of an adjective. Of a verb. Of an adverb. Of a preposition. Of a conjunction. Of an interjection. 583. What is pleonasm? 584. What is enallage? 585. What is hyperbaton?
586. Name the principal figures of rhetoric. 587. What is a simile? 588. What is a metaphor? 589. What is personification? 590. What is an allegory? 591. What is metonymy? 592. What is vision? 593. What is apostrophe? 594. What is hyperbole? 595. What is synecdoche? 596. What is irony? 597. What is antithesis? 598. What is climax?

SYNOPSIS OF GRAMMATICAL RELATIONS.

Grammatical Subject.	Modifiers of the Gram. Subject.	Grammatical Predicate.	Modifiers of the Gram. Predicate.
The Grammatical Subject of a sentence may be a noun or pronoun; a verb in the Infinitive; a clause; a phrase; or the name of any sign or letter of which anything can be affirmed.	The Subject may be modified by a noun in apposition; an adjective; a preposition with its object (adjunct); a participle; a verb in the infinitive; a clause; and sometimes an adverb.	The Grammatical Predicate of a sentence may be a verb, or the copula and its attribute.	The Grammatical Predicate may be modified by a noun in the objective case (if the verb is transitive); a verb in the infinitive; an adverb; a preposition with its object (adjunct); a clause; an adjective; a phrase; and a quoted sentence.

The subject, modified by one or more words, is called the LOGICAL SUBJECT.

The predicate, modified by one or more words, is called the LOGICAL PREDICATE.

SIMPLE SENTENCES.

LOGICAL SUBJECT.		LOGICAL PREDICATE.	
Grammatical Subject.	Modifiers of the Gram. Subject.	Grammatical Predicate.	Modifiers of the Gram. Predicate.
Ferdinand,	the king,	held	a council at Cordova.
He,	the Marquis of Cadiz,	beheld	from a distance the peril of the king.
To die	in battle	was deemed	him.
The x,	in algebraic expressions,	represents	an unknown quantity.
Franklin,	the printer,	was (a) native	of Boston.

COMPLEX SENTENCES.

Leading Proposition.	Clause.
David loved Jonathan,	who befriended him.
He always said	that discretion was the better part of valor.
He ran away from the field	before a shot was fired.

SYNOPSIS OF GRAMMATICAL RELATIONS. 275

MODIFICATION OF WORDS.

Noun, Pronoun.

A noun may be modified,—

1. By a noun in apposition; as, George, the *king*.
2. By an adjective; as, A *tall* mast.
3. By an adjunct; as, A life *of toil*.
4. By a participle; as, The sun *rising*.
5. By a clause; as, The land *that we love*.
6. By a phrase; as, Man, *made in the image of his Creator*.
7. By an adverb; as, Not us feet *only*.
8. By a verb in the infinitive; as, A time *to die*.
9. By a noun in the possessive case; as, *Lot's* wife.

A pronoun may be modified by all the above except the last two.

Verb, Participle.

A verb or participle may be modified,—

1. By a noun in the objective case, if the verb is transitive; as, The sun gives *light*.
2. By a verb in the infinitive; as, He hopes *to return*.
3. By an adjunct; as, I walk *in the grove*.
4. By a clause; as, I hope *that you are well*.
5. By an adverb; as, The wind blows *violently*.
6. By a phrase; as, *In vain* he labors.
7. By a quoted sentence; as, Bion said, "*Know thyself*."

Adjective.

An adjective may be modified,—

1. By an adverb; as, *Very* rich.
2. By a verb in the infinitive; as, Pleasant *to behold*.
3. By an adjunct; as, True *to nature*.
4. By another adjective; as, *Bright* red.
5. By a phrase; as, *In general* successful.

Adverb.

An adverb may be modified,—

1. By another adverb; as, *Most* assuredly.
2. By an adjunct; as, Agreeably *to nature*; Most *of all*.

Preposition.

A preposition may be modified,—

1. By an adverb; as, Far *beyond*.
2. By a noun in the objective case; as, Over *the hills*.
3. By a verb in the infinitive; as, About *to depart*.

Connectives.

Clauses are connected to their leading propositions,—

1. By conjunctions.
2. By adverbs.
3. By relative words and phrases.
4. By incorporation.

Classification of Sentences.

1. *Declarative*; as, I write.
2. *Interrogative*; as, Do you write?
3. *Imperative*; as, Write better.
4. *Exclamatory*; as, How fast he writes!

A Simple Sentence contains but one proposition.

A Complex Sentence consists of a leading proposition and one or more clauses.

A Compound Sentence is made up of two or more members, sometimes joined by a connecting word and sometimes not.

Clauses, &c.

Simple sentences may contain phrases and adjuncts, but not clauses.

Complex sentences may contain phrases, adjuncts, and clauses.

The members of a compound sentence may be either simple, complex, or compound elements.

Clauses are distinguished as Substantive, Adjective, and Adverbial.

Phrases are distinguished as Substantive, Adjective, and Adverbial.

Analysis of Sentences.

In analyzing a sentence,—

1. State its class.
2. State its grammatical and logical subject.
3. State its grammatical and logical predicate.
4. State its copula and attribute.
5. When there are clauses, point them out, and the leading proposition they modify.
6. Point out the parts of which the clauses are composed, and the office of each.
7. Point out the adjuncts and phrases; tell what they modify, and by what they are themselves modified.

APPENDIX.

ANALYSIS BY DIAGRAMS.

Diagrams may be advantageously used as an aid to the process of analysis. The accompanying are recommended as possessing the following merits: —

1. Each element in the sentence has a distinct sign.
2. The office of each element is distinctly shown.
3. The mutual relations of the elements may be comprehended at a glance.
4. By the use of diagrams a great saving of labor and time is effected.

The lesson should be neatly mapped out on paper by the pupil, before recitation, and handed in to the teacher as a regular exercise. In recitation, a part of the class should be employed at the blackboard, and the rest engaged in revising the work performed, or in oral analysis.

The teacher should bear in mind that diagrams are only aids to analysis, and, to be made profitable, must always be combined with oral recitations. A very little practice will suffice to familiarize the pupils with the forms.

Diagrams for Analysis.

——— = A substantive element in the nominative or objective.

▭ = A verb in the indicative or potential mode.

⌒▭ = A verb in the subjunctive mode.

⌣▭ = A verb in the infinitive mode.

|——| = A participle.

A transitive verb or participle is indicated by a diagonal line; as, ▱, ⌒▱, |⋈|. An intransitive verb is indicated by the omission of this sign.

⌒—— = A relative pronoun.

∽ = A co-ordinate conjunction.

✕ = A subordinate conjunction.

✕ = A conjunctive adverb.

\ = An adjective, an adverb, or a noun in the possessive.

/ = A predicate adjective.

═══ = Two nouns in apposition.

╲╲ ▭ = A noun or a verb modified by an adjunct.

············⌢············ = A curved line connecting the subject and predicate nominatives.

Words supplied are expressed by dotted lines.

⎧ = A curved line used to divide the logical subject
⎨   from the logical predicate, or to separate propo-
⎩   sitions.

⎫ = A brace used to connect elements of the same con-
⎬   struction.
⎭

A substantive clause or phrase is indicated by a line drawn above or below it. An adjective or an adverbial clause or phrase is indicated by its position. The method of using the diagrams can be readily learned from the models.

Simple Sentences.

1. Birds fly.   2. John reads his book.

BIRDS |FLY.|

3. Franklin was a philosopher.

FRANKLIN |WAS| PHILOSOPHER.

4. Some horses are strong.

5. Franklin, the printer, became a famous philosopher.

6. The neglected son of a tallow-chandler in Boston astonished the whole world by the discoveries of his mature age.

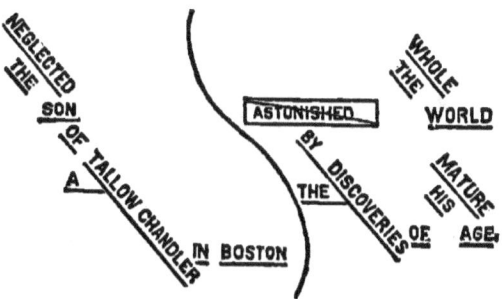

7. To steal is to break the law.

8. John and Mary recite grammar and history.

9. Tempted by pleasure, he soon forgot the lessons of his youth.

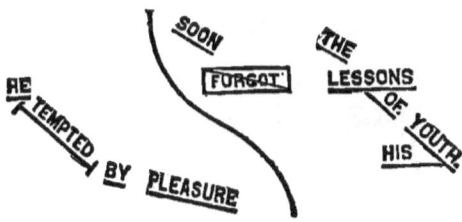

Complex Sentences.

10. You will depart with but a small retinue, said the baronet.

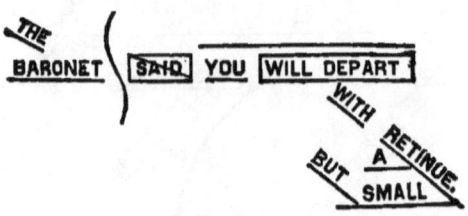

11. I will tell you what you must do.

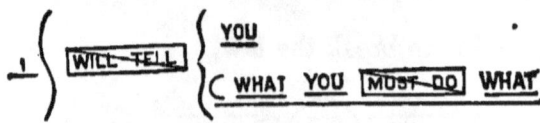

NOTE. — Divide the sign for the relative ⊂ ——, to show both its connective and substantive power. The direct object of *tell* is the substantive clause, *what you must do.* The indirect object is *you*

12. Make hay while the sun shines.

13. He owns the place where I was born.

14. If he do but touch the hills, they shall smoke.

Compound Sentences:

15. The heavens declare the glory of God, and the firmanent showeth his handiwork.

16. Alexander, being fired with ambition, determined to conquer the world; but, at last, Death overcame even him.

17. I have been young, but now am old; yet have I never seen the righteous forsaken, nor his seed begging bread.

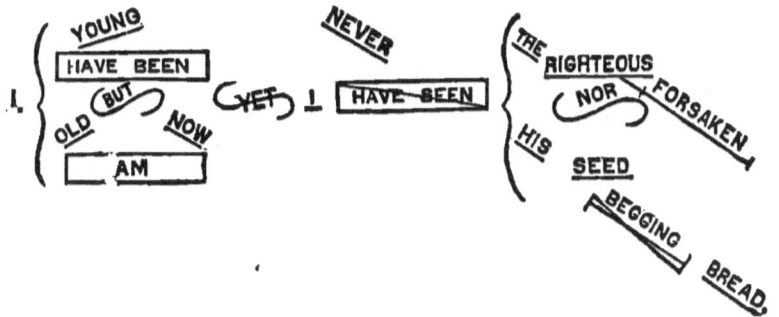

18. The book that you lent me has been mislaid, and I do not know where you can find it.

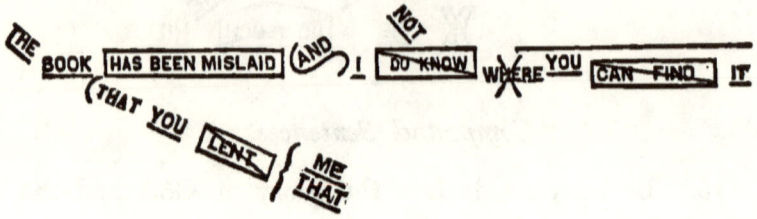

THE END.

www.ingramcontent.com/pod-product-compliance
Lightning Source LLC
Chambersburg PA
CBHW032117230426
43672CB00009B/1768